Equal Opportunities in Colleges and Universities

SRHE and Open University Press Imprint
General Editor: Heather Eggins

Equal Opportunities in Colleges and Universities

Towards Better Practices

Maureen Farish,
Joanna McPake,
Janet Powney and
Gaby Weiner

The Society for Research into Higher Education
& Open University Press

Published by SRHE and
Open University Press
Celtic Court
22 Ballmoor
Buckingham
MK18 1XW

and 1900 Frost Road, Suite 101
Bristol, PA 19007, USA

First published 1995

A catalogue record of this book is available from the British Library

ISBN 0 335 19416 8 (pb)   0 335 19417 6 (hb)

Library of Congress Cataloging-in-Publication Data

Equal opportunities in colleges and universities : towards better
  practices / Maureen Farish . . . [*et al.*].
     p.   cm.
  Includes bibliographical references and index.
  ISBN 0–335–19416–8 (pb)   ISBN 0–335–19417–6 (hb)
  1. Educational equalization—Great Britain—Case studies.
  2. Minorities—Education (Higher)—Great Britain—Case studies.
  3. Discrimination in higher education—Great Britain—Case studies.
  I. Farish, Maureen, 1941- . II. Society for Research into Higher
  Education.
  LC213.3.G7E78 1995
  370.19'342—dc20   95–5849
                                                                       CIP

Typeset by Graphicraft Typesetters Limited, Hong Kong
Printed in Great Britain by St Edmundsbury Press,
Bury St Edmunds, Suffolk

Contents

Preface

Most educational organizations claim to be in favour of equal opportunities and many advertise that they are equal opportunities employers. What do these terms mean? How are they realized in practice? In particular, what progress has been made and what increased understanding has there been of equal opportunity policy-making and practice in tertiary and higher education sectors. These sectors, for the most part, have been slower to embrace equality issues than those lower down the educational ladder, such as schools or youth organizations (Powney and Weiner, 1992). Further, while much attention has been paid to the relative absence of women, Black and minority ethnic staff in college and university hierarchies (e.g. Heward and Taylor, 1993), little attention has been devoted to the evaluation of the changes made by institutions with a commitment to reducing such inequalities.

The project which we will refer to as 'Equity and Staffing in Further and Higher Education' forms the basis for this book. It sought to address this knowledge gap by documenting the achievements of three institutions (one each from the further education, 'new' university and traditional university sectors) chosen on the basis of their stated commitment to, and track record on, implementing equal opportunities. The aim was to investigate what happens to institutional equal opportunities policies once they have been passed. In particular, the project focused on staffing issues to complement other ESRC-funded studies focusing on school curricular and classroom processes (published in Troyna and Hatcher, 1992) and to build on previous work, funded by the European Commission, on management strategies in educational institutions which enhance the promotion of women and Black and minority ethnic staff (reported in Powney and Weiner, 1992).

What policies are most likely to improve the conditions of work and promotion of under-represented groups in colleges and universities? How have such policies been initiated, developed and implemented? How can such policies be monitored and evaluated? What are the main obstacles to the successful development and embeddedness of such policies? These were some of the questions which seemed most important to our study, though attempting to get to the 'heart' of the equal opportunities policy-making process provided us with a number of technical and ethical problems, as we shall see later in this volume.

There were four members of the project team: Gaby Weiner (who was the project director) and Maureen Farish at South Bank University in London, and Joanna McPake and Janet Powney at the Scottish Council for Research in Education, based in Edinburgh. The range of research expertise of the project team enabled the project to draw on diverse research and theoretical fields (e.g. educational research, policy and textual analysis, sociological, feminist and social justice paradigms), although the project's principal identification was with the policy case study (see the Appendix for a fuller discussion of this research approach).

The project took place between 1991 and 1994, during a period of enormous change, both at institutional levels and within the fields of study related to the project. For example, during the course of the project, all the case study institutions experienced amalgamations, important changes in funding status, institutional name changes, internal restructuring and reorganization. Many of the changes were instigated by government policy orientated towards the market and most resulted in relocation of work and office space and other similar forms of disruption. Thus, while the project, in the main, was welcomed by those working in the institutions, the institutions were themselves changing. Hence, during the period of the project, equality as a policy issue seemed to be on the move *down* rather than up the policy agenda.

The book is divided into nine chapters and an appendix on research methodology. The first chapter considers the debates and controversies within the broad field of equal opportunities policy-making, focusing in particular on post-compulsory sectors of education and the trends in policy-making involving staff at all levels.

Chapters 2, 3 and 4 constitute the main case study chapters. The chapters cover similar overall themes, including background and history of the policy, equal opportunities structures and practices, and evaluations. However, they differ according to the different characteristics and emphases of the case study institutions, as do the resultant themes and areas of equal opportunity policy-making, implementation and interpretation.

Chapter 5 reports on one approach taken by the project to the analysis of the wide range of qualitative data gathered. This was to create 'snapshot' portrayals of events which point up the complexities of the equal opportunities policy-making process. In focusing on the specifics of a 'moment' in the research, the chapter brings together multiple sources of evidence. The attempt is made to bring together values, theory and practice to create new critical meanings which may be applied more generally to researching other social justice issues in the educational research context.

Chapter 6 provides an analysis of institutional policy documents, a research approach which quickly emerged as a central task of the project. The existence of extensive policy documentation on equal opportunities was a feature in each of the case study institutions. How this documentation can be 'read' or deconstructed, and the implications different formats have for the policy-making process, form the basis of this chapter.

Chapters 7 and 8 bring together the main themes and findings of the project. For example, they discuss the range of good practices revealed by the case studies, although these frequently differed according to the specific context of each organization. In investigating what happens to policy *after* it has been created, the project reveals that the policy process is far from being as 'rational' as some would suggest, and that awareness of where support and resistances are likely to occur may lead to a more sophisticated understanding and ultimately more successful implementation of equal opportunities policies.

The concluding chapter draws together the various project themes reported in the previous chapters principally for two purposes: to recapitulate the main findings of the project and to suggest new forms of practice that are likely to enhance the equity policy-making process.

We have included an appendix on methodology for those more interested in understanding the intricacies of the research process. It describes the background to the research, debates within the research team on research process and ethics, the research approach eventually adopted, how the involvement of participating institutions was negotiated, agreed ethical guidelines and so on. Also briefly considered are the ethics underpinning 'good' research practice and, in particular, those which support research into social justice issues.

Acknowledgements

This book could only have been written with the help given by many of the members of staff at our case study institutions, whom we cannot name for reasons of anonymity and confidentiality, yet who made time to talk to us about their views of equal opportunities policies within their institutions and to discuss our findings and interpretation of policy and practice. We thank them for their forbearance. Practical help was also forthcoming in a number of ways: in the arrangements of meetings and interviews, in ensuring that relevant documents were sent to us on a regular basis and in keeping us informed of policy developments. Our thanks are due to all those who took part and supported our research.

Thanks are also due to administrative staff at South Bank University and at the Scottish Council for Research in Education (especially Joan Ballantine), the Economic and Social Research Council for providing financial support for the project (grant R000233301), the project advisory group – Marjorie Bulos, Leone Burton, Rakesh Bhanot and Iram Siraj-Blatchford – for their support and helpful advice, and John Skelton and Pat Lee at the Open University Press.

Notes on Terminology

Black

We have adopted the Borough College practice of using the term 'Black' to describe people of African, Asian, Caribbean or mixed racial origin, and the practice of always using a capital letter, which in College terms is 'an expression of solidarity among groups who are subject to racism'.

'Race'

We use quotation marks to denote the problematic nature of 'race' as a concept: here it is used to indicate the broad area of racial division/difference, rather than alluding to distinct races or genetic combinations.

Section 11

Under Section 11 of the Local Government Act 1966 special funding is made available to local authorities at the discretion of the Home Office to support additional staff posts to meet the needs of 'Commonwealth immigrants' and their descendants.

masked the fact that different groups are likely to want different things (Jewson and Mason, 1986, 1989). As Cockburn (1991: 45) found in her study: 'Black women and white, women with children and without, feminists and anti-feminists varied in their hopes and fears of the policy.'

Equality programmes have also tended to be specific to particular institutions and have arisen from specific histories and sets of problems. Thus, the two major organizational contexts affecting the implementation of (and obstruction to) equal opportunity initiatives are institutional and cultural.

> [They] include structures, procedures and rules. Cultural impediments arise in discourse and interaction. They influence what men and women think and do. The two levels are interactive. Structures can be changed in the right cultural environment. But cultures predispose how people think and act.
>
> (Cockburn, 1991: 45)

Despite the disappointment expressed about past efforts at equal opportunities policy-making, there has been evidence more recently that some colleges and universities have achieved substantial improvements in their equal opportunities policies and practices. For example, in Australia in the mid-1980s equal opportunities policies led to a significant rise in the number of women in senior positions in certain universities (Jackson, 1990). Another more recent survey by the Commission of University Career Opportunity (reported in Wright, 1994) shows some progress in the UK but also considerable room for improvement.

> More than 90 per cent of United Kingdom universities have equal opportunities policies, 75 per cent have workplace nurseries, 72 per cent have guidance on fair recruitment... But only... 42 per cent provide training in equal opportunities for staff responsible for recruitment, and only 21 per cent make training compulsory.
>
> (Wright, 1994: 13)

Cottrell (1992) further suggests that the newer universities (ex-polytechnics) have had a greater commitment to equality issues citing those vice chancellors who were early signatories to the government-led Opportunity 2000, an initiative aimed at increasing the number of women in top jobs. And according to Anand (1992), ex-polytechnics are also better in terms of gender-fair representation on appointment panels and recruitment training.

Heward and Taylor suggest that the apparent resistance to change from the traditional universities is owing to more than merely tradition or inbuilt conservatism. Acceptance of the need for the 'old' universities to address discriminatory practice strikes at the heart of the elite cultures within them.

> Higher education in the UK is hierarchical with Oxbridge at the apex, large provincial and other established universities ranked above the

former polytechnics and colleges of higher education. Elite institutions maintain their position by exclusivity. Assumptions about academic merit underlie prestige ... The prestige hierarchy with Oxbridge at its apex and the values underlying it are highly resistant to change.

(Heward and Taylor, 1993: 79–80)

Equal opportunities as expressed in policy has moved higher up the institutional agenda alongside government policies to increase and widen access to higher education. It is not at all surprising that the traditional university sector has sought to buttress its elite position in higher education through distancing itself from equal opportunities considerations.

Even where equal opportunities is adopted as an institutional issue, commitment can vary as to whether the policies addressed are long or short term. Short-term policy-making involves making quick responses to procedural issues: for example, institutions producing statements of intent and codes of practice without recognizing the need for adequate resources to put policy into practice. The longer agenda has a more ambitious aim of permanently transforming the dominant (male, white, middle-class) institutional culture (Cockburn, 1989).

Not surprisingly, the longer agenda has also been likely to attract more resistance. According to Cockburn's study of organizations, male employees erected institutional obstacles to the advancement of their women colleagues, fostering 'solidarity between men' at the cultural level in order to 'sexualise, threaten, marginalise, control and divide women' (Cockburn, 1989: 215).

On a more positive note, a study by Powney and Weiner (1992) which explored equality issues concerning female and Black and minority ethnic managers from a range of educational institutions found that, despite institutional variations, a number of sound and well-tried equal opportunities practices had been put into place, aimed at counteracting discrimination at different organizational levels. A continuum of institutional adoption of equal opportunities policies and practices was identified as follows:

1. Equal opportunities is a significant part of the ethos of the institution; for example, reflected in power structures and permeating all institutional activities (*ethos*).
2. There is a genuine commitment to good equal opportunities practice (*commitment*).
3. The institution is in the process of working towards equal opportunities (*predisposition*).
4. There is some 'lip-service' given to equality issues (*lip-service*).
5. There is no evidence of any real interest in equal opportunities issues (*none*).

An institution with an ethos of equal opportunities is one where there is an awareness of the full range of obstacles barring individual progress and where every attempt has been made to remove such obstacles. For example, in the case of a further education college,

> The stated ethos of the organisation is to create a supportive, comfortable, non-hostile place where black people could meet, organise and talk openly . . . There is a large percentage of black staff in the college, in excess of 30–40% . . . Black staff are represented at those [top tier] levels . . . there are more black women than black men . . . There is a systematic staff monitoring process in the college which is explicit, public and open . . . The recruitment and'selection process is systematically adhered to with black staff members sitting on the panel.
>
> (Powney and Weiner, 1992: 29)

Also evident in the study was the comparatively greater progress made by smaller, lower status, educational institutions such as schools and further and adult education colleges, perhaps because of their relatively low status, their need to recruit from a wide range of groups in the community or their more intimate and student-oriented atmosphere. Additionally, the ex-polytechnics appeared to be moving more quickly on equality issues than the traditional university sector.

Gatekeepers of equal opportunities policies

One important feature of the spread of equal opportunities policies has been that women and Black senior staff are more likely to be allocated responsibility for equality issues or, as Yeatman (1993: 23) terms it in the context of universities, 'tagged as equity change agents'. Thus, life is made more difficult for, say, women as university managers because they are likely to become targets for those wishing to resist change, and also because of their very interest in equality issues, rendered peripheral to the most prestigious elements of academia. Thus, in the Australian context,

> To be a professor of Women's Studies; to be the only woman Dean of a country's Law Schools, where this Law School is identified with the University's bi-cultural and gender equity objectives and seen to be pioneering a 'law in context' approach; to be a Pro-Vice-Chancellor responsible for foreign students, student welfare and equal opportunity is also to be on the outer rim of academia.
>
> (Yeatman, 1993: 23)

In a UK study reported by Weiner (1993), Black managers (male and female) tended to have similar patterns of responsibility, often for both race and gender. A Black male college deputy suggested that such responsibilities further compromised his status.

> For H. there is the added factor of him having role of EOP [equal
> opportunities policies] monitor and keeping his mind at all times on
> the race dimensions in his work ... He feels he is constantly being
> watched to see whether or not he can manage.
>
> (Weiner, 1993: 14)

It seems that high visibility can be the consequence either of having specific responsibility for equal opportunities or of being a woman and/or a
member of a 'minority' institutional group in a senior position. And, as we
have seen, frequently the two come together to produce maximum visibility.

What do we mean by equal opportunities?

One of the problems with examining the effectiveness or otherwise of
equal opportunities policy-making is that the term 'equal opportunities'
itself is so elusive. It can be applied to a wide variety of contexts within
educational institutions; for instance, to staff issues (the main focus of this
book), curriculum, pedagogy, assessment, access and recruitment, priorities in funding, staff–student relations, the general work environment
and so on.

Moreover, putting aside the fact that at various times equal opportunities
has been used to address different kinds of educational or socio-economic
inequality ('race', gender, class, disability, religion, ethnicity, sexual orientation, age), there are also distinct differences in its conceptualization.

> For some, achieving equality means enabling certain under-represented
> groups to attain their rightful place in the existing social, economic
> and political order; for others it means offering radical alternatives to
> an essentially biased social and political system.
>
> (Weiner, 1986: 266)

Liberal and more radical conceptions of equal opportunities help to shape
what kinds of action need to be taken. Riley (1994) argues that strategies
for change have been premised on one of two interpretations: 'equality of
opportunity' and 'equality of outcome'.

> The liberal interpretation of equality, equality of opportunity, has
> been concerned with ensuring that the rules of the game (employ-
> ment, or access to courses, or examinations) are set out fairly. The
> assumption has been that rigorous administrative controls and for-
> malized systems will ensure that fair play takes place ...
>   The more radical conception of equality, equality of outcome, has
> been concerned with widening access (to courses, or to employment)
> through action designed to redress past imbalances. It has been an
> essentially interventionist strategy aimed at redistributing resources
> and opportunities to disadvantaged groups.
>
> (Riley, 1994: 13)

Riley elaborates on concepts of quality and inequality (the former currently more fashionable than the latter), which, she claims, are related but potentially in conflict. Quality is concerned with identifying levels and standards while equality relates to the distribution of power and resources. 'A tension exists', she argues, 'between the two which is based on values and ideology', so that 'key actors in the system can influence quality and equality outcomes in favour of different groups in the system' (Riley, 1994: 13). In our view, quality is also concerned with monitoring and maintaining performance standards; as we shall see, monitoring is an element of *equality* maintenance which is frequently omitted. As we shall also see in the case studies reported later in this book, effective equal opportunities policies certainly appear to require key actors or 'champions' who are able to intervene and divert resources from the normal channels of distribution.

Equality of opportunity is, in fact, so flexible a term that it has been used not only to address fairness in the distribution of resources, but also to embrace a notion of justice applicable to the market. Thus, one university's equal opportunities code of practice claims equal opportunities as

> essential to the efficiency and effectiveness of the University and to good relations amongst its workforce. Failure to provide equality of opportunity can carry economic costs in terms of grievances, low morale, low productivity and problems in attracting and retaining staff.
>
> (Queen's University of Belfast, 1992: 1)

Given the range of interpretation of equal opportunities as outlined above, the project team decided to draw on the various specific definitions of equal opportunities adopted by the case study institutions, and to judge progress against institutional targets as well as more widely recognized characteristics of achievement.

Equality and management issues

Despite the general under-representation of women at management levels, studies of gender and management have found that women tend to be more person-friendly, more approachable and more organized as managers (Ouston, 1993; Summers, 1993), and that their experiences as managers are likely to be different from men's. A useful summary of the research provided by Riley (1994: 94) is reproduced as Figure 1. Women as managers in education have received considerable attention in recent years, with patterns of under-representation being similar to those found for women managers generally (see, for instance, Adler *et al.*, 1993; Ozga, 1993).

Less is known about Black and minority ethnic experience. Powney and Weiner (1992) found that patterns of under-representation for non-white

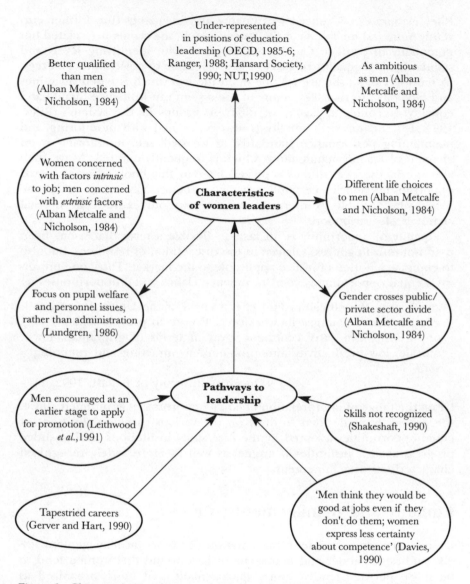

Figure 1 Characteristics of women leaders, and their pathways to leadership: a summary of research findings (from Riley, 1994: 94)

managers in educational organizations were similar to those for women, though more marked at senior levels in the funding agencies, quangos, educational administration and older universities. An illuminating example of this was the difficulty that they had in locating senior Black educational managers for their study, particularly as, according to the Commission for Racial Equality, no records have ever been kept on this. On the other hand, though relatively few in number compared with their male counterparts, white women were more identifiable in senior management positions than their Black peers.

Echoing the above study, research on the employment prospects more generally of Black men and women show that they have greater difficulty in gaining employment and find promotion less easy to obtain than their white counterparts (Grambs, 1987; Brennan and McGeevor, 1990). Black women appear to be doubly disadvantaged as they experience discrimination on gender as well as racial grounds (Al Khalifa, 1989; McKellar, 1989). Further, when they achieve senior status, women and/or Black managers report feelings of high visibility and isolation, for instance, by continual requests to be the token presence on senior committees (Bangar and McDermott, 1989). One form of racism reported by Powney and Weiner (1992) is the patronizing attitude of white colleagues who appear surprised if a Black person runs a meeting efficiently or speaks well publicly. A Black female manager commented that colleagues' 'expectations are so low that when you outstrip their expectations, they turn around and become almost a fan' (Powney and Weiner, 1992: 12).

Powney and Weiner found that racism and, to a lesser extent, sexism were as endemic in education as elsewhere. Fighting discrimination and arguing for the right to equal treatment proved a battle and a strain for many of the managers interviewed by them. However, the characteristics of racism (and sexism) were likely to be less explicit than in previous times. The operation of a colour bar in halls of residence, reported by several of the older interviewees, is now clearly illegal. Instead, more insidious racist practices have emerged, such as the more covert practice of 'losing' application forms or providing less administrative and secretarial support than that given to white managers in equivalent posts. Being 'set up to fail' was a frequent descriptor for Black senior staff (and some women managers).

Equality in organizations

Being 'set up' by management is a term used by Morgan and Knights (1991) to describe a management strategy used in the financial services sector. In this case, bank managers used policy for the advancement of women to 'set up' women workers so that they were made responsible for mounting the challenge to the 'aggressive, macho salesman' culture.

The fact that the labour market is segmented according to various socioeconomic groups and categories has not gone unnoticed by the managers of companies and institutions. In fact, according to Morgan and Knights (1991), many managers have developed an understanding of job segregation and gender dynamics generally, and have been able to use this understanding in the interests of corporate strategy. While managements may not necessarily be committed to greater equality in their organizations, following Foucault, ideologies of gender are reproduced and restructured under the 'disciplinary gaze' of management such that management is able to appropriate equal opportunities policy in its own interests.

Maguire and Weiner (1994) further suggest that the recent increased adoption of the discourse of 'masculinist managerialism' by the educational sector more generally will have severe repercussions for women's institutional positions. They point to several features that render this form of management hostile to women.

> First, it cuts across the management style most preferred by women, which tends to be more open, democratic, friendly, and collaborative, and less confrontational and competitive . . . Second, with its focus on such issues as target setting, service delivery, efficiency and 'quality', the kind of managers which such managerial cultures are likely to choose are unlikely to be those with the 'female' management styles as depicted above.

This is not to say that women managers cannot cope with target-setting or quality assurance; rather that the managerialist culture which seeks to prioritize these over professional or personal issues is likely to exclude many women.

Another issue mentioned by Maguire and Weiner is the low prioritization of equality concerns within the managerial discourse. They point out that women and Black and minority ethnic staff benefited to some extent from various equal opportunities initiatives of the mid-1980s. The fact that these avenues are now closing off because fewer such initiatives are being proposed will result in even fewer 'minority' managers in teacher and higher education in the future.

Such evident reversion to the norm of sexist and racist practices, once the policy imperative is removed, can be linked to the perceived low status of 'minority' groups generally. Cockburn asserts, rightly in our view, that status shifts occur according to the social characteristics of post holders. When (eventually) women or other minority groups achieve equivalent status to white men within organizations, the importance of those positions more generally is automatically diminished (Cockburn, 1991). In other words, the lower the proportion of white males in given posts, the lower the status of these posts. How do studies focusing on social justice issues in organizations, as outlined above, relate to more mainstream management and organizational theories and concerns?

Debates within management and organizational theory

As might be expected, there is no one overarching theory about how to implement policy effectively in educational institutions. Management and organizational theorists have put forward a plethora of explanations about why and how support for and resistance to policies are realized in practice. To choose two examples from many, Handy and Aitken (1986) and Watson (1982) concentrate on the variety of *structural* features of educational organizations. Watson suggests that effective educational organizations should be thought of as comprising seven mutually supporting yet overlapping systems (spatial, task, social, cultural, governance, economic and political), while Handy and Aitken suggests 'seven Ss' whereby effective organizations are created and maintained (strategy, structure, system, staff, skills, style and shared values). While such theorists recognize the complexity of educational organizations (Watson and Handy and Aitken focus on schools), their emphasis is on achieving consensus. They view conflict and challenge characterized, say, by 'office politics' as disruptive, inconvenient and generally undesirable. Their main concern is with the smooth running of the organization in accordance with goal or target-setting and achievement. Certainly in one of the case studies for the project, staff recognized tensions in the role of the senior manager in both maintaining the smooth running of the college and introducing new, potentially destabilizing, equal opportunities policies.

This rather functionalist position on policy-making, a dominant one in educational management, has drawn criticism from policy theorists such as Ball (1990), who see it as constituting a technology of power in which dominant perspectives and knowledges are presented as neutral and above debate or criticism. In such a way, management is a

> professional, professionalising discourse which allows its speakers and its incumbents to lay exclusive claims to certain sorts of expertise – organisational leadership and decision-making – and to a set of procedures that cast others, subordinates, as objects of that discourse and the recipients of those procedures.
>
> (Ball, 1990: 156–7)

In contrast to the structural approaches to organizations taken by those mentioned above, Ball (1987) and Hoyle (1988) focus on organizations as sites of conflict and domination cemented and buttressed by 'micro-politics'. Thus, according to Ball, the hidden agendas of organizations promote alternative, competing subcultures, which may run counter to dominant values held by policy-makers. While it is apparently centred on the routine and the uncontroversial, each educational organization constitutes an arena of struggle where conflicts are implicit and subterranean, only occasionally emerging into the open. Beneath the surface lies a layer of micro-political activity in which 'individuals and groups in organisational contexts seek to use their resources of power and influence to further their interests' (Hoyle, 1988: 88). We suggest that the chosen research methodology of the project – the policy case study – is a useful way of tapping into such webs of influence and power at institutional, group and individual levels.

Micro-political analytical frameworks have been of much interest to the project since a key research aim has been to identify the cultural under-currents of each case study institution, so that responses towards policies relating to equal opportunities might be read alongside the range of in-dividual struggles within and against the dominant power structures. We wanted to move away from simple approval or condemnation of responses to policy-making – that is, identification of 'goodies' and 'baddies' or the 'what to do' scenario – to a more sophisticated understanding of the equal opportunities policy-making process.

The project perspective

As we have seen, while attention has been paid to the relative absence of women and/or Black and minority ethnic staff in educational institutions, few evaluations, save that carried out by Cockburn, have been made of the changes embodied in institutions with well-developed equal opportunities policies and programmes. Where are the success stories? What policies and practices have been most likely to enhance the recruitment and pro-motion of under-represented groups in educational organizations? What specific processes of change have been most effective?

To answer some of these questions, the project focused on both the characteristics of equal opportunities policies in different organizational structures and how competing inter-institutional cultures have been influ-enced by history, environment and social grouping. It thus employed micro-political theoretical frameworks to explore, through the utilization of the policy case study, the specifics of how policy translates into practice. Be-cause the study was informed by, and committed to, principles of equity and justice, it also drew on debates within feminism (e.g. Weedon, 1987; Stanley and Wise, 1990; Lather, 1991) both in choosing methodology and in shaping the analysis.

Now that we have, albeit briefly, reviewed the literature on equal op-portunities policy-making as a backdrop to the project, the next three chapters report on the characteristics of each case study institution and the resultant specific themes and areas of equal opportunities policy-making. Chapter 2 focuses on Borough College, Chapter 3 on Town University and Chapter 4 on Metropolitan University.

2

Borough College Incorporated: Case Study

A day in the life

The students' equal opportunities notice board has the usual mixture of formal and less formal activities and information: deaf awareness, self-defence, an Afro-Caribbean essay writing competition, the College charter for racial equality, a public lecture on Buddhism and two pieces from the city police about 'racial abuse and crime' backed up with useful addresses and phone numbers. The deputy principal arrives with the day's edition of a national newspaper which has given generous coverage to the latest racist incident, with a blurred photograph of college security guards clustered around the gate. They had insisted that the photographer should be so far away that individuals could not be identified. The deputy has just finished dealing with some other members of the press.

She collects her coat, briefcase and heavy bag and moves around past the fish pond and library to the canteen and meeting room. On the way the deputy greets several people and there are jokes about her being a 'bag lady'.

The first meeting of the day is with the examinations *ad hoc* working group convened to 'enable exams to run smoothly'. Even early on a Monday morning the room has a rather neglected look. Discarded sheets of coloured sugar paper and cardboard lie in one corner. The group of five, including support staff, administrator and academic staff, do not seem to notice their surroundings, quickly getting down to the business of preparing a leaflet for students and a handbook for staff about exam procedures.

Only first names are used in the meeting. Everyone contributes when she or he wishes and the deputy summarizes the main points. She moves the meeting along, ensuring that the agenda, agreed at the beginning, is finished on time. At the end of the meeting the deputy suggests who should be invited to the next meeting and the others concur. The atmosphere is pleasant, relaxed and on task. Of the five people present three are women and all are white.

The main points raised that are relevant to equal opportunities issues concern the arrangements for students with visual, hearing and learning difficulties. A blind tutor has been appointed to support blind students. Mention is also made of students with other less obvious difficulties, such as epilepsy, which they do not make public, sometimes to their own disadvantage.

The deputy moves on to coffee with the lecturer responsible for all pre-vocational work in the college. They seem relaxed with each other and the meeting progresses speedily; the main issues are about implications and possible strategies in the context of uncertain future funding and some reluctance by staff to consider across-college pre-vocational initiatives. The meeting is exploratory and amiable, with both people apparently supportive of each other's ideas; at the end the lecturer summarizes points for action that have been agreed.

The deputy goes back to the staff room, which is nearly empty nowadays because it is a no smoking area. Staff stay for coffee at their own desks where they can smoke. Nearby there is an open work area of about the same size accommodating about 25 desks for staff. The union (NATFHE) notice board has a poster advertising 'Joint branch and joint union meeting on security and safety – protest about racist and murderous attacks on staff and students'. The top of the poster has a photograph of prisoners (possibly from what was Yugoslavia) standing behind barbed wire. Another notice is about a protest against the deterioration in service and increase in canteen prices. The deputy buys a sandwich from the snack bar around the corner next to the florist shop, which the college has built with funds from inner-city grants and its own funds, and established on a year's trial. Two ex-students run the shop, which offers work experience to members of the college floristry course. Back in the office, the deputy takes calls from the press and then travels by taxi a couple of miles to one of the other six sites.

The deputy has her main office in a Victorian school. She collects her post from her personal assistant, opening it on the way up to the second floor. She answers a phone call from a newspaper and patiently explains about the security cameras to be installed at the site, where some of the local residents are members of the British National Party and politically opposed and hostile to the Black members of the college. The next task is to focus briefly on the likely merger with the local adult education institute, which is going to add another 35 full-time staff and 100 or so part-time staff to the college workforce. The local authority will have to pick up the cost of any redundancies but all decisions will have to be made between December and February. The deputy makes coffee at a table in the corner of the room, popping downstairs again to wash up cups and collect the milk.

The next meeting is with the head of student services, who raises problems of having students with financial difficulties and too few skilled staff to help them. There is also a problem with the availability of telephones at the information centre and a request for the principal or the deputy to attend the next open evening. Later on the agenda is how to counteract the negative publicity from the racist incident and to think about long-term marketing strategies. All these items and the sudden availability of a student officer post result in the need for decisions to be taken by the deputy. The hour and a quarter meeting is punctuated by ten phone calls to, or from, the deputy. One asks for clarification that a reporter from the *Today* radio programme will be allowed to 'roam the site'. Another reports that a gang of youths and a pit-bull terrier have been seen outside that site – so there are phone calls to the local police to check they are informed about the situation.

A meeting with the head of personnel follows. She reports that one of the Black members of staff wishes to transfer away from the site where the trouble is. The key question raised is 'supposing there hadn't been these (racist) incidents, would we have moved him?' From personnel's point of view, the reason for the move request is crucial. An individual under stress could be allowed to move but if this is just one member of a vulnerable group then it is difficult to give this individual preferential treatment. Moving the person might start a flood of requests for transfer, which in turn would provide a model for students also wanting to avoid going to that site. On the other hand, unless the member of staff can work else-where in the college he is likely to resign. There is no easy solution to this one and the deputy will have to discuss the issues with the principal.

The deputy finishes her day in her office, writing letters and completing other administrative tasks uninterrupted (after five o'clock) by phone calls.

Introduction

The events and issues in this summarized account of a deputy principal's day at a further education college provide an evocative start to a case study about equal opportunities and staffing at this college. The deputy was shadowed from nine in the morning until the late afternoon and what was quickly apparent was her varied and intensive workload. She had to deal with large and medium scale issues in staffing, as well as curriculum, long-term strategies for the college, financial conditions of students and community relations. Matters relevant to equal opportunities are just one part of her responsibility but these are issues where the deputy's role is pivotal. It was coincidental that on the day previous to that chosen for the shadowing, a young Black student had been physically assaulted by a few of the young local white residents.

The racial incident ran contrary to the fundamental philosophy of the college and provided a test of the anti-racist policies and practices established over the years. While the deputy considered that this college had

not seen as many violent examples of racism as other colleges in neigh-
bouring boroughs, she held firmly to the college principle that staff had
the fundamental right to work in comfortable and safe conditions. This
was difficult given the number of college sites with diverse local envi-
ronments as well as different accommodation available for staff and students. On the whole working conditions were fairly spartan and all academic
staff, including the principal and deputy principal, had (as in most FE
colleges) expected to do relatively mundane tasks as well as to fulfil more
executive functions. During the day described at the beginning of this
chapter, women predominated but all of them were white except the head
of personnel. The extent to which this represents the overall staff profile
is highly pertinent to our study.

To flesh out this particular case study, we have grouped points for
elaboration under the following themes:

- The complexity and changing nature of the college.
- Equal opportunities means the right to be comfortable: development
  of policies and structures.
- Extent of success of the policies at Borough College.
- Difficulties in effecting equitable staffing.

Complexity and changing nature of the college

The variety and intensity of the deputy's workload indicated above was not
abnormal. During the period of the case study, the college had many
changes to effect and adjust to while maintaining a good quality education
in times when resources were constrained for the college as well as for
many individual students. In fact, the most significant characteristic of the
college during the course of the project was the transitory nature of its
structures as the management had to negotiate amalgamation with a sixth
form centre and then with an adult education institute (AEI). In April
1993, the college was incorporated and funded directly by the new Further
Education Funding Council (FEFC). This meant adjusting to different relationships with the borough council and taking on new responsibilities as
a more autonomous organization. Strategic planning was essential.

Each change had some impact on, among other things, equal opportunities policies and practices. The changes also required an immense amount
of time and energy in working out, for example, the use of new locations
and communications across the college as a whole, as well as in sorting out
employment conditions for staff moving from the sixth form centre and
the AEI to the college. This last exercise was extremely time-consuming
(especially for the principal and deputy principal) as the AEI had a large
number of part-time staff, many of whom were not given work in the new
structure; those who were taken on had reduced hours and some salaried

staff could not be taken on by the college and were made redundant. Most part-time (non-salaried) staff were women but of the salaried staff not given jobs, most were men.

With the mergers, the college gained more space. The college was spread across six sites when the project began and had expanded to 12 by the summer of 1993, covering much of an inner London borough. Only one of the buildings was purpose built; others included a fairly modern vacated secondary school with a pleasant and spacious assembly hall, contrasting with other sites in traditional Victorian primary 'board school' buildings with shiny brown tiles on the lower parts of the walls and stone staircases going up two floors. All the buildings were solid and would have cost a lot to modernize. Therefore access to upper floors was likely to continue to be difficult for anyone with mobility problems. The main office for the deputy principal and key post holders for equal opportunities (including disability) were on upper floors of one of these Victorian schools (which was previously the sixth form centre).

Each site had its own character although it was college practice to ensure access through a security check, either by school keepers or by a firm of external security staff hired by the college. All staff and students had identity cards to be shown on entry to college premises. Some sites were community buildings and many students and staff felt uneasy about travelling to other sites – partly because people tend to feel safe in their own localities. Thus Black staff felt safe in one locality and white staff less happy; the situation was reversed in another site with Black staff feeling very apprehensive about the minority of white racists in the locality. Facilities were variable: there was a crèche and nursery for students' children, each on a different site; a second nursery opened in 1993 on a third site for children of staff and students.

The amount of space made available through the mergers improved that aspect of working conditions but communication between sites was difficult and only possible by telephone or by travelling across the borough, often by bus, car or taxi. Many staff had to make at least one trip each day and those with a cross-college responsibility expended a lot of time and energy moving between sites and adjusting to the different requirements of each. As with most FE colleges, secretarial and administrative support for academic staff was stretched. Moreover, it was necessary to have multiple facilities, such as canteens and caretakers, to cover each site.

Each site attracted local students. Increasing numbers of the 16–19 age group had such financial difficulties that some could not afford the fare even to go to another site within the borough. About 50 per cent of the student population of about 9000 was Black and many, but not all, of the local catchment areas had a mixture of minority ethnic groups. In an area where few are affluent and most are working class, Borough College provided a wide range of non-advanced courses and qualifications many of which addressed high levels of unemployment among certain groups, especially young Black males.

Equal opportunities means the right to be comfortable: development of policies and structures

> It was reassuring to see Black staff in the office ... It's just human nature to want to see someone like yourself.
>
> (Member of Borough College support staff)

At Borough College the main purpose of the equal opportunities policies was to ensure that 'all staff and students feel safe, welcome and fully able to participate in College life' (Staff briefing pack). If the college proved a comfortable place, we viewed this as evidence of successful equal opportunities policies.

The emphasis of the research was on information accessed through senior management and staff with designated equal opportunities responsibilities. Other members of academic and support staff were also interviewed and a questionnaire was sent to all full-time academic staff, 10 per cent of the part-time academic staff and 10 per cent of the support staff. Members of the research team also attended relevant committee meetings and other events. We scrutinized current versions of equal opportunities policies related to gender, ethnicity and people with disabilities and a number of other public documents which reflect Borough College practice on equal opportunities issues. A partial staff audit was also available from the college's own monitoring procedures. As a result of publicity within the college, several people contacted us and were either subsequently interviewed, or their written comments were included as part of the evidence. And, of course, there were lots of informal conversations which helped to build up a picture of the development of equal opportunities in the college.

What emerged was a picture of a college in several transitions, building its approach to equal opportunities on the pioneer work of the Inner London Education Authority (ILEA). The impact of ILEA on the development and implementation of equal opportunities policies for teaching and support staff cannot be over-estimated. ILEA developed explicit equality and anti-discrimination policies together with guidance for putting them into effect; offered training programmes related to equality issues of gender, race, sexual orientation and disability; provided funds for the appointment of equal opportunities coordinators in ILEA institutions; and supported women already active in promoting equal opportunities, resulting in a network of women in ILEA committed to improving equality of opportunity.

The various reorganizations in the college had some implications for equitable staffing, but at the beginning of the project the most important equal opportunities structures included:

- explicit policies for language, harassment, gender, race and disability;
- cross-college coordinators for gender, race and disability located in a staff training and equality unit;

- committees for gender, race and disability accountable to the academic board;
- a principal's working group for Black staff;
- procedures for staff recruitment and appointment, and for complaints of harassment.

Consistency was facilitated by many staff having previously been ILEA employees and therefore being accustomed to debates about equal opportunities, though, as becomes apparent later, staff were not complacent about the situation.

The college appeared to work hard to promote equality in staffing policies and was relatively successful in developing an ethos supportive of those who belonged to its community. Its policies and practices removed major potential injustices but continued to explore what further needed to be done. College policy was unequivocal in requiring staff commitment to equal opportunities (as the following excerpt from the tutor handbook 1993–4 shows), requiring that all teachers working for the college:

(a) are aware of the college's commitment to equality.
(b) are thoroughly familiar with the college's equality policies . . .
(c) understand that they are required to support the college's equality policies by making them an integral part of their work.

The rest of this section looks at policies concerning language, race, gender and disability, and the structures and post holders that supported the development and implementation of these policies. All the policies were being reviewed during the period of the project to meet the changing needs of staff in the new tertiary college structure. What is significant is that staff were *re-drafting* policies. Debate had moved on to deal with slight modifications and subtleties of presentation. Staff no longer debated the necessity for policies. The exception was the initial foray into discussion of an anti-heterosexist policy; at the end of the project it had not been clearly resolved whether or not a separate policy was required.

There was clear guidance on the use of language in all college activities. Many staff at all levels were well informed and committed to equal opportunities so it was highly improbable that any public college document would contain sexist or racist language. The language used in the written policies themselves emphasized action, specifying behaviours which would be opposed: 'We are committed to taking positive action to identify and eradicate sexism and to develop equality for women throughout the College.' The titles of such policies – anti-sexism, anti-racism (and possibly in the future anti-heterosexism) – emphasized precise targets.

As we have seen, the college constructed practical equal opportunities guidelines for staff on the explicit premise that all staff had responsibility to tackle discrimination and promote equality of opportunity. Often policy statements were followed by specific issues and advice. For example:

Adequate arrangements must be made for all course members to participate. No group of people should be allowed to dominate the proceedings. No individuals should feel they are being excluded or treated with less respect . . . In doing this teachers/trainers should bear in mind that men are likely to interrupt during a conversation between a man and a woman . . . Every effort must be made to encourage and enable a person with a disability to participate fully

Guidelines also provided advice on the choice and production of materials, the use of language (e.g. 'replace mastery' with 'competence'; use 'people with disabilities' rather than 'the disabled') and general avoidance of stereotypes (e.g. 'do not assume that Black people are from overseas or that all colleagues are heterosexual'). Codes of practice made clear that discriminatory behaviour would not be tolerated in the college and procedures for making complaints or reporting incidents were available in briefing packs produced by the staff training and equality unit for academic and support staff. The packs also suggested that staff could contact the unit for further advice and support. The college established procedures to record, report and monitor incidents and occurrences which were against the college's equality policies.

Harassment

Staff (and students) were encouraged to report all instances of violence, abuse, harassment and other behaviour which appeared to contravene equality policies and codes of practice. To make the process of reporting as simple as possible an incident form on which to set out brief details of the incident was available throughout the college in site offices and libraries. The deputy principal dealt with all formally recorded incidents and equal opportunities post holders were required to report incidents even if the person experiencing violence, harassment or abuse did not wish to pursue the matter further and/or wished to remain anonymous. The relevant equality coordinator was expected to provide the individual(s) with support and advice and the head of site was also informed in case immediate action was necessary. Actions taken were monitored and referred regularly to the central management team, equal opportunities committees and academic board. The guidelines encouraged staff to take action and not to remain passive observers of any incident which might be in breach of equality policies.

Disability

Policy relevant to people with disabilities was directed primarily at students, with only limited applicability to staff. In developing the policy, members of the disability sub-committee tried to strike a balance between feasibility within existing resources and the most effective ways to encourage equal opportunities in this area. For example, the desirable practice of placing advertisements for staff vacancies in specialist publications for disabled people was acknowledged as being difficult in times of economic stringency. The policy addressed publicity and marketing, administrators, curriculum access, staffing and staff training.

Policy relevant to staff included determination to correct the historical imbalance and under-representation of people with disabilities in the workforce by establishing a recruitment target of 6 per cent of staff across all grades being people with disabilities by 1995. Candidates with disabilities who met the selection criteria were to be automatically short-listed. If appointed,

> the College will do everything in its power to provide and/or facilitate the provision of equipment adaptations and other additional support to enable candidates with disabilities to take up their appointments ... [and] will assume that once appointed staff with disabilities are progressing/developing within the organisation as quickly as their non-disabled colleagues.
>
> (Borough College Policy and Implementation Plan, May 1992)

Access to buildings was a major problem for those with physical disabilities but modifications to all sites were considered too expensive for the college. However, the disability sub-committee agreed to recommend to the academic board that an approved accommodation consultant should be engaged prior to any future building works or modifications.

Another important feature of disability policy covered staff training, primarily in relation to offering support to lecturers working directly with students with disabilities and/or learning difficulties in mainstream courses or courses specifically for students with disabilities. As the policy asserted that the integration of members of the college with disabilities was the responsibility of everyone on the staff, priority was given to the dissemination of disability awareness through training days available to all staff within the college. Organization of training as well as monitoring of the effectiveness of policy related to disabilities was the responsibility of the designated coordinator. As extra money became available to support students with disabilities, it was used for staff training and for providing special facilities, and there could also be long-term benefits for staff with disabilities.

Anti-racism

The college policy on 'race' was set out in 1985 as a policy for multi-ethnic education in line with the practice of Inner London Education Authority. Subsequently, it became a 'race equality' policy and from 1993–4 was presented in terms of targets, activities and expected outcomes. In 1985 the multi-ethnic policy had pronounced the college as unequivocally opposed to racism in all its forms, refined its terminology and urged the college to appoint more staff from minority ethnic groups.

The policy revised during 1993–4, after prolonged consultation, provided a practical framework of intent. Targets especially relevant to staff were:

- review of the college's community liaison strategy;
- continued development of the strategy for race equality at the site where there had been racist incidents;
- recommendations for a future network of persons to promote race equality initiatives in the college;
- recommendations about future ethnic monitoring of college staff.

The summary of the targets, activities and outcomes detailed above formed part of an 'Equal Opportunities: Race-Strategic Plan 1993–96', which also referred to: reviewing staff appointments procedures in terms of equal opportunities; continuing progress towards staffing targets of 30 per cent of staff at all levels being Black people by 1995; and formative use of the outcomes of the case study. It also undertook to review staff development, paying particular attention and giving priority to the development and training needs of Black staff, so that they could compete for middle and senior management positions, and to the implementation of the staff appraisal system.

Anti-sexism

College policy concerning gender has been subject to prolonged debate and revision within the relevant committee over the whole period of the project. During this time, it would have been difficult for any member of the college to have obtained a copy of the detailed policy. The revised policy completed in spring 1994 covered: marketing, publicity and the community; student admissions; the curriculum; counselling, advice and guidance; the environment; employers; the college as employer; and sexual harassment and violence. It reasserted the college's commitment to systematically identifying, combating and dismantling sexism in all its forms, redefining sexism as a process of discrimination reflecting a power relationship based on male superiority. Institutional sexism was also defined as a form of sexism whereby formal institutional structures and priorities reinforce the power relationship which perpetuates the notion of male superiority.

The college expressed the intention to review and monitor constantly for sexism all aspects of college life, including the institutional structure and all college practices and procedures. Also on the agenda was the continued development of strategies to combat sexism, including positive action programmes to deliver genuine equality to all female students and staff. These statements of intent were to be regularly reviewed and targets were to be set against each statement of intent, pertinent to staff working or wanting to work in the college. For example, the section on student admissions included advice on interviewing, monitoring admissions and enrolments; and environmental issues covered the extent to which Borough College is a comfortable and welcoming place for women, with space, facilities and security staff to support female college members. The section on the college as an employer covered advertising and appointments, work practices and procedures that might disadvantage women (probation, appraisal, career development) and devoted much attention to the issues concerning part-time and fractional staff. Short-term contracts appeared to be on the increase for certain administrative staff (most of whom are women), who thereby might have diminished entitlement to sick leave, holidays etc. There was discussion on how this might be alleviated.

A major point in the policy was that maternity pay should be comparable to sick pay and that paternity pay should be extended from 5 to 15 days for teaching staff to fall into line with support staff. Policy emphasis was on establishing good employment practices enabling staff with children to combine work and home responsibilities.

As stated earlier, this policy had been developed on assumptions that sexism favours men. Nevertheless, the statements of intent referred explicitly to two areas where men could be treated unjustly: areas of the curriculum which are not traditional for men and paternity rights. Otherwise the sex equality policy concentrated on areas likely to promote the interests of women and bring them up to equal status with male college employees.

Cross-college coordinators

The development and implementation of each of the equal opportunities policies was designated a cross-college responsibility of a senior lecturer. Coordinators for gender, 'race' and disability were based in the staff training and equality unit; each had a small budget and each was accountable to the deputy principal. There had been a permanent post (half-time) at senior lecturer level for racial equality since 1984 (then termed multi-ethnic coordinator). Similarly there had been a coordinator for gender equality since the mid-1980s (upgraded to senior lecturer in 1990) and a full-time post for disability since 1992. The job specification for each coordinator was broadly similar: advising and facilitating implementation of good practices likely to eliminate all aspects of discrimination in the college.

Equal opportunities coordination?

A coordinator was included on each appointment panel and supported appointed staff by organizing training and by being proactive on their behalf and in response to their requests. The coordinators worked in close liaison with each other, with the deputy principal to ensure that procedures were followed and with staff to ensure that the curriculum was developed to raise student awareness. The same individuals had always occupied the coordinator posts, although the gender equality coordinator had taken a year's secondment and a gap for maternity leave.

Such continuity helped the coordinators to build on their previous experience and develop knowledge and understanding in their own field of responsibility. The disability coordinator, a white male, had worked with students with special educational needs for over 20 years. The co-ordinator for racial equality, who classified himself as Black, developed his awareness and understanding of Black issues in his previous post as a lecturer in communications, writing his MA dissertation on 'race' and the curriculum. The post holder for gender, a white woman, began her career at the college while on placement for an FE qualification. She was subse-quently taken on as a part-time lecturer in 1980 and helped to write an anti-sexist policy for the college. The coordinator had specialized in gender-related work for many years.

Another factor in the development and implementation of coherent equality policies across the college was the location of the coordinators together in the staff development and equality unit. This enabled the head of staff development and the post holders for equality issues to work in close collaboration. As a group, the three special posts and head of staff development had both high visibility and a high workload. The team were kept well informed about individual initiatives as any one of the team might be the equal opportunities representative on appointments panels or other committees.

The structure outlined above was in place during the project case study. There had been a deafening silence on the future of the equal opportu-nities post holders and a perceived downgrading of equal opportunities issues in early consultation papers subsequent to the merger with the AEI. However, as a result of the consultation exercise, the gender and race posts were 'reinstated' and relocated in a new quality and equality division, though the proposal was to reduce the amount of time allowed away from teaching for the posts. The new job specifications had not been finalized by the end of the project and while it appeared that monitoring would become a major part of the newly constituted posts, it was clear that the post holders would no longer be involved in case work. The post for disability was not to be located in the same unit but was to be more closely linked with students in the new faculty of client services. As with other posts at senior management, head of school and senior lecturer level, all the equality posts were advertised for competitive application in the spring of 1994.

Equal opportunities committees and the implementation of policies

The team of coordinators did not work in isolation. There was a sub-committee for each policy reporting to the deputy principal and from

September 1992 reporting through her to the academic board. Previously the gender and race equality coordinators had been *ex officio* members of the academic board. All these committees were chaired by the deputy principal. The committees each comprised all three equality post holders, and each had representatives from technicians, administrative and learning resource staff and students; they steered and supported the coordinator in developing, implementing and monitoring equal opportunities policies. However, membership and attendance varied over the project and the latter tended to be low.

Policies developed in committee went to faculties for comment and then to the academic board for ratification. Faculties were then expected to make implementation plans with the support, if required, of the appropriate equality coordinator. This very extensive participation in the formulation of policy was seen by one member of the college as, in itself, a device by which an institution reaches people and opens up discussion: 'There is very little point in having any policy unless an extended period of formulation and consultation has taken place.'

Another important feature of the college was an association for self-identified Black staff, originally set up as a principal's working group with quasi-legal status within the college. The group acted as both a support for Black staff and a pressure group in the institution, providing a collective Black voice to inform the management. Black staff were given time to attend one meeting each term, and the group was represented at the academic board and its sub-committees and on interviewing panels – although it sometimes proved difficult to ensure that a Black member of staff could take up the working group's place on interviewing panels, especially where these were convened at short notice. The coordinator for race equality was also a member of the working group (but was not the chair). Although this was apparently not very well attended (the research team did not have access), the agenda and minutes of each meeting were circulated to all Black staff and recommendations from the working group contributed to changes in recruitment procedures over the few years leading up to the project.

Staff recruitment and development

The college's recruitment procedures attempted to ensure that qualifications required were only such as were necessary for the job. Advertisements were placed in papers likely to be read by different ethnic groups, and when application forms were submitted, ethnic monitoring and disability references were removed from application forms before short-listing so that appointments panels drew up the short list unaware of an individual's ethnicity or disability. The personnel officer was responsible for keeping records of applications, short-listing and appointments for subsequent monitoring by gender and ethnicity.

Borough College wanted to ensure that all interviewing panels included a Black member of staff. At one time the equal opportunities committees were also represented on interviewing panels. In the selection of the interviewing panel, the aim was to ensure that not all interviewers were white and male and that therefore the interviewee would feel more at ease in having at least one person of the same gender and from a minority ethnic group on the panel. Interview panel members received a set of papers for short-listed candidates and a set of criteria for each appointment. A typical question asked by one regular panel member was 'How would you incorporate equal opportunities in your day-to-day work in your department?'

Staff development received a substantial budget from the college and a staff appraisal scheme had been in place since the beginning of the academic year 1992–3. Staff development in the college included career development for individual members of staff as well as entitlement of all staff to access to a share of the resources available for staff development. Staff seeking funding for staff development were required to address equal opportunities in their application forms. The head of staff development worked with the post holders for equal opportunities to vet and support the design of staff entitlement forms and initiatives.

New staff were expected to attend an induction programme and were given a comprehensive pack of staff development materials, which included details of equal opportunities policies and guidelines for trainers and teachers. The pack also included guidelines for staff mentors and a checklist of what new staff needed to know about their jobs, their responsibilities and rights as employees, the structure of the college, personnel and college policies (including anti-racist, anti-sexist and special educational needs policies). All of these seemed designed to make the new members of staff comfortable and effective in their jobs. The briefing pack also detailed what could be expected from line managers and senior staff.

The college's overall investment in equal opportunities was therefore considerable: salaries for staff development and equality post holders, time for committees and for meetings of the Black staff working group, representation on interviewing panels, advertising budgets spread across a range of minority ethnic press, investment in induction programmes and materials and other staff development activities.

Extent of success

Did the policies work? Evidence suggests that they did. The college established codes of behaviour and procedures intolerant of overt discrimination. Policies were documented and there was clear management support, guidelines and resources to support the implementation of policies. We had originally chosen the college for its equal opportunities reputation, a view put somewhat modestly by one informant as 'this college has hitherto not been as racist as others'. Most of our informants confirmed this kind of statement – that the college was still better than most – quickly adding that there was still room for improvement. The FEFC, reporting on an inspection carried out at the beginning of the 1993–4 session, confirmed this view:

> The college is justifiably proud of its record of developing and promoting equal opportunities. Policies relating to students with learning difficulties and/or disabilities, and race and sex equality are comprehensive. They offer excellent guidance for staff and students on the achievement of good practice in all areas of the college's work. Instilling awareness of equality issues is a significant feature of the staff-development programme.

The report also commented favourably on the college's commitment to the needs of the community in providing an extensive English language programme for speakers of other languages and a substantial investment in crèche and nursery provision. However, the report also acknowledged that demand for childcare provision from those wishing to attend the college exceeded existing availability.

The explicit policies and associated practices had, according to many of the staff who talked to us, increased awareness of staff as evidenced in the cultural mix and the increased number of women throughout the college. Other practical examples of policies being effective included feedback to unsuccessful job applicants, the prompt way in which racist remarks were dealt with and resources available to support equal opportunities policies.

At the same time it was acknowledged that there were pockets of resistance among staff and that practice was variable. Policies provided useful formal statements of intent and prevented the institution or individual from practising discrimination. However, adherence to policies depended on interpretations within each faculty or section of the college and could be applied intermittently in other senses. We now provide further detail about harassment, staffing and other practices in the college to give a clearer idea of the impact of the equal opportunities policies.

Incidence of harassment

Ten incidents of harassment involving staff were reported between February 1990 and November 1993. Most of them were complaints made by students of victimization or racism by staff. There were two instances of staff being harassed: one by homophobic comments, the other by sexual harassment. Both staff and students were subject to abuse outside the college (four incidents, three of which involved physical assault by members of the public).

The procedure for complaint against harassment seemed to work sufficiently well for some individuals to use it. The year with the fewest complaints lodged was 1993, showing that the procedure did not necessarily encourage continuing floods of complaints. Three observations on the harassment figures follow.

First, not all cases of harassment are reported, possibly because of the formality of procedure underpinned by the policy. In questionnaire responses, almost half the respondents reported having experienced discrimination, but only half of these had reported this formally. Black and Asian women were most likely to have indicated on the questionnaire that they had experienced discrimination, and Black and Asian men least likely. Interestingly, one-fifth of the respondents reported that their own actions or those of staff for whom they were responsible had been challenged on the grounds of discrimination. Second, there were few formal complaints of sexism, though evidence from the questionnaire indicated that while there were some instances of sexism (15 reported in the questionnaire), people seemed disinclined to report such incidents. Third, the college's evident willingness to take action encouraged staff to follow the various recommended forms and strategies to avoid discriminatory behaviour.

Staffing

There were about 200 full-time teaching staff and about 300 part-time for the main period of this case study. In terms of ethnicity about 20 per cent of all staff were Black. At the beginning of the project the principal was aiming to achieve the borough council's target of an overall 30 per cent of staff from minority ethnic groups, to correspond with the local population. Although roughly the same numbers of men and women were employed, the distribution of women and ethnic minorities was uneven through the grades. For example, 40 per cent of administrative and clerical staff but only 15 per cent of teaching staff were Black. Additionally, faculties had uneven profiles: one had practically all white women, another had a very high proportion of Black students with a predominantly white staff.

Equal opportunities monitoring also proved uneven. There was no ethnic or gender monitoring of part-time staff and the only regular data were kept on staff ethnicity and gender in relation to the grade of full-time and fractional staff at the time of their appointment. Ethnicity of new recruits was sought voluntarily and was therefore incomplete. Maintaining a comparative record over the years proved difficult because of changes in classification. The deputy principal and 'race' post holder had agreed the classifications of existing staff based on their knowledge of staff, and used the category 'others' when undecided.

Ethnicity

The proportion of Black teaching staff remained at between 14 and 15 per cent over the period of the project. This was rather different from the dramatic increase in the proportion of Black staff, from 5.4 per cent in 1985 to nearly 15 per cent in 1993. The halt to this increase was partly accounted for by the low number of new posts and the large number of staff who were redeployed as a result of mergers – only one of the 12 lecturing staff from the sixth form centre who joined the college was Black.

Greatest gains over the nine years from 1985 to 1993 were made by the Black female group. However, there was only one Black member of staff out of 15 in the management spine, 11 out of 55 (20 per cent) at senior lecturer level, and 27 out of 192 (14 per cent) at lecturer grade. Some expressed disappointment that no additional Black staff appointments had been made on the management spine over the period of this study, as future increases were unlikely given that there were so few Black staff on the lecturing grade.

Compared with lecturing staff, there was a larger proportion of Black staff in administrative and technical support areas. Whereas Black staff made up 19.3 per cent of all staff in 1991, they comprised 28 per cent of all support staff but only 14.4 per cent of lecturing staff. None of the Black support staff in 1991 reached the top two grades of administration or the top three grades on the technicians' scale. (These monitoring figures made no reference to part-time contract staff, the greatest proportion of whom were women.)

Gender

A brief analysis of gender figures over the same period of two and a half years from 1991 shows a similar picture of imbalance in the more senior positions (Table 2.1). Although this suggests a fairly even split between male and female staff, only three of the ten senior managers in 1991 were women (all of them white). The deputy principal was a woman with a high profile in the college. The longer-term realization of the college drive towards more equality was visible in that 22 of the 39 senior lecturers in 1991 were female, three of them Black staff. By 1993, there were eight women and seven men on the management spine, which included heads of faculties: only one a Black man, and no Black women. At senior lecturer grade, there were 32 women and 23 men by 1993, including eight Black women.

There were areas of dissatisfaction about gender issues. In particular, there was the view expressed in an internal report, *Black Female Perspective* (1991), that Black female support staff remained relatively powerless. The study of the perceptions of Black female staff drew on evidence collated over one and a half years on topics such as appointments, time released from teaching for administration and code of conduct between staff and students. It indicated Black female staff's dissatisfaction with their low recognition and status within the college. Some reactions to the report

Table 2.1 Gender summary of lecturing staff (full-time and fractional posts)

	Lecturing staff		
	Female	*Male*	*All*
Black			
1991	15	13	28
1993	24	15	39
White			
1991	74	89	163
1993	116	107	223
Other			
1991	2	1	3
1993	0	2	2
All			
1991	91	103	194
1993	140	122	262

were very antagonistic: either they wanted 'to rubbish the report in male academic terms' or they adopted 'a more laid back, cool approach', which suggested that this was a normal (and therefore unthreatening) part of any college existence. Interviews with Black teaching staff for the project suggested that *Black Female Perspective* reflected aspects of reality for Black women at the college; for example, the existence of long established white networks and 'persistent and subtle forces which have a lot of power and wish to retain the status quo'. On the other hand, a white female academic suggested that the study had been a poorly researched piece and a Black lecturer reported how colleagues opposed the credibility of the report, did not feel able to talk to Black women about it and, instead, expressed their anger to white women colleagues. 'They were challenging what Black women were saying. That is precisely the problem. What Black women are saying is invalidated because Black women say it' (Black female academic).

Support staff

Data for support staff presented a different picture. Figures for 1991 and 1992 showed that there were more than twice as many female as male support staff. In March 1992, women made up 71 per cent of the total support staff, doing, for example, typing and word processing, administrative and clerical work, and library duties. Add the part-time support staff to these full-time and fractional staff, and it is apparent that there were many more females than males employed at the lower grades in the college, although some of the most senior full-time support staff posts were occupied by women.

Significantly, these figures omit any reference to services contracted out of the college, which included catering and security officers. The college undertook to ensure that contracted out services met the equal opportunities guidelines and policies of the college, but the potential effects were marked, as may be judged from the fact that before contracting out the canteen managers were all female but subsequently were predominantly male. It was also perhaps inevitable that staff in the services which had been contracted out were among the most vulnerable, as the college was obliged to accept the lowest tender. This had a special bearing on equality considerations, since most of the staff in the contracted services were Black.

No formal monitoring of staff with disabilities was carried out although there was a section for job applicants to complete (voluntarily) on the application form. The post holder for disability, other than as advisor, had no responsibility in recruitment of staff. Only two or three staff were known to the coordinator as having some kind of impairment likely to need support – two with hearing loss and another who was blind. The blind tutor, who had originally been taken on as a lecturer in English, was later employed to support blind students and was provided with extra facilities himself. An argument was put forward by several staff that students saw lecturers as role models and therefore it was as important to have some staff with disabilities as it was to have people from other underrepresented groups.

Overall the staffing patterns at Borough College confirmed stereotypical employment patterns in manual and clerical grades, with only half of the target of 30 per cent Black lecturing staff, held in the borough as being an appropriate reflection of the local population, having been achieved. Nevertheless, this was a higher proportion of Black staff than in most colleges of further education.

Part-time staff

Discussions with staff at the college and questionnaire responses gave emphasis to part-time staff in the context of equal opportunities. There had been a large increase in the numbers of part-time staff, resulting especially from the merger with the adult education institute, culminating in a total of about 500 part-timers (categorized as working from 2 to 12 hours a week). This represented the equivalent of 25 full-time staff, compared with the previous situation with 9 full-time equivalents. The sheer numbers and the temporary nature of part-time work provided problems in terms of organization and monitoring.

Converting part-time (temporary) posts to fractional (permanent) posts was prioritized for sex equality reasons, though a different equal opportunities issue emerged if posts were converted without being advertised. Part-timers did not have access to a staff development programme; neither did they have the same entitlements to pension rights and sick leave. It was difficult for part-time staff, who were spread across the various sites of the college, to feel that they could participate fully in college developments. The existence of such a large group of part-time staff is likely to constitute a major challenge to any organization with a commitment to achieving more equitable conditions of service.

Examples of equal opportunities in practice

Staff development and training

The project elicited information about the knowledge and attitude of Borough College staff to equal opportunities. It affirmed that there was little complacency about equality issues. Even when they were satisfied with policies, staff responded with demands for improved implementation and identification of gaps where discrimination was seen to persist. There was an emphasis on updating and implementing what were seen as good policies, and disability was perceived as having too low a profile. A few respondents expressed the need to explore social class equality issues and gay and lesbian rights. Most respondents supported training for staff at all levels 'from the canteen to the principal's office', including those with responsibilities for equality issues. This training, it was argued, should be partly to do with raising and maintaining levels of awareness about actual or potential discrimination, especially in more subtle forms.

Training should also provide staff with support to deal with different forms of discrimination, possibly with published guidelines, with those who had experienced such training cascading it outwards both to their colleagues and to trainers. Just over half of those who responded to the questionnaire indicated that they had received training in equal opportunities. However, the training varied in quality from a single talk or a session during an induction course to more sustained workshops in recruitment and interview techniques or an extensive programme of training. Topics had included awareness raising in relation to disability, race and gender, and workshop sessions on how to deal with racism or sexual harassment at work.

Seventy per cent of questionnaire respondents agreed that one of the tasks of the staff training and equality unit was that it 'should meet the needs of women and black staff in terms of personal career development'. However, it was suggested that this goal had not yet been met; neither were there effective monitoring procedures. Staff who disagreed with this position argued that women were already adequately served and it was men who were being disadvantaged. The language in which some of these 'negative' replies were couched suggests that certain individuals (mostly white males) felt strongly that women and Black staff attracted sufficient, if not too much, attention compared with other staff.

Respondents had three views of the usefulness of equal opportunities post holders: supporters of current approaches to equal opportunities; those who disapproved of the concept of separate post holders; and those who approved the concept but deemed the present state of affairs unsatisfactory. Over half the respondents supported post holders and their role, seeing important gains from active efforts to promote change, and a rise in the profile and status of equal opportunities. It was perceived as essential to have individuals responsible and accountable for equal opportunities policies, who would coordinate action and provide staff development. Being available to take up complaints and to advise other college staff and students was another feature of the role. Most positively,

the gender, disability and race committee have met, discussed, changed, implemented many issues . . . need a senior lecturer for each area to carry it further into management. Senior lecturers have been experts, committed and positive in their work.

(Black female lecturer)

Some thought that the post holders had too low a profile and were not sufficiently proactive because of insufficient time and power, and because of their marginality from the college management structure. Monitoring and rigorous research into the effectiveness of equal opportunities policies were perceived as lacking in the college, particularly in pin-pointing key issues in future college policy developments.

Other staff considered the equal opportunities posts to be divisive, in that their impact on different groups was variable. Such views may be summarized by the following comment:

Appointing staff to these posts has a two-fold negative effect:

1. It is tokenism which encourages compliance – 'We have dealt with *equality* because we have a policy and we have a post.'
2. The post holders are perceived by other staff as not having much to do, causing resentment.

(White male senior lecturer)

Some asserted that individuals labelled with responsibility for equality issues acted as a brake to other staff devising and assessing policy and change – it was not seen as their problem.

The equality committees at Borough College were key in formulating and pursuing the implementation of equal opportunities policies and in maintaining a high profile for equal opportunities. Topics discussed at gender committee meetings provide evidence of the range of interests:

- the perceived need for a policy on anti-heterosexism;
- withdrawal of the gender representative (along with other equal opportunities post holders) from the governors working party, staff recruitment, curriculum standards and pastoral committees;
- 'traditional' sex-role recruitment patterns of students;

- preparations to mark International Women's Day;
- opportunities for work shadowing women managers;
- reinstatement of equal opportunities representatives on appointment panels;
- staff appraisal;
- maternity entitlement.

The committee structure was also criticized by staff on several counts:

- there were too few resources to support the members;
- committees had not always been effective and had usually been isolated from the rest of the college, providing little feedback;
- committees could be marginalized, especially as their membership had few staff at senior grades.

The areas that generated most staff comment were related to conditions of employment – recruitment, interviewing, promotion and support for career development – with the acknowledgement that the college had already implemented sensitive staff recruitment procedures.

Difficulties in effecting equitable staffing

Overall, staff felt that the paperwork had been done but issues were being kept at a safe distance. *Black Female Perspective*, policy statements and academic board minutes were generally seen as 'documents which talk about people, their perceptions, attitudes and upbringing'. Black staff who had been at the college for a long time claimed weariness from the constant struggle against racism; a member of teaching staff realized on her return from the West Indies that she was 'tired of this whole issue. Over there my colour did not need debate.'

Initiatives, such as the Black staff group, seemed to have both advantages and disadvantages. One woman felt that if she attended she was showing her white friends that they were different. However, if Black staff did not go to the group, Black colleagues might shun them as 'coconuts' (Black on the outside, white in the middle). One informant, a Black female lecturer, suggested that many Black staff take refuge in not talking to other people about their concerns. Criticism of the Black group also came from those precluded by colour from attending the group: the group was perceived as 'a bit like the Masons; this built another barrier but we should break down barriers'.

While they have undoubtedly been reduced by explicit college policies, what remains uncertain is whether racism and sexism have been driven underground and become subtle, or whether they would have been challenged by staff without the policy framework. For example, feelings about the *Black Female Perspective* report ran so high that one male lecturer, who had never been known to attend meetings outside his teaching hours, felt compelled to stay behind for the open meeting!

Thus, on the one hand, Borough College could be judged as having good equal opportunities policies in terms of language, recruitment, staff from a mixture of ethnic groups and training on gender and race issues. On the other hand, it was sometimes difficult to obtain copies of equality policies, at least two administrators were of the impression that policies ignored practical issues such as flexi-time and there was still the fact that senior administrative positions were predominantly occupied by white female staff, with Afro-Caribbeans and Asians in more junior posts. Crèche facilities newly established on one site would not meet the needs of many staff. The crèche was for term time only and therefore inadequate for full-time support staff who work all year round. Moreover, the facilities were expensive (£50–70 per week) and therefore beyond the means of lower paid administrative staff and part-timers.

Some of the features of institutional culture which were 'enabling' and/ or 'disabling' in promoting equal opportunities at Borough College were identified by the project and are shown in Table 2.2 (see p. 36). This short list suggests that on the plus side there are policies, procedures and practices which promote equitable staffing and that equal opportunities policies which challenge and threaten established practices can expect opposition.

Shifting forwards, not backwards

Borough College is not new to equal opportunities activities but it became clear during the project that even when basic principles were agreed and provided the basis for action, new issues emerged. Constant vigilance had to be maintained to avoid policy slippage. It was as if there is a continuing spiral and reformation, revisiting similar issues, such as recruitment, staff development and appraisal, from a point further on each time. Features identified by the project as conducive to progress in equality at Borough College are:

- the role of senior management;
- structures which require and facilitate good practice;
- a balance between staff dedicated to equality initiatives and expectations that all staff were responsible;
- monitoring procedures;
- allocation of resources to support equality;
- understanding that implementation of policies would change the incidence and focus of discrimination and conflict but not dissipate them entirely.

We now consider each of these in turn.

Table 2.2 Features of institutional culture

Enabling	Disabling
Institution's history.	Mergers and restructuring increased workload of people key in equity at the college.
Explicit policies affecting everyone in organization: all students, support staff, teaching staff.	Lack of systematic monitoring of staff in post, staff development, promotion.
Language for discourse on equality.	
Posts with specific responsibilities latterly supported within each faculty. Several 'champions'.	Assumptions and not debate about ways to increase equality issues.
	Lack of formal power for equality committees.
Commitment/coherent, coordinated policies across race/gender/sex-orientation/disability.	Increasing financial stringency threatens many activities/posts designed to discourage discrimination and increase equality.
Supported by senior management team.	
In-house training/staff development for all staff.	EO 'a profession', a career track.
	Staff profile still reflects inequality.
Black staff support group recognized by management.	Insufficient childcare facilities.
Some childcare facilities.	Many sites and dispersed staff and student population with many peripatetic staff. Not 'a campus'. Makes networking difficult for individuals and cost of running so many buildings expensive.
Procedures (designed for equity) in recruitment, interviewing and promotion as well as dealing with incidents of discrimination and harassment.	
	Many buildings inappropriate for large numbers of part-time staff with little voice.
Student profile of mixed ethnic groups a spur to match the staff profile.	Buildings mainly inaccessible to people with substantial physical disabilities.
Large number of staff committed to enhancing equality.	Senior manager responsible for equality and equality training also has many other commitments.
	EO post holders' lack of access to management information and decision-making.

Commitment of senior management

Senior management appears committed to ongoing development in matters concerning equal opportunities and to making that commitment explicit in publicly accessible policies and documents. At Borough College, 'clout' for this was attached to the deputy principal's office. As a member of college advisory group for this project said, 'an important criterion is access to resources and access to a power-base.'

However, if this is primarily the remit of one person only, the policy is vulnerable on three counts: resources, conflicts of interest and change of personnel. Tension has thus existed between commitment to equal opportunities and the smooth running of the institution. Commitment also has to be matched by sufficient resources to implement and to maintain the momentum of further development. While staff felt that the progress of equality was relatively safe with the current senior management (principal and deputy principal), there could be no guarantee that any eventual successors would take the same position.

Supporting structures

Equal opportunities can (should) be built into an organization's structures to facilitate good practice. These include sub-committees and staff to lead policy-making as well as appropriate means of dissemination of policies and methods of implementing them. Structures can facilitate or inhibit change, whatever stage of policy-making or implementation is involved.

Borough College had developed sub-committees and working parties to develop policy and strategy. Some staff still expressed the belief that policies were being formulated and debated only by select groups of people – the governing body and the gender committee – who were 'preaching to the committed'. But, in fact, policies and structures were precursors of procedures which have had a real impact on equality in the college. The way staff were treated when they applied for job or promotion, shortlisting and interview procedures, how complaints were dealt with – these were the kinds of events which seemed to determine the ethos of the college.

However, the existence of structures at one time is no guarantee for the future; structures can be amended fairly quickly. How can staff ensure that their organization does not move backwards?

Role of post holders for equal opportunities

In promoting activity concerned with enhancing equality for staff at the college, ILEA and subsequently the borough council and the college itself supported the appointment of staff specifically for the task. The post holders clearly stimulated thinking as well as dealing with reports of discrimination or inequity affecting staff. Each of these post holders had been a champion for a designated area – gender, race, disability – but they had also worked collaboratively with the head of staff development.

However, the appointment of specialist posts for equality could be perceived as inherently contradictory to ensuring that equality is everyone's concern and is concerned with everyday practices and procedures in college life. The danger in the latter approach is that 'everyone's responsibility' becomes 'no one's responsibility', yet at the point when this project ceased, the college was moving into a new phase whereby additional responsibility for equity was being devolved to faculties. This offered practical recognition of college policy that, for equity measures to be effective, responsibility has to be shared.

Monitoring and evaluation

Effective monitoring procedures were essential for the implementation of the policies agreed by the college. Each of the sub-committees directly concerned with equality issues included monitoring as part of its remit but as far as staff were concerned these analyses were incomplete. For example, part-time staff were an important part of the college, yet they were neglected in monitoring.

Allocation of resources

Resources are rarely thought to be sufficient. As we have seen, Borough College contributed a substantial part of its resources to equality issues. Staff development had a budget, part of which was allocated to equal opportunities as a separate budget for each post holder. Much of the resource available was in the form of *time* given by the deputy principal, equal opportunities post holders, the head of staff development and members of the various committees.

However, only the post holders had specified hours allocated to spend in this area. The job specification for the deputy principal (and from now on for other senior members of staff) included responsibility for equal opportunities but members of the various committees had no time specifically allocated to these activities. The dilemma seemed to be that the time required for equal opportunities related tasks seemed to increase, not decrease, in a successful organization. This suggests a need to monitor the actual time and money that is likely to be devoted to equal opportunities issues and to ensure that it is kept available.

Continuous struggle

Increasing awareness and action on implementing equal opportunities are not necessarily accompanied by a diminution of conflict in the organization; rather the reverse seems to be the case. Only when issues are on the overt institutional agenda can they be openly addressed. As a senior member of Borough College put it,

> Formulation of policy is the device itself by which an institution reaches people and opens up discussion . . . It is also useful to find out who is for and against that particular policy. It provides a diagnostic process which can lead to useful staff development activities.

At the same time, staff increase their expectations of what equal opportunities can mean in practice; as policies become successfully implemented and routine, so staff feel secure enough to ask for more and policies become outdated.

Concluding comments

Borough College, in our view, demonstrated a high level of awareness of the necessary policy and practices likely to enhance equality of staffing. The language of discussion was sophisticated and considerable resources were designated to support equal opportunities. There were few instances of overt discrimination and there were clear procedures for dealing with any that did occur. Nevertheless, even this college, with so many of the staff committed to equality of opportunity for staff (and students), could not relax. The college exemplified the continuing tensions and struggles facing staff committed to developing and working in an environment which had an ethos designed to be supportive of everyone belonging to that community. New difficulties were always emerging, stimulated by internal dissatisfactions or by external constraints and change.

Equal opportunities policies are concerned with identity, power and justice, and affect some of the most vulnerable individuals and groups in society as well as those who are less vulnerable but denied access to positions for reasons irrelevant to their qualifications and other specifications for employment. Borough College had policies and practices which removed major potential injustices and it continued to explore what else needed to be, and could be, done.

3

Town University: Case Study

Few researchers are granted the privilege of admittance to the 'inner sanctum' of a university. However, it was indicative of the dynamic ethos of Town University that at the research team's first meeting with two of its most senior managers, we were offered the chance to use an unusual research strategy, that of 'work shadowing' or 'tracking' the senior manager. During the several days that the shadowing took place, windows were opened on to a range of meetings, with revealing insights into relationships and strategies. We were able to record many chance encounters and informal meetings and were much impressed by the sense of awareness and understanding of equality issues that permeated discussions and actions within the university.

Equal opportunities practices appeared to be the norm and *unexceptional* for those working there. The strong commitment to policy appeared to create a culture of discussion, argument and, more significantly, *high expectations* – expectations which, perhaps inevitably, also produced high levels of dissatisfaction with certain aspects of university equal opportunities policy. People were surprised to learn that other higher education institutions did not enjoy a mix of policy and practice similar to that currently operating at Town University. Indeed, we were sometimes chastised by staff at the university for failing to recognize sexist language and behaviour. For example, after a meeting between the university and a local college to discuss possible amalgamation, we were urged to note the gender-specific language: 'Did you notice they [college staff] referred to Mr this and Mrs that?' Despite our awareness of a possible intention to create a good impression in front of the project team the remarks served to demonstrate the worth of much routine institutional business.

It also became clear to us that a committed and enthusiastic senior management team is helpful in developing workable equal opportunities policies and practices. At Town University, there appeared to be close consultation between the most involved senior managers and staff from the earliest stages of policy formulation. For example, one meeting we attended dealt with the combined launch of the equal opportunity, language and sex harassment policies. It was evident at the meeting that exhaustive discussion between senior management and the equal opportunities officers involved had preceded the meeting. Thus, from the outset, Town University presented us with an exciting case study opportunity, not only because of its reputation concerning equal opportunities but also because of its apparent institutional vigour.

Town University

The Town University is a 'new' university located in a busy county town close to important national transport systems. The university buildings occupy several sites close to the centre of town, less than a mile from a major British Rail junction. The buildings are situated less than ten minutes' walk from each other, although it has been recognized by the university that a campus criss-crossed by major roadways provides an obstacle to further expansion. The geographic centre of the university is, in fact, a very busy roundabout which is often difficult to negotiate quickly and safely. Hence, one recently relocated service experienced a reduction in student numbers when it moved to a building immediately adjacent to the roundabout.

The university has a high profile in the town as it continues to expand. However, the close proximity of the various centres presents an impression of intimacy and of a close-knit community. Thus, despite some difficulties of access to certain buildings, the location seems to encourage relatively easy communication between different groups of staff and students.

Before we examine the major themes arising from the case study, it should be noted that during the 18-month period of the project, there were several structural changes to the university. The most significant change followed the March 1992 Further and Higher Education Act, which abolished the division between the traditional universities and polytechnics. A unitary system of higher education was established and the polytechnic changed name and corporate status to become a university. The university also underwent substantial restructuring of academic and support services, with changes to the management structure which included the 'harmonization' of contracts for different staff groups. Additionally, several building projects necessitated relocation of departments, causing widespread disruption to staff and students. Although these changes may seem somewhat marginal to implementation of equal opportunities, it is important to note the institutional context of change within which people worked during the course of the case study.

The findings and outcomes of the Town University case study are presented here as a series of themes:

- history of 'champions', significant impact of senior management;
- wide-ranging policy structure for employment, gender, 'race' and language;
- outcomes and impact of equal opportunities policies;
- structures which support equal opportunities;
- rhetoric versus reality;
- policy priorities.

History of 'champions'

The development of equal opportunities at Town University illustrates the importance of the 'champion' in effective policy-making. The previous vice chancellor had started the ball rolling from his appointment in 1983, since when equal opportunities policy and practice has had a sustained history at the university. Certainly, for both students and staff, gender and racial equality have been 'live' issues for at least ten years. Initiatives on gender and 'race' have, however, developed in parallel, resulting in different outcomes and commitments. We therefore briefly examine the separate development of equal opportunities policies relating to 'race' and gender from a historical perspective in order to understand present structures and practices.

In 1985 the Race Equality Unit (REQU) was established using Section 11 funding and employing eight 'race' equality staff. The unit had the remit of expanding, for minority ethnic staff and students, research opportunities, student and staff development, access to higher education and curriculum development. In 1990, the REQU was closed in accordance with the 'permeation' model of change whereby its six permanent staff were transferred to the faculties, taking their equal opportunity remit with them. A further eight Section 11 posts were created in the faculties to promote minority ethnic access to a variety of disciplines. The Centre for Racial Equality (CRE) was established in 1990, primarily to offer specialist advice and counselling to students. It continues the work of the REQU and is an important focus, in the university, for 'race' equality issues. Notably, the university (when a polytechnic) was the first higher education institution to introduce ethnic monitoring.

The previous vice chancellor also initiated moves towards eradicating gender inequality within the university. Soon after his appointment, he sponsored an internal report on the conditions and needs of women in the institution. Subsequently, the Equal Opportunities Committee (EOC) was constituted to spearhead policy initiatives in employment, language and sexual harassment. Inevitably, there have been problems in progress towards equal opportunities for women since, as the internal study produced in 1988 pointed out, 'a movement for equality once embarked on is so disturbing'. Indeed, in 1987, the EOC resigned *en masse* in protest at the management's perceived lack of commitment to equal opportunities.

At this point, an independent researcher was invited to examine the sex equality policy process and to make recommendations for future development. This third internal report meticulously and exhaustively traced the apparently tortuous process of equal opportunity policy-making through various committees and commented at length on the relatively disadvantaged position of women within the institution. Key recommendations from that report, such as the creation of a Women's Unit, have since been implemented by the university. The report also remarked on the 'poverty of the statistics' available and the difficulties of obtaining accurate information on women's position in the institution. As a consequence, the university's personnel section now regularly monitors staff by age, disability, sex, ethnicity and job description. The university has continued to prioritize gender issues, by, for example, the secondment of a full-time officer to deal with sex harassment issues.

At Town University responsibility for the development and implementation of equal opportunity policies lies at the most senior management levels and this has brought enormous benefits to the policy-making process. An illustration of how important this can be is the arrangements made for the launch of three policy documents – on equal opportunity, sexual harassment and language. A briefing meeting was held for the relevant equal opportunity representatives to discuss the launch and it was decided that recommendations would be made to the EOC about sending information on the policies to all university staff together with a personal memo from the vice chancellor. The memo was an unusual procedure, used in this case to emphasize the serious nature of the policies. Significantly, the vice chancellor was involved in the briefing discussion and had also been present at previous meetings, at which the fine details of policy and procedure were argued through.

Thus the vice chancellor's specific role in the university and his evident personal commitment to equal opportunities enabled swift and immediate action and decisions to be taken for promoting equal opportunities. It is unlikely that many other vice chancellors are as actively involved in such detailed aspects of policy-making, and there is no doubt that such commitment is one reason for the very high profile of equality issues in the university and nationally. However, the duties of senior management are not always compatible with the aims of equal opportunity policies. For example, it might be difficult to combine the perceived necessity for firm, efficient management with the visible promotion of equal opportunities which aims to give a voice to 'minority' and less powerful groups. At present what seems to be happening is that, at Town University, strategy on equal opportunities simultaneously 'enables' and 'disables' those very groups for which the policies are created.

The power and influence of senior management certainly enables policy to be transformed into visible changes in practice. Other less powerful policy-actors, excluded from the formulation of policy, expressed frustration that their views and expertise are not acknowledged, nor their efforts duly rewarded. For example, initiatives may be blocked for reasons that are unclear to some staff because of management influence at senior committee level. 'We were moving to a vote but it was clear the chair wanted it retained. He stated "this committee is advisory to me, therefore I will make the decisions", and no vote was taken. We thought, why bother with discussions?' (Female EOC member).

Wide range of policies

Town University is a recognized 'brand leader' in the field of equal opportunities, rightly so in our view, and is one of only a handful of higher education institutions in the UK that operate, and strive to implement, advanced equal opportunity strategies and developments. Policy dissemination and implementation has also been a key to continuing good practice. Equal opportunities affect staff in the university through wide-ranging means, including:

- mission statement;
- equal opportunity policy;
- policies for language and academic affairs;
- employment policies;
- sex harassment/harassment policy and procedures;
- Women's Unit and women's officers;
- Centre for Women in Technology, Design and Manufacture;
- Centre for Racial Equality;
- Centre for Professional Ethics;
- charter for management;
- equal opportunity committee structure;
- committed senior management team;
- in-house expertise for staff training.

Attempts have been made to deliver equal opportunities in the context of a 'comfortable environment'. This has led to a raised level of awareness of equal opportunity issues among staff, as the following comments illustrate.

I have worked at other universities and [the University] does have a greater awareness of equal opportunities.

(Female senior administrator)

Equal opportunities is a good system here. Each person is regarded on merit and because of the equal opportunities everybody who wants promotion has the chance to apply.

(Female administrator)

We now expand on three specific areas to illuminate policy-making at Town University: employment, language and sexual harassment.

Employment policies

Initially motivated by reports of the disadvantages experienced by part-time women workers, the university has a range of employment policies aimed at eradicating inequality. As early as 1987, it was acknowledged that the terms and conditions for part-time staff were inadequate, and since then job-sharing, flexible working and career break schemes have been in operation, designed to support those who are unable to work full-time.

While these employment policies are mostly effective, there is evidence that both new applicants and existing staff need better information about the availability and flexibility of these policies. For example, the *job-share scheme* has caused some confusion, largely because of different interpretations about how it might operate. For example, when one half of a job-share partnership became vacant, personnel wanted it to remain a job-share though the manager involved held different views:

> [I was] told that I have to advertise the 0.5 of her job share, when in fact I have got someone in the other 0.5 of the job share who wants it because she wants to be full-time . . . I want to look at the idea that a job-share post is a full-time post. If something happens to the job-share partnership, the remaining person ought to be given the option of altering their proportion.
>
> (Female senior manager)

Additionally, some posts appear to lend themselves more easily to job-sharing than others, as this example concerning a vacancy for a computer programmer indicates.

> The programmer working on this programme – it's like all the knowledge is in his head . . . the question is, how can you transfer all somebody's thought processes into somebody else half-time? It's like knitting a jumper with somebody else – you knit a row and they knit a row. How do you keep up with the pattern?
>
> (Female senior manager)

In theory, all posts at the university may be considered as job-shares, though a post can be designated unsuitable with the permission of the vice chancellor and it seems difficult for senior managers to job-share in the organization currently. Information regarding job-sharing is written into all advertisements for posts, and also on the application form.

The *career break scheme* has raised concerns about how posts are funded:

> If you've got to keep posts vacant for people for a period of time, and you completely restructure the polytechnic [university] in the meantime, where do they come back to? Who's got the budget for it? . . . The career break scheme was put into operation about two or three years ago, so we're . . . just getting people coming back off career breaks. We're only just realizing the impact of some of the problems . . . those

issues keep coming back on the agenda . . . they do raise more issues to solve.

(Female senior manager)

Maternity leave is a particular career break issue that raises questions about how systematically to fund and provide cover because 'effectively you've got to pay someone's salary twice'. In this case, the university has resolved the situation by resort to 'contingency' funds: 'I know there are certain pots of money that are there and I know can be drawn on, for example if someone wants maternity leave' (Female personnel officer).

The *flexible hours policy* is also open to different interpretation. For example, personnel services was able to reorganize work timetables without loss of salary in the case of a member of staff with medical problems. 'Can you see it is a very practical role not just academic debating, a personnel role but with good practice related to my feelings about equal opportunity. It is good practice and fairness towards all clients' (Female personnel officer).

Language policy

The language policy, which is now viewed as a central plank in the university's overall strategy, was developed from a 'non-gender specific terminology' policy agreed in 1987. From 1992 onwards, 'use of appropriate language both reflects the University Mission Statement and supports relationships of mutual respect' (Language policy document, 1992).

The stated aim of the policy is to eradicate any bias in written and spoken forms of language and communication. Thus the code of practice which constitutes the core of the policy is mainly concerned with identifying non-discriminatory terminology; for instance, by suggesting alternative terms which recognize the different positioning of various groups within the university. It covers gender, 'race' and ethnicity, religion, people with disabilities, and lesbians and gay men, and offers guidance and interpretation, such as suggesting that 'black British people' should be substituted for 'second generation immigrants'. ' "Second generation immigrants" . . . is a meaningless contradiction in terms, sometimes used as a euphemism for "black" and always indicating that the speaker does not accept the equal status of black people born in Britain.'

Also included is a section specifically relating to university documentation for use either internally or externally. For example, the use of individual titles such as Mr, Mrs, Ms, Professor or Doctor internally is considered unnecessarily hierarchical and inequitable. For correspondence outside the university, it is suggested that academic and individual titles should be used only on request if not to do so would be 'detrimental to the standing' of the university.

Heightened awareness of the importance of language in everyday practice was evident, particularly in the case of sexist or similarly discriminatory language, which was often challenged at meetings. Significantly, the university has also developed a sophisticated understanding of language in terms of 'race' and ethnicity. It is ahead of bodies such as the Commission for Racial Equality (CRE), which uses 'ethnic minority' as an all-embracing term to encompass all racial differences other than white. The university has reversed the words, creating the term 'minority ethnic' to emphasize the fact that 'everyone belongs to an ethnic group'.

While the university shows understanding of non-racist terminology, there is some doubt about the extent of its general use around the university, despite the fact that the language policy was distributed to all heads of department and services in 1991 with the request that it be 'displayed on a relevant notice board'. More recently, it was decided that the equal opportunities booklet, which includes the language policy, was to be distributed individually to all staff. Nevertheless, the policy still has its detractors: 'Well, look at the language policy, for example. It has been written and discussed. OK! They produced it but nothing happened. Who knows about it? Who is monitoring it?' (Female lecturer).

Policy on harassment

The progress made by the university in the development of its sexual harassment policy is particularly innovative. Certainly, at various times, the university's policies and practices have drawn the attention of the local and national press.

The sexual harassment officer (SHO) is a 'named person' who 'gives people direction' and who investigates and reports cases of sexual harassment on behalf of the panel, presenting any recommendations for action directly to the vice chancellor (as chair of the equal opportunities committee). In 1992, the SHO's post became full-time, though still seconded, with the brief of 'assist[ing] the Vice Chancellor with cases of sexual harassment and develop[ing] policy in this area'. Significantly, the post was underpinned with relatively generous resources for training, and subsequently the SHO has gained recognition nationally for harassment issues.

The SHO keeps a systematic record of all cases and circulates regular reports of work undertaken. While there were only a handful of complaints prior to the appointment of the SHO, during 1990–1 the number increased to 35, all but one from women. The highest proportion of complaints came from staff about the behaviour of colleagues. Complaints rose to 75 during the academic year 1991–2, and to 89 in 1992–3, ranging from sexual assault to distribution of obscene material through electronic mail. Computer abuse was identified as a particular problem and addressed through written and/or verbal warnings from the vice chancellor, with a resultant decrease in such complaints.

The complaints procedure for sexual harassment was as follows.

- Panel is drawn from male and female representatives of personnel services and teaching staff. Because of work pressure, most complaints are investigated by the chair of the panel, with advice from other panel members as and where appropriate.
- Department heads are required to report any complaints to the chair of the panel.
- Complainants can approach any member of the panel direct, although in practice it is the chair who is involved in investigations and who reports to the vice chancellor in conjunction with other panel members.
- Reports and recommendations are presented to the vice chancellor by the SHO. 'I can only report and advise – it is up to the vice chancellor to act.'
- Disciplinary action is taken on approval of the vice chancellor where a complaint is upheld. This can take different forms, including an undertaking not to repeat behaviour and/or a formal apology.

As we have seen, sexual harassment has had a high profile in the university, being viewed as the most highly prioritized aspect of equal opportunity policy. It has had a particularly strong impact on some staff. A male senior manager has been 'amazed' at the number of cases of harassment reported:

I would have put myself in the category of being prepared to accept that there was some sexual harassment going on but that it would be relatively modest in terms of numbers of incidents . . . in terms of the diversity of cases we have had to deal with I have been really amazed at the spread of activity.

The rise in number of cases since the introduction of the procedures has been unexpectedly steep and confirms, it would seem, the need for greater emphasis on formal action regarding harassment. However, not unexpectedly, there has also been some criticism of the policy, much of it related to perceived deficiencies in understanding of definitions and procedures, lack of awareness more generally and opposition from male staff, some of whom feel 'collectively vulnerable'. 'A lot of it is ignorance, they tend to think that sexual harassment is calling people love and I am trying to spoil their fun' (SHO).

On a more formal level, while agreeing in principle with the policy, trade union members have raised concerns about the excessive power of the vice chancellor in policy creation and implementation. Moreover, some aspects of the policy have been perceived as involving unfair practices, the most serious being: 'allegations [that] can be made or be considered by a committee or individuals without the person who is being accused of sexual harassment knowing anything about it' (Male trade union representative). This view, concerning the rights of, and appropriate action for, those accused of sexual harassment, was echoed in the ethics audit carried out in the university during 1992, which concluded that 'it is inappropriate to leave these decisions to one arbitrator'. The response to these criticisms was that while they may be valid, the vice chancellor (as chief executive) needs to be closely involved since, under the articles of government for the university, he is charged personally with any decisions that might lead to the suspension of a member of staff. In practice, however, where action has needed to be taken, others have been involved, such as heads of department.

There has also been some discussion within the university about the contradictions of needing strong and often directive leadership for a policy that aims to empower under-represented groups. The case for strong leadership was succinctly summarized as follows:

> To carry out the job properly there is a need for power and authority. He [the Vice Chancellor] is being pushed hard all the time and needs to maintain strong authority. He is part of the male ethos but comes in for strong criticism because of his stance over sexual harassment.
> (SHO)

On the other hand, some staff have felt intimidated because of their perception of the public exercise of the complaints procedure – despite assertions of confidentiality and secrecy. The impression gained is that 'everyone knows what is going on' (Female administrator).

Staff have also expressed concern about the outcome of sexual harassment procedures in that complainants are likely to suffer damaging effects whether or not cases are proven, and requested more explanation and training on sexual harassment issues. For example, there seem to be no guidelines for staff on how to deal with or recognize sexual harassment when it occurs. Neither has counselling or support been available for staff compelled to leave because of sexual harassment, whether victims or perpetrators. 'There is little help from management in terms of explanation or training with regards to implementing harassment procedures' (Female campus services staff member). It would seem, therefore, that while the policy is strong, training is weaker, with the current two-hour training course for managers judged as insufficient. Members of the sexual harassment panel, in contrast, have received extensive training. These particular sets of concerns illustrate the high level of staff expectation operating at the university such that managers are expected to be proactive in dealing with sexual harassment. This has also led to policy being invoked as an example of management 'bullying'.

If there are some doubts about the mechanisms and ethics of existing procedures, there is still general agreement that the policy is a good one, even though some reorganization, say, to diminish the concentration of power in one person is necessary. The policy has undoubtedly raised awareness of sexual harassment issues in the university: 'Most of the complaints were probably from women and I must watch my step – jobs can be lost because of sex harassment and even if a person is proved innocent a stigma still remains' (Male campus services staff member). While increased pressure of work has meant there has been little time available for the SHO to publicize the principles and procedures of the policy, it is clear that the university has made exceptional progress since its inception.

The original sex harassment policy led, perhaps inevitably, to questions being raised about whether other forms of harassment (for example, on racial issues) should be included, or whether the harassment policy needed to be altogether broader. For example, 'Do we perhaps need a harassment policy full stop? People harass each other at work all the time – it's really got nothing to do with race or gender; it's perhaps something to do with personality and power' (Female senior manager).

A new, broader policy has recently been introduced, intended to 'cascade easily' across gender, sexuality, race and disability. The argument for this new approach is given in the university statement on harassment:

> Harassment is behaviour which is unwanted, offensive to the recipient or others, and which is not justified by the professional and/or working relationship. Harassment often involves the abuse of power. Although harassment is most commonly sexual or racial, people may be harassed for other reasons, such as disability or age, or simply because someone takes a personal dislike to them. Incitement to engage in unwanted behaviour including language also constitutes harassment.

The final policy document also includes short definitions of individual areas of harassment. For example, 'Racial harassment is unwanted behaviour of a hostile or offensive nature or expression of one racial or ethnic origin against another person' (Harassment policy). The race and gender advisory groups also wanted the university to appoint a racial harassment officer with expertise in race relations to parallel the work by the SHO and to support implementation of the harassment policy generally. In the end, the eventual structure was built round the current SHO, now retitled harassment officer, whose responsibilities expanded to include chairing the panel and coordinating complaints and action for all harassment complaints.

In the first four months of the new policy, 21 complaints of general harassment were received. Several referred to 'mixed' harassment, racial harassment apparently now being acknowledged as part of the expanded policy.

Policy impact

What impact have these policies and structures had and what are the outcomes of the plethora of policies for staff groups, namely those with disabilities, who are from minority ethnic groups and/or who are women?

Disability issues

Disability has also been a focus of the project, though not as highly prioritized as 'race' and gender. Records from 1993 show that 14 members of staff were registered as disabled at Town University, in addition to two employed in response to a government directive that people with disabilities should be assigned to certain posts, e.g. as car park attendants. There are also likely to be other staff who have not, for various reasons, declared their disability and, in this, the picture at this university does not appear to be much different from others.

Evidence of university awareness of the needs of those with disabilities has, nevertheless, emerged throughout the project, including a detailed survey of access and mobility within the university and practical equipment being made available to support members of staff with disabilities. Significantly, all documents for university meetings are also printed in Braille.

Minority ethnicity

According to the most recent monitoring data available (1993), minority ethnic staff (as defined by recorded ethnicity) represented 3 per cent (56; 32 women, 24 men) of the total staff (1580). There were 20 minority ethnic teaching staff, employed mainly as senior lecturers (nine) and lecturers (eight), representing 3.5 per cent of total teaching staff (566). The university as of 1994 had two minority ethnic heads of department, out of 64.

In 1993, campus services employed the largest number of people in one department (281), representing 17 per cent of the total staff. It also had the highest concentration of minority ethnic staff in one department, particularly when compared with the academic side of the university. There were 18 minority ethnic staff (6 per cent of all campus services staff), of whom 16 were cleaners. Other minority ethnic staff have tended to be scattered across a variety of departments.

The university has expressed its concern about the relatively low numbers of minority ethnic staff at the university; however, it is difficult to tell to what degree this pattern is reflected elsewhere in other universities since, at the time of writing, no such data are available. The problem of identifying 'norms' or recruitment targets has also been an issue. Should the university's minority ethnic population reflect local, county or national patterns? The 1991 Census shows that minority ethnic groups represented 5.5 per cent of the total population of Britain, with most concentrated in the South East, West Midlands and North West England. In the county in which Town University is located, the proportion was 4.4 per cent, though the university's local community had a higher concentration (10.3 per cent). Groups originating from the Indian sub-continent formed the largest proportion (6.5 per cent) and were also the largest minority ethnic group employed by the university (32 per cent of total minority ethnic staff).

How can the university increase its proportion of minority ethnic staff, given that it may be recruiting from a relatively small pool of minority ethnic groups in comparison, for example, with the more heavily populated areas in the large cities? Personnel services has endeavoured to increase minority ratios – for example, by advertising all posts in the national press and by targeting the national 'ethnic' press – although this has, to date, yielded disappointing results. It also regularly distributes details of job vacancies to local community organizations and groups, and monitors all job applications, short lists and appointments according to sex, ethnicity, registered and non-registered disability.

One possible reason for the relatively low uptake of jobs by minority ethnic groups suggested by a member of staff is that applicants from these groups may have different education and employment histories compared with 'standard' group qualifications and experiences. Since each advertised post attracts a deluge of applicants, the strategies used to sift applicants might well be drawing rather too heavily on conventional qualifications as selection criteria, to the disadvantage of some minority ethnic applicants.

The university has indicated awareness of this possibility by committing itself to a review of the application form and more highly prioritizing the needs of minority ethnic groups in the job application process. In 1993, the appointment of a Black, female head of personnel services seemed to indicate continuing awareness of the issues and commitment to future improvements.

Women

Town University comprises 64 departments of varying size listed as having a head or director. Fourteen of these are headed by women, including the head of personnel services, the university secretary and two faculty deans, all of whom are members of the senior management team. The senior management team comprises seven women from a total of 21, and the more senior university executive team contains three women out of a total of 11. The number of women managers at such senior levels is relatively high compared to other similar institutions in the UK, despite women's continuing minority status in relation to their male colleagues.

Other patterns of gender inequality also remain. In 1993, the Women's Unit produced an internal report fully detailing the staffing and employment issues of women at the university, on which the project was able to draw. At that time, women represented 47 per cent of the total staff at the university, with over half (51 per cent) of female workers employed in such 'traditional' female occupations as cleaners, catering staff, library staff, clerks, typists and administrative assistants. Indeed, categories of staff such as clerical assistant, clerk, typist, receptionist, administrative assistant and personal assistant were all *exclusively* female. The report pointed out that many of these occupations were part-time or temporary or involved job-sharing, all characteristic of women's rather than men's work. It further detailed the subordinate position of female manual workers in relation to male manual workers. For example, 92 per cent of female manual workers were employed at the lowest grades, mainly as part-time staff, while three-quarters of the men, who overall held 28 per cent of manual jobs, were employed in the three top graded manual posts. More recently, the university has attempted to alter these employment patterns by promoting women to higher grade posts, as caretakers, for instance.

Similar gendered patterns have been evident in relation to teaching staff. While there is a strong female presence at senior management levels, there are still far fewer women managers than men: 'the higher the grade the fewer the number of women in post' (Women's Unit, 1993). In 1993, women represented 32 per cent of university teaching staff (readers, principal lecturers, senior lecturers and lecturers) although, at that time, there were no female readers and only ten female principal lecturers (14 per cent) out of a total of 71.

This is, nevertheless, a significant improvement on staff patterns recorded in 1987; from 11 per cent (31) women senior lecturers in 1987 to 31 per cent (105) in 1993, and from 32 per cent (23) women lecturers to 48 per cent (61). However, problems still remain in terms of the generally differing career paths of male and female lecturing staff. For example, in comparing lecturers' salaries, the Women's Unit found that 'men on average reach the same career point at age 36–40 as women do at age 51–55', though clearly extra-university factors have a significant impact here. Figures for 1992 showed 17 per cent of management posts held by women compared with 83 per cent held by men, with an analysis by age showing, as in the case of teaching staff, that men are appointed to management at a younger age compared with women.

Interestingly, there was considerable variation in staffing patterns *between* departments, with some favouring women and others favouring men. Those that had a high concentration of female staff (nine departments) were likely to have a female head of department. For example, all midwifery teaching staff and the head of department were female and social work and health departments employed an approximately equal balance of male and female staff. At the other end of the scale, 11 departments had relatively few female teaching staff, with most at lower grades than men. For example, business information and management had 24 teaching staff, of which only two were female senior lecturers. The chemistry department had 17 academics, of whom only one was a woman, at lecturer level. Computing and electronics had 46 academics, of whom only seven were women. And the department of public policy had 24 academics, of whom only two were women, who were at lecturer level.

While the departments mentioned above are clearly affected by cultural and gendered values about their specific subject areas – some are perceived more as women's subjects and some more as men's – this situation presents a difficult problem for the university. The departments with the greatest gender segregation illustrate the persistence of traditional gender divisions within the professions linked to their departments. The concentration of women in administrative and manual posts also reflects similar gender divisions within the national labour market.

Town University appears to have rather more control over appointments to senior management, and claims to have tried to appoint women to senior management positions where possible. It has also made some progress in appointing women to senior committees, such as the senior management team. Nevertheless, despite all these endeavours, conspicuous differences still remain. A main issue for many of the female heads of department, as a senior woman manager observed, is that of having to deal with the largely male level of staff immediately below them, which frequently leaves them feeling vulnerable and exposed. 'X had to cope with a line of male principal lecturers and there was a kind of barrier . . . There is this macho style of I say–you do . . . It was a deterrent to me. Was I going to have to be macho as well?' (Senior woman manager). Senior women in the university have also reported feeling isolated because of what they regard as 'excluding' male behaviour:

The . . . thing I find difficult is the way in which men deal with each other, they trade with each other – which women just don't do . . . If they have gone into an agreement with each other outside a meeting they'll stick to it inside the meeting. I find that very difficult, because it means that you possibly get worse solutions than if the thing was open . . . Nobody challenges it. I actually think it's unhealthy.

(Senior woman manager)

Any positive policy of promoting women into senior positions seems inevitably to precipitate counter-reactions. Sexist attitudes continue to persist within the university, with the consequence that women may not be perceived as having achieved high office legitimately:

It appears that some women have individual treatment and apparently get to the top by a fluke . . . women of high profile have enough problems in the university and it does not help the issue if people comment 'she got there through equal opportunities, therefore she is no good'.

(Female administrator)

The situation at the university illustrates the perpetual dilemma that women face as they strive to make progress in a male-dominated environment, and seems surprisingly resistant to change despite policies committed to redressing organizational gender imbalances.

Structures supporting equal opportunities

Equal opportunities policies within the university operate through a system of committees and designated posts, the responsibilities and management structure of which are often very different. Posts include:

- equal opportunities advisors (five) based in the faculties and accountable to the dean;
- sexual harassment (now harassment) officer reporting directly to the vice chancellor;
- Centre for Race Equality (head of centre and two administrators) with the head of centre accountable to the head of programmes;
- Women's Unit comprising two women officers on a job-share, accountable to the dean with responsibility for women's affairs in the university.

These differently located posts are buttressed by the EOC and three advisory groups for disability, gender and 'race'. This complex set of structures, while comprehensive, inevitably leads to some policy fragmentation and unevenness. This is best illustrated by examining four different structures: the Centre for Racial Equality, the Women's Unit, the EOC and the Centre for Professional Ethics.

Centre for Race Equality

The Race Equality Unit (REQU) was established in 1986 following a survey that established that there were racist attitudes in the institution. The results were never revealed but the 'situation was pretty bad' (Ex-REQU worker). The unit employed six equality workers mainly for the benefit of the students, but also attached to faculties as subject teachers and as part of the faculty management team. Five of the six REQU members came from minority ethnic backgrounds.

During its five years of existence REQU's main achievements involved developments relating to access for students. Links were established with local community groups and ethnic monitoring was introduced for staff and students. REQU staff pioneered a code of practice on racial equality which was adopted in 1987, and also developed a range of multi-cultural curriculum and access projects. It was a decision of the previous vice chancellor that REQU should not be involved in employment issues. The unit was, nevertheless, able to organize staff development days for course admissions staff, although these were 'marked by a high non-attendance rate' (REQU, 1990).

REQU had more success with courses for staff responsible for recruitment, particularly after a compulsory requirement to attend these courses was introduced. However, the unit lacked a strategic plan and clear objectives and targets: 'Equal opportunities, anti-racism or multi-culturalism – what we were expected to permeate the institution with I don't quite know. The idea was to get these issues raised and for people to take them seriously' (Female ex-REQU worker).

With the ending of Section 11 funding in 1990, it was decided to devolve REQU staff to the faculties. The five years of REQU revealed both the negative and positive sides of working as a separate unit. Faculties tended to pass any 'race' problems to the unit, simultaneously shedding responsibility for tackling these problems themselves. As a consequence, REQU became ghettoized: 'We were becoming isolated. We were identified as the people who dealt with black problems, therefore send them to REQU' (Female ex-REQU worker).

Faculty devolvement likewise had its negative side: isolation for some of the ex-REQU staff after the supportive culture of the unit. 'Race' is always a sensitive issue, and Black staff in a predominantly white organization found considerable difficulty in questioning harassment or prejudice in the wider context of the faculty. 'There is a colour blind attitude which can be quite painful at times' (Female ex-REQU worker). Nevertheless, a positive outcome of the demise of REQU was the creation of the Centre for Race Equality (CRE), with the key objective of raising awareness of racial issues within the university as 'part of the institution's wider commitment to equal opportunity' (Corporate plan, 1993). It has inherited from REQU an emphasis on students rather than staff and offers advice on grievance and disciplinary procedures, enrolment and counselling as well as resources for students, i.e. journals and leaflets. Important REQU links have continued with local community groups, through liaison with local radio and community outreach.

The CRE has dealt with several cases of racial harassment since its inception, mainly on behalf of students, but unlike with sexual harassment cases, no records have been kept as 'most cases were sorted out at the very initial level' (Female head of centre). Despite strong lobbying from the race and gender advisory groups to the Equal Opportunities Committee, there seems to have been a failure to adopt procedures to counter racial harassment which parallel those for sexual harassment. This may have been because of unevenness of organizational structure of equal opportunities or because of the split development of equal opportunities policies in which 'race', gender and disability have had very different development trajectories. Moreover, while the SHO and the Women's Unit are responsible directly to the vice chancellor and dean respectively, the CRE is answerable to a rather more 'lowly' departmental head. This has been perceived as indicative of the lower priority of 'race' issues in the university generally.

Overall, then, the response to the various 'race' equality structures has been mixed. As already pointed out, there are comparatively few minority ethnic staff (3 per cent) in the university, scattered across the institution. 'There is a feeling that there is no problem with race' (Female lecturer). There has been little evidence of extensive racial awareness or acknowledgement of racial issues in meetings observed for the project. For example, in the shadowing exercise there was frequent reference to gender, sexual harassment, disability and associated language policy but not to 'race' issues. When requested, personnel services did not have local minority ethnic population figures to hand. This fairly subdued internal profile contrasts markedly with the stronger pressure from local 'race' equality organizations which see 'race' rather than gender as the key issue for the local community and the university. This imbalance is recognized within the university:

> Race issues I find difficult because I don't know enough about them. It's as simple as that . . . We work hard at it, but we don't know as much about race as we do about sex. We are under-represented in terms of minority groups on the staff. So I suppose institutionally we just don't know as much. We've got quite a way to go.
>
> (Male senior manager)

Women's officers and Women's Unit

The Women's Unit is the consequence of a long history of campaigning and researching women's issues at the university. The post of women's officer was created in 1992 and currently two women share the post. One of the women officers, with extensive knowledge of equal opportunity development in local government, reflected on the importance of hands-on experience in her appointment: 'It is important that it was me. I am a non-academic appointment with practical experience of implementing policy.'

The unit has responsibility mainly for women staff; the students union has its own women's officer catering to student needs. Initially, four areas of development were identified by the unit: advertising and recruitment, data collection, academic affairs and curriculum issues. One of its first tasks was to collect information on 'good practice', i.e. examples of how women's issues are represented in the curriculum, and on any specific arrangements to support and encourage women students and staff.

To maintain links with women in the university and alleviate some individual concerns, the unit produced a booklet, *The Women's Handbook*, containing a wide range of information on health and safety, legal matters, local facilities, equal opportunities, 'race', disability and sexual harassment together with relevant internal telephone numbers.

Progress has also been made in gathering data on the position of women in the university. The 1993 Women's Unit report focused on employment and other related concerns of women staff and also scrutinized recruitment, job application and promotion patterns with recommendations, some of which have now been acted upon, such as revisions to the application form. The report drew attention to the partial effectiveness of language policy, making the point that some staff still seemed unaware of language issues.

Most of the report's recommendations were accepted by personnel services as both practical and achievable. The report also drew criticism for being too narrow and not 'radical enough', say, compared to earlier reports. However, the conditions in which the various reports were written have been different. In contrast to a report commissioned from an independent researcher who had an open brief that allowed her wide access to key meetings and documents, the Women's Unit has not enjoyed such 'freedom' or been able to give equivalent time to its investigations. However, such criticism may be indicative of the Women's Unit's perceived position as *outside* the main structures of the university.

A plus for the women's officers has been the strength and importance of informal, personal networks which seem to have laid the foundations for contact systems and goodwill within the university. Early in the project, anxiety was expressed about the difficulties of obtaining information direct from various university departments: 'I find things out because of my other networks. Might be because I am new but it could be quite easy to be marginalized.'

The original exclusion of the Women's Unit from important parts of the equal opportunities decision-making process does seem to have undermined its proactive role. The unit is represented on various committees but its sphere of influence seems to be restricted to the formal equal opportunity 'circuit'. The unit's task, it would seem, is to implement agreed policy rather than challenge or innovate. Notwithstanding this, the existence of the unit is evidence that women's issues are taken seriously in the university, which is one of the first higher education institutions to create posts specifically for women's issues. The Women's Unit also complements and works closely with other areas of equal opportunity, dividing up various areas of work as appropriate; for example, with the SHO. One of the women's officers admitted, 'I'm quite glad I don't have sex harassment as well. I could spend all my time doing just that.'

Although the Women's Unit wants to keep its separate identity, there appears to be some uncertainty about the future and its potential marginalization. This contrasts with the positioning of the other university gender post (for sexual harassment), which has been centrally located and administered, with the added advantage of enthusiastic patronage from the university's most senior manager.

Nevertheless, in the Women's Unit's first two years of existence it has clearly done much work in a relatively short time. An increasingly heavy workload, however, is a major problem.

There is somebody new every week seeking help ... I cannot take on all the individual problems so I try to deflect some responsibility back to departments. It is part of what I am trying to do here: trying to create a climate, get people used to a mental checklist that includes equal opportunities.

Equal Opportunities Committee structure

Equal opportunities within the university is underpinned by the Equal Opportunities Committee (EOC) and three advisory groups representing disability, gender and 'race' issues. The EOC was created in 1985 and a new membership structure was agreed in March 1992. A previous report from an EOC working group had expressed concern that since the time of the departure of REQU staff to the faculties, committee membership had become unrepresentative. As a consequence, membership was reviewed and the present structure of 25 members agreed; but the new structure seemed to favour deans and the vice chancellor. The new formula seems to have had a 'disempowering' effect. Imbalance in membership is also exacerbated by the fact that because of the way the membership is designated, equal opportunity 'activists' of the university no longer have a voice on the committee.

The main objective of the EOC is to develop policy from issues raised through the advisory groups. However, there is currently some confusion about the committee's exact role, given its advisory status in relation to the vice chancellor. Is it a discussion group or a policy-making forum? The present EOC appears to have opted for the former by encouraging discussion such that 'every word and phrase goes backwards and forwards and the whole thing goes on and on' (EOC member).

Some staff have been concerned about the impact of too much bureaucracy or 'proceduralism' on the work of the committee: 'At every one of those meetings, I've felt frustrated – in fact very frustrated – by the proceduralism. I've never come across proceduralism like it' (Male senior manager). Perhaps this comment illustrates an unrealistic expectation of the EOC's role in the university's decision-making structure and a misplaced faith in the ability of such committees to arrive at speedy decisions:

> Committees can raise expectations but very often cannot deliver because they do not have their handle on the resource lever . . . people in a line management role with specific responsibilities have to discharge those responsibilities and committees give advice and monitor . . . There have been such diverse opinions in the [EOC] that I think on some issues it is impossible to say that it could ever come to a conclusion.
>
> (Male senior manager)

Despite such frustrations, 'diverse opinions' clearly have a place in raising awareness about equality issues. However, the ability to offer 'diverse opinions' tends to be restricted to those articulate, brave and knowledgeable enough to speak up at the often large EOC meetings. For example, at one meeting observed for the project, administrative and manual staff representatives did not speak at all, most of the debate being conducted by the deans and other senior academics. As has been noted,

The very formal structure of the meetings does little to foster creative discussions or the kind of supportive environment which enables issues to be explored without individuals finding themselves open to criticism. People feel inhibited in this way, and may therefore feel unable to speak their minds or ask questions.

(Equalities staff working group, 1993)

As we have seen, the EOC is advisory to the vice chancellor and also chaired by the vice chancellor. The vice chancellor is therefore the identifiable architect of equal opportunity policies. We found that staff at all levels of the university acknowledged and appreciated the personal commitment and involvement of senior management, often against prevailing political and higher education trends. One reason the university has achieved a reputation for equal opportunities development is precisely because the vice chancellor, as an individual, has revealed a dedication to pursuing equality goals and an ability to use the authority vested in his position to guide policy.

None the less, there is a paradox arising out of the wide range of management powers at one person's disposal. This concentration of power can inhibit discussion within the university, particularly on sensitive issues. As a member of the EOC commented, 'On the one hand it is useful having the vice chancellor chairing the committee but on the other he controls every situation' (Female senior academic). Some staff appeared uncomfortable with the vice chancellor as chair of the EOC, and with the potential for manipulation of the agenda and discrimination against dissenting individuals. On the other hand, the buck clearly stops with the chief executive, so committee discussion must necessarily be 'advisory'. As the vice chancellor pointed out,

We would seek views generally through the EOC but at the end of the day a decision about the organization and the management of the institution under our articles of government has to be mine . . . it is me who has to decide the organizational structure. That sounds a bit despotic but I think it is highly unlikely that I am going to say we will do this despite what the EOC has said.

In contrast to members of the EOC, members of the less formal advisory groups are more likely to be equal opportunity activists, co-opted for their 'expertise' in specific areas. The advisory groups discuss issues of disability, gender and 'race' respectively, and then make recommendations to the EOC. Each advisory group draws its membership (approximately 15) from all sections of university staff and students. In practice, while notionally 'unrepresentative', the nomination procedure is flexible such that interested 'experts' can be invited to join. Moreover, the nature of this forum may help to counteract any 'exclusions' from the EOC.

The ability to co-opt has been important for the advisory groups. For example, the disability advisory group co-opted representatives from property services, who were able to help in its audit of university buildings;

by encouraging men to join, the gender advisory group has made great efforts to balance the sex ratio of its membership and thus reduce the perception of it as a women's group. Overall, it has been difficult to attract student representation on any of the groups, though students seem even less willing to join the disability group, perhaps 'because it is less politic-ized and maybe less interesting than gender or race'.

The principal role of the three advisory groups is to provide expertise in specific areas and report regularly to the EOC. Meetings are held two or three times a term depending on whether there is a perceived need to progress particular issues more speedily. In contrast to the more formal EOC, advisory group meetings seem relaxed and flexible and there is gen-erally open, frank discussion. One clear advantage of such groups is that equal opportunity issues are discussed in depth before recommendations are made or decisions taken.

Nevertheless, some concern was expressed about the appropriateness of the dean's position as advisory group chair. It was again suggested that 'ordinary' staff or students might feel inhibited about raising particular issues of concern during meetings, similar criticisms of deans on advisory groups as were made of the vice chancellor's position on the EOC: 'the whole idea of equal opportunity is to have grass roots representation, people must be there because of interest not because of position' (Female senior academic). Yet deans, as members of the executive and manage-ment teams, clearly have access to central decision-making committees and can therefore be proactive on behalf of the advisory groups. Accord-ingly, deans were appointed as chairs of the groups in order to make the groups work better.

Fragmentation of effort is another concern. The existing structure does not seem to facilitate cross-fertilization of ideas and action between the three advisory groups. While each group was engaged for at least two years in discussing codes of practice relevant to its area, group representatives had difficulty in meeting and therefore found it impossible to coordinate the three eventual, very different codes. As a consequence, the disabilities advisory group was seen as more effective and practical than the other groups, largely because disability needs seemed easier to identify.

Centre for Professional Ethics

During 1992, Town University launched the first ever audit of ethics and values in a British university. The aim of the six-month's audit was to examine professional ethics and identify shared values across the institu-tion. The audit highlighted the need for an 'explicit code of values' arising from the university's mission statement. The recommendations from the report suggest how 'best practice' can be developed and how areas of 'ethical conflict' can be resolved. The recommendations represented

> an attempt to encourage a University management style and culture
> in which recognition of and respect for all members of its community

is the paramount value and where a climate of genuine trust, participation in decision making and collaboration is fostered. The assumption then is that good and fair ethical practice will naturally evolve
and become the norm.

(Ethics and Values Audit (EVA), 1992)

These aims are not too far removed, we suggest, from those conventionally considered relevant to equal opportunities policies and practices.
Indeed, it has been suggested that 'the ethics audit is the umbrella term
that takes on board very many issues within equal opportunities' (Female
EVA project leader).

The Ethics Audit Report concluded that Town University has an adequate equal opportunities structure but that there is need for a review of
practice to ensure more effective implementation of policy. There was also
some criticism of the sexual harassment policy, and recommendations
that investigative procedures and decisions should be the responsibility
of a group of people rather than 'an unfair burden' for one person. Once
again, attention was drawn to the powers of responsibility vested in the
vice chancellor under the university articles of government, a concern
which the vice chancellor acknowledged: 'I think what people are doing
is rightly flagging up that there may be too much power in the hands of
an individual. But I have not had any specific suggestions that power has
been misused to date.' There seemed to be an awareness, at least at senior
management level, that broad issues of ethics and values might prove a
useful future approach in the development of equality practices: 'I think
it [ethics and values] is the next step, especially as some of the issues in
equal opportunities keep raising different questions . . . there is a next
step which is on to these softer issues' (Female senior manager).

Established in January 1993, at the same time the Ethics and Values
Report came out, a year later the Centre for Professional Ethics had two
(female) professors, seven research fellows, four academic staff and 14
part-time PhD students and a major international research project on
genetic counselling. Significantly, the head of centre also chairs the ethics
committee, yet another committee advisory to the vice chancellor.

At the time of writing, the ethics committee is discussing a code of
ethics for professional behaviour within the university, possibly providing
better links between ethics and equal opportunities initiatives. However,
there is no mention of ethics or values in the most recent university report
on equality issues (Equality Issues, 1993), which clarifies future objectives
for the university, and little evidence of formal collaboration between
those involved with ethics and those involved with equal opportunities.

Rhetoric and reality

During the course of the case study, the project team were inevitably made
aware of the rhetoric of policy implementation; observation of its practice

proved more difficult to ascertain. However, one particular phase of policy change highlighted for us some of the problems of translating equal opportunities policy into practice.

The staff review and restructuring exercise particularly influenced people's conceptions of what equal opportunities should mean in practice. Administrative and campus services staff, who were interviewed at a time when both groups were experiencing major restructuring in their respective departments, were clearly sensitive to and dissatisfied with proposed changes in employment status. Equal opportunities was seen to be threatened by new sets of practices within higher education, the consequence of enforced self-funding and entrepreneurialism. Town University anticipated this shift in institutional emphasis by creating a structure review group aimed at producing a 'flatter', more efficient line-management structure with an accompanying redistribution of staff.

The university claimed that it has adopted a methodology of restructuring which promotes fairness and enables staff to be redeployed on the basis of achieving the closest match in terms of former responsibility, with guaranteed protection of salary should a lower grade be decided upon: restructuring 'will provide a first step towards job evaluation which is seen as important in the pursuit of equal opportunities policies and high staff morale' (University corporate plan).

Those in charge of the review suggested that tensions felt by staff were less related to the restructuring than to how details were communicated to staff. 'Staff may not be appropriately informed of things they need to know to be effective. They may not be, or may feel they are not, adequately involved in decision making' (Corporate plan, 1993). Staff drew the attention of the project team to the apparent paradox between the university restructuring exercise and perceptions of equality. When questioned about their experience of equal opportunities, for example, administrative and manual staff expressed strong concern about inequalities in the staff restructuring exercise, as the following set of quotes shows.

> The restructuring exercise . . . has particular implications for women in the University, affecting the way they progress.
>
> (Women's officer)

> There is now more work and less staff.
>
> (Female campus services staff member)

> I have been made up to 'acting' . . . I wish to improve myself but the review might cut my job and I would slide down again. Management should be more truthful because staff feel vulnerable not knowing what the new grades will be. I might have to re-apply for my job with no guarantee of success.
>
> (Male campus services staff member)

> Staff are frightened to complain and feel under pressure because of the risk of losing their jobs.
>
> (Female campus services staff member)

The review, though necessary, is like cracking a nut with a steam roller. All become victim.

(Male campus service staff member)

Top-down policy implementation has taken the main brunt of the blame: 'it was implementation from above that caused the problems' (Male campus services staff member). Understandably, senior management feels that it is in the front line for criticism whatever policy it presents. 'Even the introduction of what we would regard as very important policies, like equal opportunity, are sometimes opposed on the grounds that it is changing the jobs individuals do' (Male senior manager).

The key point we want to make here is that disaffected staff explicitly pointed to the inadequacy of their own personal experience of the restructuring exercise as measured against equal opportunities policies in the university. In their view, the practice of restructuring did not live up to the spirit of the equal opportunities policies. In the view of management, part of the problem was that the university had inherited a range of different contractual obligations affecting manual staff on incorporation, and was now attempting to tackle resultant staffing problems in the light of equal opportunities and other policy requirements. Thus the restructuring exercise was seen to be in the best interests of the staff, though this view, inevitably, was not held by staff.

Nevertheless, Town University has produced a range of diverse, and in some instances innovative, equal opportunities practices, such as:

- Statistical procedures to monitor staff recruitment, aiming to improve the recruitment and promotion of under-represented groups.
- Attention to the needs of staff with disabilities across the university.
- Continual review and updating of university documents. New initiatives such as the equalities staff working group demonstrate that the university is fully aware of the need for constant review of how policies are working and how they might be improved.
- High standard and well-resourced staff development.
- Emphasis on employment policies with sufficient resources to allow for flexibility in recruitment.
- Creative 'mix' of equal opportunities policies and practices, with exceptional progress made in the field of sexual harassment/harassment, and in non-discriminatory and inclusive language.
- Committee structure which involves staff at different levels and sectors of the university yet provides direct links with management.
- Embeddedness of equal opportunities in formal university structures.
- Enhanced profile of women's issues, with an evident commitment to promoting and appointing women to senior positions.
- Committed management team determined to create a university ethos in which equality practices flourish.

Inevitably tensions have arisen between the policy as it is written and how it then becomes embedded in the practice and ethos of the institution. Such tensions include:

- Fragmentation in the development of equal opportunity policy policies with evidence of different equality groups acting independently of each other.
- Differences in priority of equality issues such that women's issues appear to have a far higher profile in the university. In contrast racial awareness appears to be less well developed.

However, differences in emphasis should also be seen in the context of the particular history and the split development of equal opportunities policy within the university. Such differences should be built upon, it is argued, as different groups move towards a common aim:

The internal workings of an organization in relation to equal opportunities, ethics and values need to be addressed now because of what is going on externally. If we get that balance it is something to do with the common good and the society we live in ... There comes a time when it is not necessary to have positive discrimination because of gender or race, you just have to have justice and fairness.

(Senior woman academic)

The uneven development of some policies may relate more to the specific academic culture of higher education than to different interest groups or deficiencies in effort on the part of the university. A recently appointed female member of staff suggested that when compared to the more managerial culture of local authorities, the culture of the university appeared more resistant to change. What is needed, she claimed, is a shift in management culture:

In my previous [local authority] job people were sacked for contravening policy and procedures and everybody knew clearly what to do ... I was surprised and shocked by the different culture of the university where equal opportunity initiatives are continually questioned. This is a very political institution and it is difficult to resolve equal opportunity issues in that atmosphere. [At my previous job] someone was sacked for racist remarks and anti-racism was ingrained in our behaviour ... Now I find myself slipping back and putting people into categories.

The apparent lack of consistency of policy-making has been acknowledged as a problem for the university. Recently, an 'umbrella' committee, the equalities staff working group, was formed to generate a more consistent approach to equal opportunities at staff level. Its membership is drawn from all the equality initiatives in the university and it discusses the viability of the range of current staff equal opportunity structures and practices.

The development of a 'corporate strategy' which strengthens existing equal opportunity structures yet preserves the diversity of separate initiatives seems to be at least a partial resolution to this tension. Integral to this is the emphasis on ethics and values, suggesting new and advanced ways forward for equal opportunities practice. Inevitably, 'working towards equality', will always make demands for further change. As the vice chancellor put it, 'Once you have reached a situation you realize you can still do better . . . you find there is a new horizon.'

4

Metropolitan University:
Case Study

Introduction: four views on Metropolitan University's equal opportunities policy

On a wet and windy day in May 1993, four members of staff in one faculty at Metropolitan University were asked by one of the project researchers for their views on equal opportunities within the university.

The dean of the faculty, a man who had been working at Metropolitan University since the late 1960s, felt that considerable progress had been made in recent years. The first time equal opportunities issues had ever been raised in the university, he recalled, was some 15 or 20 years ago, when the identification of women members of staff by the titles 'Miss' or 'Mrs' in the academic directory was questioned by a member of staff, who was met with ridicule. Since then, he felt that awareness of the issues had increased considerably; in particular, there had been moves to censure sexist language practices, to encourage more women undergraduates to take courses in science and engineering, and to ensure that the number of female staff appointments increased. He felt, however, that adopting a positive discrimination strategy would be counter-productive, as few members of staff would support this move, and also because 'there are still very powerful senior management and lay individuals who are instinctively opposed to equal opportunities: they find it difficult to grasp that this is a serious issue.' An additional argument against positive discrimination, he thought, was that it was possible that overemphasizing equal opportunities issues might prevent the best applicants from getting jobs.

A female professor, recently appointed in the faculty, took a different view. Although the university claimed concern about the lack of female undergraduates on science and technology courses, she said, there was no thoroughgoing support for equal opportunities in this institution, and no attempt to ensure female representation on university committees. There were no female heads of department, no female deans, no women in the senior management group, and thus women had no say in resource allocation. In her view, the university still had a long way to go in ensuring equality for all staff, despite a belief that everything necessary to secure this had been done.

A part-time male lecturer, who had been in the university for a number of years, felt that his views of the situation typified those of most ordinary members of staff. He felt comfortable with the current policy on equal opportunities, although most staff had shown little interest in the developments and there had been some resistance to change.

In contrast, a female research assistant on a temporary contract in the university expressed anger at the day-to-day behaviour of colleagues and particularly at the 'jocular' sexist remarks of male colleagues, designed to 'score points' and to ensure that the 'correct' messages were conveyed. Her view of the university's equal opportunities policy was that it was extremely disappointing.

Subsequently, the research team remarked on the range of perspectives expressed in one institution on a single day. It was chance that these particular four people were interviewed, yet in a number of ways their views seemed to epitomize those of staff across the university. To explain such differences of opinion, we needed to take into account the particular historical and local influences on the development of equal opportunities issues at Metropolitan University, and also the reasons for the ways in which the particular policies and practices adopted there had evolved.

The account of our findings at Metropolitan University thus involves: history and the current position of equal opportunities at Metropolitan University; equal opportunities policy, practices and structures; and campaigns on specific issues.

Equal opportunities at Metropolitan University: history and the current position

Metropolitan University: a brief description

Metropolitan University is a large institution in Scotland. Created in the 1960s after a merger between a science and technology college and a business college, the university has maintained a marked focus on science and technology, although recently the business, arts and social sciences faculties have also become more prominent, and an education faculty has been added, as a result of a merger in 1993. The university has a long history of commitment to equal opportunities for students: one of the principal founding colleges was created in the nineteenth century to provide higher vocational education for working men *and women*, and sought practical ways to further these aims by arranging night classes and part-time courses for working students. Today, the university maintains an innovative approach to student recruitment, targeting inner-city schools, developing programmes to encourage women to take up science and engineering, and running a range of courses to help potential mature students prepare to return to study.

The university is located in one of the larger Scottish cities, and is housed in a number of buildings from various periods of the university's history, some dating back to the nineteenth century. Most of the buildings are relatively recent, representing a range of 'modern' institutional architectural styles. Despite the university's city centre location, considerable effort has been made to create a 'campus' feel, and one long-term aim of the institution is to occupy all buildings within a designated boundary. In all, there are now five faculties: arts and social studies, business school, science, engineering, and education.

Equal opportunities for women

As noted above, the university has its roots in an early nineteenth-century college of science and technology founded to provide practical education in these fields for skilled workers of both sexes; in the early days there were roughly equal numbers of men and women attending mainly evening classes. By the 1960s, however, there were few part-time or evening courses, and men were in the majority in both student and staff bodies. One staff member who had worked in the university since the 1960s commented:

> The situation was not a very progressive one in the sixties: the university's bias towards science and technology meant that there was a predominantly male culture. There were some female students in the science faculty, but there were very few – as far as I am aware – in technology; and furthermore, the all-male staff there thought in terms of an all-male student body.
>
> (Senior academic)

More recently, there have been moves to redress the balance somewhat. In the academic year 1992–3, 59 per cent of the university's full-time students (undergraduate and postgraduate) were male and 41 per cent female, before the merger with the college of education. The overall balance changed markedly as a result of the merger (in April 1993), however, after which 53 per cent of the students were male and 47 per cent female, a slightly more balanced mix than the Scottish national average of 55 per cent male and 45 per cent female (SOED, 1992).

Moves to achieve equal opportunities for female staff date back to the early 1980s. Concern among a small group of female academic staff about the position of female staff led the only female professor at the time to research the position of women in the university, focusing principally on the information available from payroll data comparing the years 1979–80 and 1983–4, and also on a 'snapshot' view of the staff situation on one day in 1985. The findings, published in an internal report in 1985, identified the following key issues for the university:

- prevalence of sex segregation in relation to the types of work commonly carried out by men and women;
- considerably weaker promotion prospects for women than for men, in relation to high level posts;
- absence of flexible working arrangements and job-share possibilities;
- absence of childcare provision;
- lack of equality in terms of employment for women, compared with men;
- need for equal opportunities monitoring to establish the extent of discrimination against women and the effectiveness of moves to counter this;
- need for the university to draw up a code of practice which would define the institution's responsibilities in relation to equal opportunities.

The 'Metropolitan Report' concluded:

> This picture of the Metropolitan University workforce shows real inequality in the position of women compared with the position of men. The majority of women are employed in 'women's' jobs with low pay and limited prospects for promotion or transfer. The majority of women are on the lowest grade in their category of work, and their prospects of promotion are even worse . . . Whilst there has been some increase in the number of academic departments that employ women as contract research staff, there has been no real change in the numbers or the distribution of women lecturers in the different departments or faculties of the University. Their degree of inequality is best illustrated by the level of their pay. Earning on average only 60% as much as men for working full-time, women at Metropolitan University do worse than women in the country as a whole.

These findings were not accepted by the university as a whole. Methodology and the report's 'balance' drew particular criticism. Nevertheless, it led to a number of developments in the university. A women's pressure group, now known as the Programme of Opportunities for Women (POW), which was formed by female staff in the early 1980s to draw attention to inequalities in women's position in the university and to raise the profile of women's work and women's achievements, drew strength from the publication of the report. The group is still active, constituting one of the principal forces pressing for change in the area of equal opportunities in the university.

Another development set in motion by the report has been the gradual reassessment of a number of practices and procedures in the personnel department. Monitoring of appointments by gender was introduced in 1988 and the statistics are reported to relevant university committees on a yearly basis. The personnel department has also been responsible for the drafting of an equal opportunities policy, which, after a fairly lengthy period of consultation, revision and expansion to take into account additional issues relating to equal opportunities (such as sexual and racial harassment) that were beginning to come to the fore nationally, was formally adopted by the university in September 1992. Subsequently, the department has sought – and finally won – funding for an equal opportunities officer to coordinate implementation of the policy. The officer was appointed in February 1994, after the case study had ended. It is important to note that this was the first full-time appointment of its kind in a Scottish university.

Other issues raised by the report still remain. There has been considerable debate about childcare provision but, at the time of writing, none was yet available. Flexible work arrangements and job-sharing, though theoretically possible, appeared to be limited in practice. The degree to which sex segregation existed in relation to employment, and the extent to which women may be excluded from senior posts, remain controversial issues in the university, and consequently no further initiatives have been undertaken.

Describing the current position of women at Metropolitan University is a complex task. Analysis of the figures emerging from the monitoring exercise described above shows that in the academic year 1991–2 women made up approximately 46 per cent of the university's staff overall. However, when the figure is broken down, various imbalances between the positions of women and men emerge. For example, 34 per cent of full-time and 97 per cent of part-time staff are women. There are also marked differences in the proportions of the sexes in the various categories of staff employed: while clerical and manual staff are overwhelmingly female (96 and 77 per cent respectively), the proportion of women in the academic sector is low (10 per cent), reflecting the university's focus on science and technology and the 'traditional' predominance of male academics in these fields. It is also clear that comparatively few women reach the highest grades in the sectors in which they work.

The 1991–2 figures, however, represent an improvement on the position of women in 1985, as described in the internal report. The number and proportion of women working in the university overall rose from approximately 40 to approximately 46 per cent, with increases in every sector. The number of women in the highest grades of each sector also rose over this period.

Interpretation of these statistics within the university has varied widely. Supporters of the university's stance on equal opportunities have argued that there is strong evidence to support the claim that equality of opportunity for women is being taken more seriously, and that gradual gains are being made as a result. Those taking this position pointed to the fact that it will take time for the larger number of women being appointed in the university to reach the highest grades in their sectors. Critics, on the other hand, have pointed to the continuing existence of marked inequalities between the sexes as evidence that much remains to be achieved, and that current policies and practices are ineffective.

Equal opportunities and 'race'

In contrast to gender issues, the question of 'race' has had a much lower profile in the university, almost certainly because of the very small numbers of Black staff and staff from minority ethnic backgrounds. There has been neither a report such as the one described above in relation to issues affecting women in the university, nor a pressure group to raise awareness of the position of Black staff and staff from minority ethnic backgrounds. Indeed, the precise number of Black members of staff and of staff from minority ethnic backgrounds is not known, as records are not kept. In the course of the project, researchers did not speak to any Black members of staff or staff from minority ethnic backgrounds, as none fell into the categories of staff interviewed. Occasionally, however, issues relating to 'race' were raised (by white members of staff) in the course of the research, suggesting that there is some peripheral interest in this aspect of equal opportunities.

Equal opportunities and disability

Disability is another area which has received relatively little attention, particularly in relation to staff, though the university has played an active part in the identification of students with certain learning difficulties – such as dyslexia – and in providing support for those affected. An attempt by the personnel department to initiate monitoring of staff with disabilities was abandoned when it became clear that some people known to have disabilities refused to identify themselves in this way. As with race issues, disability issues were occasionally raised by (apparently) able-bodied members of staff in the course of the research, indicating a degree of awareness – though marginal – that such issues might be included within the remit of equal opportunities. However, even when disability was discussed, the most common response was to point out the inappropriate design of the university buildings for wheelchair users, and the expense of rectifying the situation. Again, there has been little pressure to promote the perspectives of staff with disabilities, and there has been no history of awareness raising on this issue. The researchers did not speak to any members of staff with disabilities (as far as we are aware) in the course of the research, as, once again, none fell into the categories of staff interviewed.

University perspectives on equal opportunities

Views about the meaning of equal opportunities within the university vary considerably: the research team identified two contrasting perspectives.

One, most frequently expressed by male members of staff, and particularly by those in management positions, was that equal opportunities is already practised widely in the university, in that all appointments and promotions are made on the basis of merit and ability, following open, democratic procedures. In support of this, they pointed to the increasing numbers of women in all sectors of the university over the past decade. This perspective emphasizes positive aspects of the current situation but fails to consider less favourable aspects, such as the evidence that, in proportion to the numbers of women in the university generally, few women are being promoted into the highest grades within their sector.

In contrast, many of the women to whom we spoke, and also some of the men, took an alternative view: that the institution was dominated by a white, male, academic culture which it was extremely difficult to challenge. They argued that much of what had already been achieved in relation to equal opportunities had been done solely in order to promote the image of the university, rather than to bring about real changes, pointing to the low numbers of women in senior positions in all sectors of the university and arguing that concrete strategies – such as 'targeting' – were needed to combat discrimination.

In addition to these two perspectives, staff attitudes towards equal opportunities veered between apathy and hostility. The anonymity of the questionnaire circulated to staff in the second year of the project enabled some to express their reservations about the issue:

> If the university was to enforce its equal opportunities policy, it stands perhaps to lose out on recruiting the best staff available – enhancing people's prospects of promotion on the basis of sex, colour, disability is discriminatory. Will the thought police come and get me now?
>
> (Questionnaire respondent)

However, it was difficult to quantify the extent of this feeling, as most of the people to whom we spoke either had a specific role in promoting equal opportunities or were expecting to have to voice a view on this issue, since they were aware of the aims of the project.

Developments in the course of the project

A number of changes to the institution occurred during the course of the project, some of which had a bearing on the way in which equal opportunities issues were viewed and interpreted. Chief among these were:

- the merger with the college of education;
- the formal adoption of the equal opportunities policy;
- developments which came about in response to a number of campaigns with an equal opportunities focus;
- changes to the structures supporting equal opportunities in the university.

Probably the most significant change for the university as a whole, occurring in the course of the research, was the merger with the college of education in the city. At the time of writing it is difficult to assess in any detail the impact that the newly acquired faculty has made on the university as a whole, though it is clear that the somewhat different traditions of the college and, in particular, the higher proportion of female members of staff and students are likely to point up certain contrasts in style and approach between the older faculties and the newer one.

Another significant change was the adoption of the equal opportunities policy in September 1992. The researchers monitored the progress of the policy as it approached adoption and subsequent developments, key among which has been the decision to fund a new post of equal opportunities officer, with responsibility for coordinating the various initiatives designed to bring about the implementation of the policy.

At the same time, there were a number of campaigns supporting equality of opportunity for women. For example, the women's pressure group, POW, demanded improved monitoring of employment statistics relating to women staff, the development of staff training aimed specifically at women, more research in academic departments into gender issues and the setting up of a women's resource centre. A group supporting childcare provision for university staff was also active during this period.

In terms of the structures supporting equal opportunities, developments in the course of the research included the formal establishment of the vice principal's responsibility to court (the university's governing body) for overseeing equal opportunities. As a consequence, regular meetings were set up between the vice principal and POW in order to draw the attention of the university management group to issues which POW wished to raise. This has gone some way towards integrating the POW perspective into the university mainstream, though the group itself remains a pressure group and there is no obligation on the university management group to act on any of POW's recommendations.

The impression gained of developments in equal opportunities over the lifetime of the project has been one of gradual and somewhat cautious progress towards both the principles and the practice of equal opportunities. However, it was also clear that though significant numbers of staff members supported this progress, there was considerable opposition both from those openly hostile to the concept of equal opportunities and from those who simply see no reason for change.

In summary, factors supporting the university's progress during this period include:

• groups and individuals committed to the establishment of an equal opportunities policy and its implementation;
• a certain momentum to developments once the equal opportunities policy was adopted;
• a degree of institutional support for the principles of equal opportunities;

- a degree of general goodwill among staff towards the principles of equal opportunities;
- political and social changes outside the university supporting the increased participation of women at all levels of the workforce.

Factors hindering the university's progress during this period include:

- haphazard connections between those pressing for changes to policy and practice and those making decisions relating to policy and practice;
- a degree of institutional inertia;
- relatively low priority on the agendas of senior managers;
- hostility towards equal opportunities among some individuals and groups;
- lack of interest and awareness among many members of staff in relation to equal opportunities;
- political and social changes outside the university hindering the full participation of women and minority groups in the workforce.

The interplay between factors supporting change and those hindering will emerge in greater detail in subsequent sections.

The equal opportunities policy

Developing the policy

At the start of the case study, an equal opportunities policy, drafted by the personnel department, had been circulated to the key university committees and discussed by a range of different decision-making groups, such as the university management group, the staff committee, the unions and the POW committee. The policy was close to formal adoption in December 1991 when new guidelines relating to equal opportunities policy were issued by the Committee of Vice Chancellors and Principals (CVCP), recommending, among other things, that universities should incorporate sexual and racial harassment policies into more general policy statements relating to employment rights. Accordingly, the university's policy was withdrawn from circulation, and additional sections relating to sexual and racial harassment were added. Other minor changes were also made to the policy in the light of the CVCP guidelines, and the new policy began its tour of the relevant committees early in 1992. The content of the policy is discussed briefly below.

Equal opportunities in employment rights

This is a short one-page document, consisting of a boxed policy statement followed by a list of more detailed principles on which implementation is to be based. The language of the document is formal, identical to that of most of the other administrative documents which frame the university's practice in a number of areas. The terms of reference for the policy are wide: a long list of groups who might potentially suffer discrimination is included, and the principal aspects of employment practices – selection, training, appraisal and promotion – are covered. Responsibility for the upholding of the policy is vested both in the university and its employees in general terms, and also more specifically in the staff involved in selection, management and supervision of other staff. Implementation of the policy is to involve publicizing the policy, monitoring areas in which discrimination potentially might occur and providing training for staff with responsibility for appointments, staff training, appraisal and promotions. Disciplinary procedures are to constitute the force behind the policy if discrimination is found to have occurred.

The focus of the policy is primarily legalistic. Distinctions are made between types of discrimination which are currently illegal and those which, though undesirable, are not proscribed by law. The style is quasi-legal too: general principles are stated and sanctions listed, but the ways in which these principles are to be interpreted are left vague. Only when specific cases are brought for adjudication can the precise meanings of phrases be established, such as: 'Wherever possible all posts will be advertised *as widely as possible* and be designed to encourage applications from *relevant* groups' (emphasis added). Similarly, specific recommendations as to how equality of opportunity is to be achieved are not included in the policy.

The sexual and racial harassment policies

These policies provide a detailed description of what constitutes sexual and racial harassment and describe both formal and informal procedures which victims of harassment can follow. Various ways of dealing with complaints are outlined, including seeking advice, referring the matter to one's immediate manager and making a formal complaint. The methods for implementing the policies are not included in the policy document.

Progress of the policy towards adoption

The policy document was circulated over a period of approximately six months in 1992, and discussed widely. At a staff committee meeting observed for the project, debate was relatively limited: apart from a discussion relating to the appropriateness of the term 'gender' (as opposed to 'sex'), there was no dissent from the draft of the policy. A representative of the personnel department with responsibility for piloting the policy through to adoption confirmed that this was typical of responses at all the committees at which this draft policy was discussed.

At a POW meeting shortly after the policy was formally adopted, at which the final form of the policy was presented, discussion of the document focused on the implementation of the sexual harassment policy, details of which were not included in the policy document itself. As a result of this the need was identified for training of designated advisors, wide dissemination of the names of designated advisors and the development of complaint mechanisms.

The statement that those who made malicious accusations of sexual harassment would also be subject to disciplinary procedures provoked considerable outrage among some members of the group. It was felt that this was tantamount to a warning to women to consider the consequences very carefully before making a complaint and would deter many women with genuine complaints from coming forward. It was argued that there was considerably less danger of men suffering from malicious complaints than there was of women continuing to suffer sexual harassment in silence because of a lack of confidence in the procedures. Furthermore, it was argued (and subsequently confirmed) that no other university policy contained this type of clause. It was decided to investigate the effects of the statement when the policy came up for annual review after adoption.

Adoption and subsequent developments

The policy was formally adopted in September 1992, though this was not made widely known at the time. The personnel department, charged with implementing the policy, had decided against publicity, for two reasons. First, the department was keen to secure the appointment of an equal opportunities officer who would be responsible for coordinating the various initiatives designed to implement the policy. Second, it was felt that until staff had been trained to implement the policy, it would be counterproductive to risk raising expectations before the university was in a position to fulfil them.

Nevertheless, despite a lack of awareness of the content of the policy, there were still strong views on aspects of its implementation (whether or not staff knew that these were planned), as we discovered when we studied questionnaire responses about the appropriateness of appointing an equal opportunities officer. The personnel department was aware that views on the subject were decidedly mixed, and that considerable lobbying would be required in order to succeed in getting funding for the post. Questionnaire responses revealed the extent to which such an appointment was likely to be controversial.

Those opposed to the post had a variety of reasons. Some were against the appointment of an equal opportunities officer for pragmatic reasons: the money could be better spent elsewhere, particularly as (according to several among this group of respondents) the university was already too bureaucratic.

We already have too many 'overhead' posts. This would mean one less lecturer.

To single out [equal opportunities] by creating a post when staff throughout the university are overworked would invite criticism.

Others held the view that there was no need for an equal opportunities officer because the university was already operating in a non-discriminatory way – or at least that there was no evidence that this was not the case:

Staff in positions of authority/influence if properly recruited should have enough decency and common sense to make just decisions.

Some, while clearly supporting the principle of equal opportunities, felt that the appointment of an officer would not be the best way of implementing the policy. Rather it might detract from a more widespread assumption of responsibility for the issue:

The responsibility for equal opportunities must not be monitored by one person. The subject is too important.

The key to equal opportunities is the appointment of a greater number of women and minority groups as both academic and other staff. The key influence here is the attitudes and values of head of department. An equal opportunities officer may look good but have little power or influence.

Those in favour of an equal opportunities officer argued that there was a need for someone with a specific brief to raise awareness about equal opportunities issues, to coordinate initiatives and to evaluate the success of the policy:

It is an issue which the university must be seen to take seriously. Awareness among staff is so low that an appointment is necessary to make sure that the issue is put on the agenda and given systematic attention.

Promotion of EO is the responsibility of all staff; but unless it is monitored by an individual with specific responsibility, there is a danger that the success of equal opportunities is not evaluated.

In the light of this diversity of views, it is perhaps not surprising that it took the personnel department a year to succeed in having funding allocated for the post. Consequently, other aspects of the implementation were delayed, such as the training of staff with the responsibility for the implementation of the policy. Because of the delay in implementation of the policy, it was also necessary to postpone the review of the policy, originally planned for a year after the policy had been adopted.

Practices relating to equal opportunities

Equity in existing practices

It will be clear from the above account that the formal equal opportunities policy had little impact on the day-to-day organization of the university. Nevertheless, a strong theme running through a number of our interviews with staff was that the kinds of practices most likely to be affected by the policy – appointments, promotions and other decision-making procedures – were already egalitarian, and that in effect the policy simply codified what was already practised.

The research team observed several different events relating to staff appointments and promotions involving the 'decision-makers' in the university – in order to investigate the basis for the claim that existing practices supported equal opportunities for all staff.

Appointments

One research strategy was to follow one academic appointment from the advertising of the post to the final decision to appoint the successful candidate. The complexity of the process by which a decision is made about an appointment emerged very clearly in the course of this particular aspect of the research. First, there is the question of the criteria which are used to decide the most suitable applicant for the post. These are described briefly in the published job advertisement and in more detail in the particulars sent to applicants. But over the course of the short-leeting and during the interviews, other criteria, not mentioned in the recruitment literature, emerged as factors likely to affect the appointment. Chief among these, from the equal opportunities perspective, was an age preference (for candidates in their early to mid 30s), which appeared to the researchers to have some influence in determining the short leet, and which may, in fact, have been a factor in the final choice of candidate. Operating age criteria would seem to contravene the principles of equal opportunities – and, as may be recalled, the university's policy specifically outlaws discrimination in appointments or promotions on the grounds of age.

The chair of the short-leeting panel specifically raised this point, however, and the panel offered the following justification for preferring candidates from this age group:

- younger candidates did not have enough practical experience in the field to be able to fulfil the demands of the post adequately;
- the age profile of the department was from mid 40s onwards, and it was important to bring in younger staff with new ideas and approaches.

Discussion with other interviewees (unconnected with this particular appointment) raised an additional issue in relation to the age of candidates for appointments: older and more experienced candidates cost more.

Though I believe that appointments are made in the spirit of equal opportunities, it may be funding rather than principles which determine whether one appoints or promotes an experienced (but relatively expensive) candidate rather than a less experienced (and therefore cheaper) one.

(Senior academic)

The appointments panel appeared, indirectly, to be operating according to this principle, as it was stated at one point that the key to the appointment was 'potential'. Indeed, this statement seemed to come at an influential point in the final discussion over which candidate to appoint: until then, the panel seemed to favour a candidate in his 40s, possibly the most experienced of the four final candidates, but subsequently there was a change of course and eventually the youngest candidate was selected.

It will be clear from this discussion that the operation of age criteria in determining the appropriate candidate for this post cannot be seen as a simple instance of discrimination, as the reasons for preferring candidates from a particular age group have a degree of validity. For example, if it is appropriate for employers to state that they welcome applications from women or members of certain minority groups which are under-represented in their organization, is it also appropriate to target under-represented age groups? The question of the cost of an appointment is also a difficult issue. It is not only the salary costs which come into consideration in this context but also, as another interviewee pointed out, the additional costs which staff with disabilities may incur: 'If the appointment of disabled staff requires extensive additional resources, this may be controversial with other members of staff' (Senior academic).

What seems problematic is not so much the rationale given to support what might be interpreted as discriminatory criteria, but rather the lack of debate and, ultimately, of clear guidelines or training for staff engaged in making decisions about appointments. Asked what he would see as appropriate training for his job, a head of department said:

I feel that equal opportunities training in my responsibilities as a manager, particularly in relation to appointments, would be appropriate. The key areas on which I feel I need guidance are age and disability. Gender and 'race' are more straightforward in terms of determining how to avoid discrimination: they simply shouldn't be taken into the equation of the job. Disability is particularly problematic, given that small budgets and building constraints make it difficult to appoint people with specific disabilities.

It seems that it is the unwritten 'rules' which decision-makers have to apply that raise the most problematic issues in relation to equal opportunities in the university.

A second issue which emerged from the appointments procedure was the ways in which the members of the panel identified the strengths and

Table 4.1 Candidates' strengths and weaknesses

Candidate	Strengths	Weaknesses
1	Strong research profile. High standard of practical skills required in the field. Broad experience. European contacts.	Referees had not replied. Teaching competence unknown.
2	Strong teaching profile. Good standard of practical skills required in this field. 'Home-grown product' (i.e. had been a student in the university and returned to tutor there). Candidate with the most 'potential'.	No research experience. No European contacts. 'Low-key' performance at interview. Long association with the university could be problematic.
3	Very strong interview performance. Stimulating speaker, likely to motivate students. Attractive personality.	Lacked clear ideas about teaching or research. Lacked intellectual depth.
4	More 'insightful' than the other candidates. A scholarly approach.	Weak presentation to department. Seemed inarticulate and uncomfortable in interview – would not motivate students.

weaknesses of the candidates and related these to the criteria for the post. Clearly, all appointments involve a compromise between the demands of the post to be filled and the abilities of the candidates who apply. In many cases, of course, the mismatch is quite apparent. As we were not present at the time of the long-leeting, we cannot say exactly what the criteria were for rejecting candidates at this stage, but it is likely that relevant deficiencies included inappropriate qualifications, lack of relevant experience in the field, failure to address the criteria stated in the particulars and other quite basic inadequacies of this type. At the interview stage, however, the situation seems more complicated. We were told that on principle all those who reached the interview stage should be appointable. So what is it, in the final analysis, that influences the decision to choose one out of a short leet of suitable candidates? Table 4.1 shows the strengths and weaknesses (as identified by the appointments panel) of each of the candidates for the post.

Each candidate had different strengths and weaknesses, but how were these weighted against each other? It emerged that strength in either teaching or research was going to be the key factor in making the decision. This led to the elimination of candidates 3 and 4. Candidates 1 and 2 seemed to be mirror images of each other: candidate 1, some ten years older than candidate 2 (who fell into the 'optimum age' category of early to mid 30s), had considerable professional experience in the field before making the decision to become an academic and becoming involved in research work, in which this candidate was also now highly accomplished. Candidate 2 had less professional experience and none at all of research, but had considerable teaching expertise. In addition, because candidate 2 had studied and worked in the university for some time, this candidate's work was known in much greater depth by the department than was the case with the others. In the end, teaching expertise, plus the department's familiarity with candidate 2's work and 'potential' – a term which was never defined very clearly – won out against the professional and research experience of candidate 1. But for an outside observer it was not easy to identify why the decision went this way. It seemed that unwritten rules came into play, and therefore it was difficult to establish whether subtle forms of discrimination were taking place or not.

Finally, we were made aware of many small and possibly insignificant – but also possibly influential – aspects of the interviews which might or might not have a bearing on the equality of opportunity offered to each of the candidates. These are shown in Table 4.2, in which instances from the interviews are noted, with the issues they raise alongside.

The researchers found no evidence to suggest that the appointment made at the end of this process was based on discrimination of any kind. The issue that we are raising here is the scope, when guidelines are not laid down and procedures are not systematized, for unintentional discrimination. Though staff frequently and vehemently rejected the possibility that the democratic practices of the university could be manipulated in this way, others revealed the relative ease with which prejudice might be justified:

> There may still be a number of people with doubts about employing women, disabled members of staff or members of staff from minority ethnic backgrounds. If a department has a bad experience employing someone from such a group then it is not surprising that they would feel apprehensive about appointing someone from a similar background a second time.
>
> (Senior academic)

Promotions

The research team attended three academic review meetings which determine whether probationary lecturers will have their probation 'confirmed' (in other words whether they become recognized as fully qualified lecturers and are confirmed in their posts), and which members of staff will be

Table 4.2 Some issues raised by the interview procedure

Instances from the interviews observed	*Issues raised*
Candidates were not always asked the same questions. Sometimes, the reason for this was to get at the different histories and areas of experience which each candidate had; but sometimes, it was not easy to see why different questions should be asked. For example only candidate 3 was asked to discuss strengths and weaknesses of the university department concerned with the appointment. All candidates were asked to devise an interdepartmental project, but only with candidate 4 was the other department specified (and unfortunately it was clearly a field of which this candidate had no knowledge).	How easy is it to compare candidates if they have not been asked the same questions?
The following characteristics of interviewee responses may have been influential in giving the impression of a 'good' interviewee: • eye contact; • length of time the candidate speaks, in answer to one question; • keeping one's response positive at all times; • committing oneself in one's answers; • engaging in dialogue with the interviewers.	Do male and female candidates have different styles in interview? Do candidates from minority ethnic backgrounds have different styles in interview? If so, how aware of these different styles are members of appointments panels, and how do they respond to them?
Candidates 1 and 3 were 'good' interviewees – relaxed, confident, talkative, engaging. Candidate 3 was particularly attractive – one of the panel described himself as having been 'swept along' by the flow of the conversation. Candidate 2 was described as 'low-key', 'diffident' and 'introspective'. Candidate 4 seemed nervous and defensive throughout.	What strategies do interviewers have for candidates who are nervous or don't come over well – both to relax them at the interview and to assess contribution appropriately afterwards?
Members of the panel related interview 'performance' to candidates' ability to motivate and inspire students.	To what extent does 'performance' at interview relate to the candidate's ability to do the job in question?

promoted and/or receive additional pay increments in recognition of good work.

There were two key features of these meetings which bear indirectly on issues relating to equal opportunities. The first was an undercurrent of certain tensions in the course of the review process, relating to ways in which the university was changing in response to various external pressures. The second was, once more, the extent to which unwritten rules applied to the decisions made. Each of these factors is considered in turn below.

In the 1980s, universities were urged to become more market conscious and to investigate ways in which the services they provided could be made profitable. Methods for doing this included encouraging more foreign students to apply and promoting the expertise of university staff in various fields in industrial and business contexts where 'market' consultancy rates could be charged. But such moves could frequently provoke controversy within the institutions, and, even though it was probable that the fiercest clashes were over by the time the research team became involved with the university, it was clear that tensions lingered and resurfaced from time to time.

An example of this emerged at one review panel meeting. The case concerned a lecturer seeking promotion to senior lecturer not on academic grounds but rather on the excellence of his entrepreneurial skills. This provoked what the panel itself described as a 'clash of cultures' between, on the one hand, the conventional academic criteria of research and scholarly publications and, on the other, the activities of the centre which attracted funds and gave the university considerable outside publicity and credit. Eventually a compromise was reached: the decision made was to promote the lecturer, but with advice to publish in more conventional academic ways. The panel also made recommendations to examine further the issue of culture clash and to develop guidelines to be applied in other cases of this nature.

Another controversial issue – of much longer standing – was the need to place equal emphasis on teaching and administrative skills as on research and publications, which had traditionally been seen as the benchmark for promotion. Academic staff had been debating this issue for a number of years, but it became a more pressing issue in the late 1980s, as a result of government pressure for greater 'productivity' in universities. In addition, questions about the quality of university teaching were being raised nationally, and university inspections were being piloted during the case study period. In recognition of the importance of encouraging staff to develop their teaching skills, and also of the considerable administrative demands made on some members of staff, in relation to the increased numbers of students, it had been decided that excellence in teaching or in administration should be regarded as equivalent to excellence in research as a promotion criterion. The formula established was that excellence in one of the three criteria and competence in the other two were the appropriate qualifications for promotion.

However, this formula also provoked resistance, which again emerged from time to time in more or less covert ways. For example, in considering the case of a lecturer who had been appointed head of a unit within the university providing a particular service for students, and who, as a result of the considerable administrative duties involved in this task, had no time for research, it was clear that members of the review panel felt that he could not be promoted without a longer publications list. It was nevertheless recognized that the request for promotion was based on the lecturer's excellence in administration. However, unlike excellence in research, of which the panel had experience, excellence in administration was something with which it was not very familiar. In this case, no compromise was reached: the lecturer was to be informed that he had no chance of becoming a senior lecturer while he held this post.

These two cases seemed to illustrate the extent to which it was possible for those involved in making decisions about promotions to resist new or controversial views on the nature of academic work. Neither of these cases had equality implications, as both the lecturers were male, white and unaffected by disability. But in a more fundamental sense, they do raise issues related to equal opportunities, in that staff were being given one message about criteria for promotion (that research, teaching and administrative skills were equally important, and that entrepreneurialism was of considerable importance) while those responsible for making decisions about promotions were applying a different, more traditional, set of criteria. Thus lecturers who resisted the new order and maintained a research focus were better placed for promotion.

It was suggested that women might be disadvantaged by this state of affairs, in that it was possible that women, traditionally encouraged to take up 'supportive' roles within an academic department, might have been side-tracked into administrative work that would not enable them to be promoted. We found little evidence of this, though it was not possible to conduct exhaustive investigations in every department in every faculty.

As with appointments, the extent to which unwritten rules played a part in the ways in which decisions about promotions were made seemed problematic. There appeared to be considerably fewer written criteria in relation to promotions than there were for appointments (where every advertised post has a job description). The *Handbook for Academic Staff* set down in detail the procedures which review panels were to adopt but provided very little in the way of criteria for establishing the promotability of candidates. The following, from the *Handbook*, demonstrates the difficulties well:

> In the case of proposals for promotion to Reader, the Review Panels will in particular examine the candidate's report in the duties that are normally called for in a senior member of academic staff in the areas of scholarship, particularly teaching, administration and research. The Panels will expect a candidate to have shown an exceptional and distinguished contribution of both innovation and dissemination in

at least one of these areas of scholarship and to have demonstrated more than satisfactory performance in the others.

'Exceptional', 'distinguished', 'innovation', 'dissemination' and 'satisfactory' are not defined, and are thus left open to the panels' own interpretation.

What, then, are the unwritten rules? As outsiders, it was difficult for us to be alert to the nuance of every turn of phrase, and in none of the presentations of cases were the signals as blatant as that suggested by a senior member of staff:

> There are 'codes' which heads of department use on recommendation forms – for example 'very reliable at handling examination results' probably means (if there is no additional comment) that the candidate does not have a good track record in research.

Nevertheless, the way the panels handled the cases seemed to indicate that the members were astute at picking up the signals as to which candidates the faculty wanted to promote and which were not favoured contenders. Extended discussion was reserved for those whose cases were not being recommended and, though there was some attempt in these cases to search for evidence supporting the candidates, ultimately the discussion led to the construction of a case against them. Effectively, this seemed to imply that decisions about promotions had taken place at an earlier stage, and that the role of the panels was to ensure that such decisions were fair.

This is not to suggest that such a system is necessarily unreasonable or inherently discriminatory. The review panel meetings were already long and considerable documentation was involved. All candidates for promotion had to be interviewed beforehand, and the dean discussed the decisions with all concerned afterwards. However, without guidelines or written criteria for promotion, the devolution of the moment of decision-making to internal, unscrutinized meetings of senior faculty members raises the risk of discrimination. Possible ways in which the faculty was able to subvert the university's criteria for promotion were put forward as follows:

> Is there a shared understanding of what a 'promotable' candidate is? Not totally, but there are historical issues which it is important to be aware of. In the past, this faculty was perceived to be a 'teaching faculty' and was therefore very weak. The current dean has had a clear strategy of moving to become a 'research faculty' as the way to gain a stronger position in the university. Thus those professors who emphasized research became central in decision-making, and those who have followed a research strategy have been more successful in promotions.
>
> (Senior academic)

This may be the stuff of institutional politics, but what if the male dean, the male vice deans and the male heads of department had decided not to promote women? Would this decision be challenged anywhere further down the line? As with appointments, the likelihood of such discriminatory attitudes prevailing may be remote, but it seems important to ensure that the opportunities for prejudice to influence decisions relating to promotion are minimized.

Significantly, the University Review Committee had recommended the development of guidelines to establish criteria to be used in determining the promotability of candidates. In the past, it would seem that there has been a high degree of consensus about the criteria for promotion, but now this was being challenged in a number of ways. Guidelines on equal opportunities seemed to merit similar attention, in our view.

Structures supporting equal opportunities

Developing structures

Structural support for equal opportunities was somewhat diffuse at the beginning of the case study. However a number of changes occurred in the course of the research which indicated a gradual strengthening of support. The most substantial development was the appointment of an equal opportunities officer after the project had ended. Prior to this appointment, in the absence of a post holder for equal opportunities, a number of different people took on aspects of this role. These included the vice principal, the personnel department and the POW committee.

The vice principal

Ultimate responsibility for equal opportunities rested with the vice principal, for whom it was only one of a great many. In addition the post holder changes every two years. The vice principal in post from September 1992 onwards was ambivalent about whether the vice principal should have this responsibility:

All senior officers have a portfolio of responsibilities and this one seems to happen to have fallen to the vice principal. In a number of ways, however, the vice principal is not the most suitable officer, as the office is a two-year appointment which would seem to be a handicap in achieving anything in this area. It takes some time to get to know the issues and by the time this has happened, the person filling the office has little time left to get anything done. When the equal opportunities officer has been appointed, his or her job will be to brief the senior officer efficiently and quickly; the existence of an EO officer will ensure continuity of information.

Despite these doubts, this vice principal could point to a number of achievements in the course of his term of office. In addition to supporting

the personnel department's bid for the appointment of an equal opportunities officer, and also to his role in securing agreement for childcare
facilities to be provided by the university, an important development over
this period was the establishment of a more systematic reporting mechanism between the vice principal and the POW committee. His intention
was that the convener of the POW committee should meet him regularly
in advance of staff committee meetings (which take place quarterly). Thus
issues raised by the POW committee could be channelled via the vice
principal into the mainstream committee structure, through the staff
committee. The vice principal commented:

> The vice principal's role is to direct POW to the appropriate fora [*sic*]
> for debate in relation to the issues the group raises – for example,
> staff committee. In fact, there will now be a regular report from POW
> to the staff committee, and this is an appropriate system. Ideally equal
> opportunities issues concerning staff should be initiated either by the
> personnel office or by POW and then directed to staff committee.

Thus, although the amount of time which the vice principal could spend
on issues relating to equal opportunities was clearly limited, the significance of his contribution both in promoting developments in this area
and in facilitating links seems clear.

The personnel department

The personnel department acknowledged responsibility for equal opportunities in issues relating to employment rights. It had taken on the work
of drafting the equal opportunities policy and of piloting the policy through
the various committees. Subsequently, it was the personnel department
which fought for and won funding for the post of equal opportunities
officer, as it was recognized that implementing the policy would involve
considerably greater resources than had previously been required and the
personnel department did not have the scope to provide these. Thus the
appointment of an equal opportunities officer was seen as a way of allo-
cating the tasks to one full-time coordinator, responsible to the director
of personnel.

The POW committee

The POW committee acted as a pressure group campaigning for a range
of women's issues. Membership of the committee represented a range of
groups from the academic and academic-related sectors of the university.
Some members were co-opted, while others were nominated representatives from, for example, each of the faculties and a variety of administrative sections. The POW committee was set up in the university to promote

women's interests throughout the university, in a number of different ways:

- supporting academic courses and research into gender issues;
- supporting the establishment of the Women's Development Training Group, with a focus on management training for female staff;
- promoting non-traditional subject areas for female students and special courses for women returning to work;
- encouraging women to play a larger part in the university's decision-making bodies (court and senate);
- monitoring employment and promotion statistics for women in the university;
- enhancing the image of women in the university and beyond, such as by organizing International Women's Day events, nominating female honorary graduands, monitoring the representation of women in university publications and prospectuses etc.;
- supporting practical initiatives for women, such as the establishment of childcare facilities for staff, a women's resource centre etc.

However, as a pressure group, the POW committee could not take the place of a formally constituted equal opportunities committee, and of course had no brief to promote aspects of equal opportunities other than those which affected women in the university. There was some debate among members of the POW committee as to whether the committee was more effective as a pressure group than would be the case if it were incorporated into the university's committee structure. The former route might ensure that the committee had greater power to bring about change. However, such a move might also limit the range of issues POW was able to address, and reduce the influence which members had over a range of committees and senior members of staff in the university.

Senior managers similarly felt that POW had greater scope outside the mainstream of university decision-making structures:

If you had a programme of action for women reporting to a point, you would be disturbing the managerial system in the university, or rather creating a focus which was broad across the whole university, but which didn't really have a direct line function.

(Senior manager)

The Programme of Opportunities for Women committee is not an integral part of the decision-making process in the university. It operates effectively as a ginger group and does not have a reporting mechanism . . . It has been suggested that POW should become a sub-committee of staff committee, but this would not be appropriate as POW's interests are wider than simply reporting to staff committee.

(Senior manager)

Nevertheless, while the decision to remain a pressure group may have been the appropriate one, the absence of a central committee to address the full range of equal opportunities issues in the university seemed to represent a gap in the support structure. The role of the POW committee appeared limited, both because of its focus exclusively on gender issues and because of its status as a pressure group without any guaranteed forum.

Campaigns on specific issues related to equal opportunities

Range of campaigns

During the time that the research team was involved with the university, a number of campaigns promoting aspects of equal opportunities were launched or under way. Many of these were generated by the POW committee, members of which were involved in moves to increase the number of female honorary graduands, to encourage women to take degrees in science and engineering, and to argue for more comprehensive gender monitoring, including target-setting. It was not possible for us to investigate all these campaigns in detail. Instead, in this section, we have focused on two contrasting campaigns: one to establish a childcare facility in the university for children of members of staff working in the university; and one to promote the use of what is termed in the university 'gender-free language' (or non-sexist language) in official university publications and other public settings within the university.

Childcare group

Childcare provision for the children of members of staff was one of the recommendations made by the 1985 report on the position of women in the university. Subsequently a group campaigning for such provision was formed to put pressure on senior managers to consider the issue. However, initially the group had little success. From the point of view of group members, their failure to raise interest in the issue was because of two factors. First, the university's senior managers were all men, many of whom belonged to a generation which had assumed that wives would take responsibility for providing childcare. Second, the group recognized that in order for campaigns of this nature to work, it was essential to have a 'champion' among the ranks of the senior managers who would take responsibility for keeping the issue on the agenda. In the early years, before equal opportunities became the responsibility of the vice principal, there was no way of identifying a member of the senior management team who might automatically assume the responsibility; nor did it prove possible to arouse an altruistic interest in any of the senior managers of the time.

The situation changed in the course of the case study in that a newly appointed principal undertook to promote the childcare issue by appointing a 'task force' headed by the vice principal elect to investigate the issue in depth. The task force surveyed both students and staff in the university to identify the extent of likely demand for childcare facilities. The results were encouraging in that they showed that demand was likely to be high (well over 100 children under the age of five, and additional demand for after-school and holiday provision for primary school aged children). However, there were also a number of problems. First, estimating the costs of provision was a particularly complex task. Second, it proved difficult to find suitable premises and suitable carers. Third, doubts as to the viability of the enterprise were raised by those who held that parents would prefer to send their children to childminders or nurseries near their own homes rather than subject them to a long journey into the city centre and home again each day.

These factors played a part in delaying further the establishment of a childcare facility in the university, and some of the issues had not been resolved by the end of the case study, although the task force had succeeded in winning a firm agreement to incorporate a childcare facility into a new building project which the university was about to undertake. Staff held different views on this. Some believed that the thoroughness with which the issue was being investigated pointed to the university's commitment to providing childcare, despite the complexity of the situation, and that a facility would be established eventually. Others asserted that the problems raised were minor, and that if the senior managers of the university were genuinely in favour of providing a childcare facility, they would have overcome them long before. It was suggested that we might compare the logistics, costs and subsidies of setting up childcare provision with those relating to the establishment of new sports facilities in the university, though this was not feasible.

Gender-free language

The campaign to encourage the use of 'gender-free' language was also promoted by POW. Guidelines were devised by staff from the linguistics department, at the instigation of the committee, and in 1991 a leaflet giving details of linguistic practices deemed to be discriminatory (such as the use of generic *he* to include women, gender-specific terms such as *chairman*, also used generically, and other terms of a similar nature), explanations as to why such usage was considered discriminatory and suggestions promoting 'gender-free' alternatives was widely circulated throughout the university. The use of gender-free language, as was stated in the leaflet, had the formal support of both the university court and senate.

It is difficult to assess the impact of such a leaflet. Evidence of change can, on the whole, only be anecdotal. One senior member of staff referred specifically to the leaflet and said that he felt changes had occurred as a result: 'I feel there has been a marked decline in the use of generic *he* in recent years.' However, though unable to carry out a systematic analysis of all university documents, we noted several instances of 'inappropriate' generic usages, most frequently of *chairman* in a range of documents which appeared after the circulation of the leaflet (e.g. the 1993–4 university calendar still uses the term to refer to those chairing convocation, court and senate).

We included an item in the questionnaire about the gender-free language leaflet and its effects on linguistic practice. Half the respondents denied receiving a copy of the leaflet. Of those who said thay had received the leaflet, 18 per cent (6 per cent of all those who replied) reported that they had changed their language habits as a result. Responses revealed that staff had widely differing views on the subject and it was clear that some people had found the leaflet offensive or threatening:

> Unlike languages such as French, there is no gender attached to nouns in the English language. Anyone who objects to words such as 'chairman' etc. has a personality problem and should seek help. My wife is a professional woman who competes with men as an *equal* and believes this is utter nonsense.

> I think universities should deal with education not mind altering.

Others simply did not see that the issue was relevant to them:

> [These guidelines] don't apply in my subject.

> I do not believe in the concept.

> The situation does not arise very often when teaching technical subjects.

Some respondents indicated that they accepted the principles behind the move to gender-free language, but that they took issue with some of the recommendations:

> I try to avoid obvious and harmful gender bias (i.e. referring to a head of department in terms of what 'he' might do) but am not prepared to use 'politically correct' terminology such as 'chair' etc.

> Already believed firmly in 'equal opportunities', but also believe that you cannot prescribe an entire 'politically correct' language/vocabulary – styles change and different situations demand different responses.

A number of those who said that they had not changed the way that they spoke or wrote explained that this was because they had already made moves to avoid terms that were potentially offensive:

> I have not changed the way I write as a result of the guidelines as such. More generally I have tried to avoid some unnecessary use of

words considered to have a gender connotation where a practical alternative is available.

Already sought to employ gender-free language and ethnic/racial and sexual evaluation terms – the leaflet acts as a constant useful reminder to do better.

Some indicated that the leaflet had acted as a stimulus to reviewing their linguistic practices and that they now made a conscious effort to avoid inappropriate usage:

I now think of neutral words as opposed to referring to male dominated nouns.

I tend to use plurals and avoid him/her.

It is clear that the issue is likely to remain controversial, particularly because of the fact that it is interpreted as a symbolic question rather than one of practical concern (in that the use of terminology which excludes women contributes to their under-representation in the workforce in general and in particular at senior level). As the proponents of gender-free language in fact support both these arguments (as well as arguing that exclusive terminology is directly discriminatory, they also believe it is necessary to change the way people think, by changing the way they speak, in order to prevent such discrimination), it is unlikely that opposition to the new terminology will diminish in the near future among individual members of staff.

The failure of official university publications to follow guidelines which have been officially approved, however, reflects the absence of effective monitoring of equality initiatives once they have been adopted. The histories of both campaigns show the difficulties involved in trying to bring about changes in a large institution, particularly in the absence of institutional support and resources.

Summary and conclusions

Summary

The case study of Metropolitan University focused on three areas relating to equitable staffing policies and practices: the formal adoption of the university's equal opportunities policy; an analysis of practices with a bearing on equitable staffing policies; and the development of structures to support equality of opportunity for staff in the university. In addition, the researchers considered the impact of some of the campaigns promoting aspects of equal opportunities at the time of the research.

The *university's equal opportunities policy*, developed by the personnel department in consultation with a range of university committees, employment

rights and measures to combat sexual and racial harassment. We characterized it as a 'first-time round' policy in that it presents a general statement of good intentions in relation to equal opportunities and makes few
specific recommendations for change. It seemed clear that only after the
policy had been widely publicized and staff had become aware of the
impact the policy was likely to have on their work would the kinds of
changes required begin to be discussed.

We also focused on aspects of *practice* – appointments and promotions
– which were central to the policy though they had not at the time been
affected by it. We found little evidence of discrimination at observed
meetings at which appointments and promotions were discussed; but we
did note the absence of specific criteria to determine candidates' 'ability'
and 'merit' and, in contrast, the extent to which unwritten rules or 'consensus' as to what these consisted of played a part in the decision-making
process. We also came across situations in which the consensus view clashed
with other aspects of the changing culture and politics of university life.
We thus became aware of the power of the consensus to resist change.

We explored the *structures* which supported equal opportunities in the
university. In particular, we considered the Programme of Opportunities
for Women, campaigning actively on a number of issues of relevance to
women in the university; and a group campaigning for childcare provision
for university staff and students. Neither of these groups, however, was
formally incorporated within the university's committee structure, and
consequently access to decision-making bodies seemed somewhat haphazard. The personnel department had responsibility for the development of the equal opportunities policy and its implementation, but was
limited in the extent to which the department could become actively
involved in this work when there were no additional funds allocated for
the task.

During the research a number of changes to these structures were made.
The vice principal elect was appointed leader of a task force with the job
of solving the childcare issue. As a result of this initiative, the campaign
group was able to present recommendations to the various decision-making
bodies involved in making provision, and ultimately succeeded in securing
agreement for purpose-built accommodation in a current building project.
When the vice principal elect took over as vice principal, he assumed
formal responsibility for equal opportunities at senior management level,
and made arrangements for regular meetings with the POW committee as
a way of channelling the views of the committee into the university's staff
committee. Later, the personnel department succeeded in winning funding for the appointment of an equal opportunities officer who would take
over responsibility for the implementation of the policy. All these changes
resulted in equal opportunities having a higher profile in the university
than previously. However, it was still the case at the end of the research
period that there was no direct access to decision-making bodies for many
of those engaged in equal opportunities work.

Conclusions

Metropolitan University is an institution still in the early stages of developing an equal opportunities policy and of analysing existing practices from an equal opportunities perspective. Evidence of the progress made includes the adoption of the equal opportunities policy and the start of moves to ensure its implementation – most notably in the appointment of an equal opportunities officer. In addition, the strengthening of the structures which support equal opportunities in the institution has improved access to decision-making committees. This has had at least one concrete outcome to date, in that the involvement of the vice principal elect in the task force set up to identify ways of making provision for childcare can be seen as a factor contributing to the long-awaited decision to establish an on-site nursery. It is, nevertheless, the case that further structural changes would be required to ensure that those engaged in work promoting equal opportunities have direct access to decision-making in the university.

It is clear that the changes made are key steps in any institution's move towards ensuring that the principles of equal opportunities are incorporated into all relevant practices. Yet, as the diverse views expressed by staff at the start of this chapter indicate, whatever initiatives an institution takes to promote equal opportunities are bound to be seen as controversial.

We have seen that the university has taken a cautious approach to innovation and that the development of a consensus is felt to be of considerable importance when changes are proposed. There are advantages and disadvantages to this procedure. The length of time that it takes for decisions to be made, and the delay between making a decision and implementing it, can be deeply frustrating for those actively promoting a particular issue. There is a risk of momentum being lost and cynicism setting in, and it is important to take into account the likelihood, for example, of losing female staff or staff from minority groups if conditions of work and the ethos of the institution are felt to be unfavourable and unpromising and the likelihood of change seems remote.

At the same time, this approach ensures that controversy is kept to a minimum and that rash decisions are not taken. It may well be the case that in seeking to avoid the alienation of particular groups and to obtain the agreement of all, there is a greater chance of the policy being successfully implemented in the long run. What is gained and what is lost by this approach has to be carefully judged.

5

Critical Moments and
Illuminative Insights

How can the complexity and 'messiness' of policy-making be described and portrayed? We have shown how equal opportunities policy developed in each of the case study institutions, and how historical and institutional factors meshed with equality issues. The policy case study format enabled us to present our findings to the different institutions involved in what, we hoped, was a coherent and accessible way. However, in our original research proposal we had also promised to generate theories about the policy change process as well as providing analyses of policy decisions and effectiveness.

The aim of this chapter is to describe a particular approach taken to the analysis of the wide range of project data gathered. We present three extracts from the data with the aim of creating critical meanings which illuminate gender and other aspects of equal opportunities policy and which also may be applied more generally to researching social justice issues in education.

Theoretical framework

We adopt a micro-political perspective of social relations, as we have seen in Chapter 1. We also draw on feminist post-structuralist and standpoint theories because they have proved useful to recognizing the importance of 'agency' as well as structure in the production of gendered practices.

In the context of education, feminist post-structuralism moves beyond the female-as-deficient or female-as-victim models, as Jones suggests, by providing 'new possibilities for understanding girls' socialisation or the "production of girls", which go beyond seeing girls primarily as "disadvantaged" and socialised within oppressive patriarchal structures' (Jones, 1993: 157). Briefly, post-structuralism relies on a number of central ideas. First, it views *language* as the common factor in any analysis of social organizations, power and individual consciousness. It is in language that our subjectivity as well as social organizations are defined, contested and constructed:

> The assumption that subjectivity is constructed implies that it is not innate, not genetically determined, but socially produced . . . Language is not the expression of unique individuality: it constructs the individual's subjectivity in ways which are socially specific.
>
> (Weedon, 1987: 21)

Post-structuralism assumes that meaning is constructed within language and is not guaranteed by what the author intends. Thus, any analysis of, say, the impact of policy documents or management rhetoric necessarily needs to consider interpretation as well as intentionality or impact.

Post-structuralism also takes *universals* and *truths* to be problematic and open to scrutiny, arising out of specific historical changes. It seeks to analyse in what ways those ideas have become *universal* or *normalizing* – hence, as Ball (1990: 2) argues, 'the idea of a judgement [is] based on what is normal and thus what is abnormal.' It uses the principle of *discourse* to show how power relationships and subjectivity are constituted. Discourses are structuring mechanisms for social institutions, modes of thought and individual subjectivities. They are, according to Foucault, 'practices that systematically form the objects of which they speak . . . Discourses are not about objects; they do not identify objects, they constitute them and in the process of doing so conceal their own invention' (Foucault, 1974: 49).

Thus each individual actively takes up discourses, say within the lecture theatre, classroom or family, through which he or she is shaped. According to Weedon (1987: 105), how people feel about themselves or their power to act is constantly in flux, a consequence both of their own meaning-making and of various discourses that attempt to fix meaning, once and for all.

> A constant battle is being waged for the subjectivity of every individual – a battle in which real interests are at stake, for example, gender-based social power . . . Common sense and the liberal-humanist tradition upon which it is founded suggest that every individual possesses an unchanging essence of subjectivity . . . [Yet] the battle for the meaning of gendered subjectivity and the many attempts made by conflicting discourses to fix meaning once and for all is doomed to failure.

As a reverse or counter discourse, feminism positions itself to challenge such meaning-making, enabling the production of new, resistant discourses which reveal how power is exercised through discourse, how oppression works and how resistances might be possible. Additionally, embedded in feminist perspectives on research, and more widely, is the search for more equitable and gender-conscious practices and processes which also engage with social justice and injustice, from a standpoint or vantage point of being feminist and female. This may be viewed as more (or differently) illuminating than other vantage points (Harding, 1990; see also Hill Collins,

1990, for discussion of a Black, feminist vantage point). Smith argues that such standpoint theory has crucial cultural as well as empirical consequences for women by 'taking up the standpoint of women as an experience of being, of society, of social and personal process which must be given form and expression within the culture' (Smith, 1978: 294).

Further, Harding (1990: 97) suggests that unlike empiricism, which still holds to a faith in the 'scientific' approaches to research, feminist standpoint theory provides the possibility of a critique of research claims to the truth.

> The feminist standpoint theorists are unambivalently opposed to the idea that a-historical principles of enquiry can ensure ever more perfect representations of the world. They challenge the possibility of such a 'science machine' or algorithm for producing true representations.

Although currently popular, standpoint theory has nevertheless drawn criticism since it is quite obvious that certain standpoints, such as those of white, academic, middle-class feminists, have clear predominance over others, such as the 'silenced feminist standpoints' of Black and lesbian feminist epistemology (Stanley and Wise, 1990). Accusations that standpoint theory is essentialist and involves reification of women's experience are, however, denied by Harding:

> But standpoint theory does not require any kind of feminine essentialism, as this frequently mentioned critique supposes. It *analyzes* the essentialism that androcentrism assigns to women, locates its historical conditions, and proposes ways to counter it.
>
> (Harding, 1990: 99)

Thus, moving away from the universals of liberal and radical feminism, social relations are viewed in terms of plurality and diversity rather than unity and consensus, enabling an articulation of alternative, more effective ways of thinking about or acting on issues of gender (Scott, 1990).

Critical moments

How have micro-political, post-structuralist and feminist standpoint theories influenced the Equity and Staffing Project and the analysis of its findings? Clearly they provided the main framework for the research team's development of ideas about project organization and also for the identification of particular policy factors that we focused on and developed. Such debates also helped in the selection of research methodology and, in particular, in our reporting of the case studies. However, in seeking to identify and portray the complexity of how equal opportunities policy is experienced by individuals and groups at different organizational levels, we needed an additional analytical framework to that offered by the policy case study.

We turned to a particular form of analysis which utilizes the notion of the *critical incident*. According to Tripp (1994: 24), an incident is held to be critical when it marks 'a significant turning-point or change in life of a person or an institution . . . or in some social phenomena'. Tripp identifies the importance of *analysis* in marking off the 'critical' from the 'typical'.

> The vast majority of critical incidents, however, are not at all dramatic or obvious: they are mostly straightforward accounts of the very commonplace events that occur in routine professional practice which are critical in the rather different sense that they are indicative of underlying trends, motives and structures. These incidents appear to be 'typical' rather than 'critical' at first sight, but are rendered critical through analysis.
>
> (Tripp, 1994: 24–5)

Tripp used the notion of critical incident to help teachers improve on their professional practice through problem-solving. Magda Lewis, a North American feminist and academic, developed a somewhat similar analytic approach in her notion of the 'pedagogical moment' which arises in a specific context when all the elements affecting the classroom (psychological, social and sexual) come together 'in ways that create the specifics of the moment'. These elements may include the social location of the teacher and students, the political climate in which they work, the personalities and profiles of individuals in the classroom and so on. Lewis uses such moments, which she sees as transformative, to enable greater understandings of the gendered context of the classroom, and to develop 'an interpretive framework for creating a counter-hegemony' (Lewis, 1990: 487).

Following on from Tripp and Lewis, we offer the suggestion of the 'research moment' in which crucial elements affecting any piece of research – for example, the social location, the researcher and the researched, the political and institutional climate in which they both operate, the issues which provide the research focus – come together at a particular conjuncture to illuminate, in the case of our research, the equal opportunities policy process. The two stages in the creation of a critical incident offered by Tripp (1994) will be replicated here: first, the observation and description of the phenomenon (the production of the incident); and second, the explanation which can be applied in the wider social or professional context.

Our development of the research moment as a unit of analysis, deriving from understandings generated by feminist and other debates concerning research and praxis, seems to us particularly useful. It allows us to move away from the more usual 'pattern identification' aim of research to focus on the minutiae and complexities of trying to turn written equal opportunities policies into viable practices which are, in turn, able to challenge and eradicate existing inequalities.

Thus, we rework selected extracts from the data by utilizing the concept of 'research moment'. Three selections from the data are considered. Two occur in the same case study institution at about the same time and involve the same researcher. The first reports on the tracking of the senior manager (A) and the second describes an interview with a newly appointed women's officer (B). The third involves interviews with four members of staff (male dean, H; female professor, J; male, part-time lecturer, K; female research assistant, L) in the same institution on the same day.

Research moment 1: tracking the boss

The decision to track a senior member of staff arose because A suggested that a useful way of getting to know the institution would be to follow him around for a few days. As chief executive, he would be able to guarantee access to certain major policy-making committees and introduce the researcher to the main actors within the institution. The project team discussed this proposal and decided, on balance, that it would offer a useful means of entry into the organization.

In the researcher's account of the meetings she attended and observed, A emerges as a power-player *par excellence*. He seeks to exert what control he can over the research process while simultaneously aligning himself with the aims of the project, using the research arena to display his institutional authority and using the researcher as a confidante-debriefer-therapist. He appears to revel in being the object of research: 'I [the researcher] was introduced to several people and each time he explained the research background and said "she is shadowing *me* for a few days." [Another member of staff] made a joke about David Lodge.'

On the day in question, the field notes indicate that the pre-arranged timetable has been changed as A has decided that his earliest meetings of the day are 'too sensitive' for the researcher to attend. The first meeting that the researcher is allowed to attend is over lunch with the three male solicitors for the institution. A speaks confidently about the success of the institution's policy on sexual harassment and urges more simplicity in the solicitors' advice. After the meeting, he debriefs with the researcher, as the field notes record:

> Pompous weren't they? Very gender-specific in their language – all about 'he' and 'him'. [Researcher's note: I am ashamed to report I had not noticed.] I asked A if the input about summaries of advice was deliberate. A: 'Yes, it was a deliberate criticism. After all we are an exceptional customer – not many small town solicitors would have such a prestigious and wealthy customer . . . need to be brought up to the mark. As you will see I am mischievous sometimes, I like to wind people up.'

In her notes, the researcher reflects on whether gender, disability and employment were deliberately included in the conversation for her benefit.

The researcher's second meeting of the day is with A and a male senior manager Y, concerning the institution's '*Charter for Management*', which identifies some of the values underpinning the mission statement and which was put together at a recent heads of department conference (both mission statement and charter include strong equal opportunities elements). A takes firm control of the meeting from the start, despite claiming that 'we operate a cabinet government style of decision making'. While Y affirms that the charter is 'an excellent, spontaneous leap forward', he queries the main body of staff's commitment to it and also its authorship. He suggests that

> those who agree will abide by it willingly but others with doubts might feel they must abide by it or else. There are some cynical people who might suggest it smacks of McCarthyism or is part of appraisal . . . We must have ownership of this policy – not use it as a stick to beat those who don't agree . . . Did you put in this bit about 'using resources effectively, efficiently'? Sounds a bit like you.

A denies his input to this particular part of the document but agrees that perhaps there is not wholehearted support as there have been visible absences at follow-up meetings and women appeared to find it more difficult to raise issues (a point suggested by Y). However, A goes on to deny any problems of gender relations, instead pointing to the breadth of the charter's aims: 'I don't think it was a gender problem. This charter may, of course, set up expectations and it does have a long agenda.' This gains the agreement of Y – 'Yes, I'm impressed' – and the meeting comes to a close in a relaxed manner. (The other two meetings of the day are with public relations over a new institutional logo and with union representatives over a course that is likely to be cut – certainly a sign of the times!)

Research moment 2: talking to the feminist

The interview with the newly appointed (part-time, three days a week) women's officer B takes place in a busy part of the institution. The field notes from the interview suggest that B's perspective on the project and policy-making is substantially different from A's. A newcomer to the institution and still able to take a relatively dispassionate view of its workings, she is far more concerned with the day-to-day practices related to the equal opportunities policy, and, through networking with women and her relatively low status, appears far more aware of the resistances and setbacks to implementation. The interview is built around the researcher's prepared questions.

B has considerable experience of equal opportunities (having held a similar job elsewhere working for a local authority) and has decided, in consultation with A and the (female) dean responsible for 'women's affairs', to focus on staffing issues. She concentrates in particular on recruitment and advertising; monitoring, for instance, where women are in the organization; and staff support. In terms of staff,

> If there is a pattern to these problems [work-related] I can take them up as a problem that seems to be affecting women. [They] can come to me because [they] do not feel able to approach – feel reticent – feel it may have consequences for them in their working lives.

Another female member of staff has been seconded for 12 hours a week in order to deal with sexual harassment, which releases B to deal with other matters. At present, B tends to see 'manual and teaching staff' rather than administrators, who, she suggests, have female colleagues with whom they share their problems. She also tries to alert colleagues to problems related to their departments.

> I cannot take all individual problems so I try to deflect the responsibility back on to departments – try to say to people – you clearly have a problem in your department, try to raise the issue there . . . You need to take that further – get people used to a mental checklist that includes equal opportunities.

While B feels supported by her line-manager (the only woman dean at the time) she works outside the main faculty structure and therefore experiences difficulties in communication and gaining information. She uses informal networking with women in the institution to overcome marginality but perceives that she is still viewed with suspicion by some. 'It depends on e.o. and what involvement in e.o. in the past. I think people are a little wary of me, or my post. Always some people who will not change . . . who will not change views . . . some more aware than others.' She intends to address equal opportunities structurally as individual initiatives appear to have had little success. She has noticed

> keen and interested [people who] . . . are floundering around . . . are despondent and burnt out by constantly nagging away at e.o. issues . . . The experience and the history of gender issues has largely been because of the vitality and commitment of individual women who have taken things on . . . it saps them, they say 'I don't want to do this any more, I'm sick and tired of sticking my head above the parapet.'

Despite the existence of a 'race unit' in the institution for a number of years, B claims that racial inequality has been given little attention and that gender and racial issues have had different institutional histories. Moreover, while she commends the institution for its policy and commitment to equal opportunities, she worries about lack of resources (when appointed, she had no budget or administrative support and now believes that all her resource comes out of A's 'slush fund') and about her role in effective implementation:

> There is a reluctance to see that the receivers of the policy might be reluctant to take this forward if there is an element of imposition . . . My paranoid view is that people will say 'It is hopeless, we can't do anything about women's issues, we have a woman's officer and she has done absolutely nothing.'

Research moment 3: differing perceptions of policy

This research moment revisits the four individual interviews mentioned at the beginning of Chapter 4. As was noted, they all took place on the same wet and windy day, in the same university building. The interviews had been arranged by the main case study researcher, who gained access to staff via the dean of faculty. Another member of the research team did the interviewing using a semi-structured interview schedule covering knowledge of, and involvement and sympathy with, the institution's equal opportunities policy. The interviews took place in the interviewees' rooms or rooms of their own choosing, and each seemed willing to be interviewed. All were polite and all, though having cleared time to be interviewed, were clearly busy. They had been provided with a copy of the questions before the interview.

One of the most prominent features of this research moment is its illumination of the potential for 'fragmentation' of research subjects. For example, all the interviewees are white; two are relatively high status (male dean (H), female professor (J)) and two relatively low (male, semi-retired, part-time lecturer (K), young, female, research assistant (L)); two are male (H and K) and two female (J and L); two are long-established staff members (H and K) and two are relatively new (J and L); one (L) is much younger than the other three.

What also comes through strongly in this research moment is that each interviewee, rather than revealing any hidden 'truth' or new perspective on the equal opportunities policy, appears swiftly to take up a position, to 'claim an identity' (MacLure, 1993), in relation to equal opportunities and in relation to the university. Thus, K identifies himself both as a long-time staff member and as having views typical of the institution as a whole – though he feels perhaps that he is rather more advanced in his thinking about equality issues than some of his colleagues in the all-male department in which he works. As the field notes report,

> K would think that his view on equal opportunities is shared by the university, and [he] is fairly comfortable with the current e.o.

policy ... In the main most staff have been fairly indifferent ... While changes have occurred, there are lecturers who are less open to influence than K. But then, K is probably less responsive than he would like to be.

In contrast, L presents herself as quite angry, in particular, about the day-to-day behaviour of colleagues and would like more done about the 'jocular' sexist remarks of male colleague whereby 'points are still scored and the "correct" message sent' and understood! She is already 'way ahead of the language guidelines provided' and is very disappointed in her lack of involvement in equal opportunities policy-making. She identifies most with being female, young and on a temporary contract; so overall, although 'L regards herself as receptive and interested in any [equal opportunities] development', her view of the university equal opportunities policy is that it is 'disappointing'.

Most noticeable in the interviews of K and L is how relatively unknowledgeable they are about policy compared with H (male dean) and J (female professor). H presents himself as a well respected, hard working and long-standing member of the university with a good research record. He is very aware of the 'still very powerful senior management and lay individuals who are instinctively rather than intellectually opposed to e.o. Most can deal with women on court only if they can flirt ... [they] cannot cope with those who "talk back"'. Yet H has managed to help ease or 'nod through' official policy and support the activities of various feminists in his faculty. He is the only one of those interviewed to provide an overview of how equal opportunities had developed over the years – as a result of the variable efforts of the three university principals. For instance, he remembers that the gender-specific language booklet created 'real "rage" among some lay members of court'. H reasons that though considerable progress has been made by the university, there are still major problems and 'it is still not taken as seriously as it should be'.

Finally, J appears to have the most sophisticated and knowledgeable perception of the strengths and limitations of the institution's equal opportunities policy. She reports that though there is little overt discrimination against women, there are only three female professors, no female heads of department or deans and no women in the senior management group. There is also no thoroughgoing support of equal opportunities, no proper monitoring and no attempt made to ensure female representation on the important university committees: 'thus women have no purchase over resource allocation'. Not surprisingly, J finds the university culture strongly male, middle aged and middle class.

Despite this catalogue of poor practice and 'want of a system', J does not appear as angry as L – perhaps because she has moved, at least to some degree, through the 'glass ceiling' and feels less vulnerable to the day-to-day sexism of male colleagues. As to her view on the university's equal opportunities policy, she intimates that there is a degree of smugness at higher levels: 'It's a bit of a "curate's egg"'. There are some good things happening but the university still has a long way to go.'

Research moments: discussion

The research moments suggest that even when actively involved with identical policies and implementation, actors are *positioned differently* within the policy discourse as gendered and powerful or powerless subjects. Thus, for A (research moment 1) it would seem that the main objective is to put policy into place, with a tendency to gloss over any 'dissension in the ranks'. On the other hand, B (research moment 2) takes the policy for granted: what matter to her are the day-to-day gains and resistances, and how she can support women members of staff. From B's description of former attempts at institutional change, there is certainly disappointment and frustration, and also exhaustion and despair from those who had been involved – and some disillusion about the lack of depth of equal opportunities policies in general. Her difficult task is to make policies work better in the future.

Both A and B show a tendency to *prioritize gender* over other inequalities and to see all women as having the *same* kinds of problems. In B's case, her prioritization of gender is not surprising given that she is the women's officer. However, it is not clear whether she appreciates that she is likely to be asked to take up other issues as well as sexism on behalf of women (for example, concerning racism and disability) if she is to support the full range of female staff at the university.

Inequalities of power within both policy discourse and the research process are also clearly visible. When Y (research moment 1) seeks to raise problems about the reception of the policy, i.e. the non-participation of women staff members or possible accusations of McCarthyism from 'cynics', A steamrollers him, overlaying his own meaning and assuming control of the discourse. Similarly at another level, A attempts to dictate and control the research agenda and to place boundaries round the enquiry. In contrast, B remains unaware of the power play at senior levels, marginal as she is to the mainstream working of the institution. Significantly, while B has little autonomy, having been 'told' to make herself available to the researcher, her lower status and *feminist vantage point* (or *standpoint*) give her a greater insight into any likely resistance and hostility towards the policy. She rather than A will know whether or not it is really working.

The utilization of *structural inequality* within the policy discourse is also significant here: the status of A as white, male and senior (and full-time) enables him to push through policy (it must be remembered that this institution has a high profile nationally on equal opportunities issues). Simultaneously, it puts him at an advantage in relation to other subordinate members of staff and in particular *vis-à-vis* the female researcher and the women's officer – despite his overt stance on increasing equality within the institution. Certainly, his practice and his rhetoric seem inconsistent, though perhaps this is inevitable in any policy context where high levels of responsibility and visibility render senior managers vulnerable, if in different ways from those lower down the hierarchy. On the other hand, power relations seem more *equally distributed* (or at least more reciprocal) between the female actors at various levels in the institution, i.e. the woman dean, the researcher, women's officer and other women involved with the policy.

The third research moment focuses less on the policy-makers and 'activators' of policy than on the receivers and interpreters of policy – though it is acknowledged that within the policy discourse meaning-making is highly complex. As in the previous research moments, the interviewees' knowledge of policy, their support of, resistance to, identification with and criticism of policy, all seem closely related to their immediate professional and personal contexts – and to their multiple realities. The two female interviewees (J and L) would, no doubt, have identified themselves as feminist, if asked. Yet their perception of the policy and its actual (or potential) impact on their immediate circumstances, their bargaining power in the market place, their differential positioning in the power/knowledge practices within the policy discourse all serve to highlight their *differences* rather than their shared interests. However, it is apparent that the two women's shared experience of sexist practices enables them to offer a sharper perspective on the 'problem' of inequality than their male colleagues.

The two male interviewees (H and K), in contrast, portray themselves as more detached, more 'rational', more distanced from equal opportunities concerns. They both assert that it was vociferous feminists in their faculty and outside the university who had raised the stakes and/or created the fuss. They, themselves, seem frozen on the sidelines: able to act only in offering or withdrawing their support. As dean, H appears to have a genuine commitment to enhancing equality within the university, yet it seems to be related more to *altruism* than to any deeply felt passion for challenging existing practices or material conditions that might affect *him*.

In fact, what most unites the two male interviewees is their concern to dismiss 'positive action', which is not mentioned by either of the female interviewees. In K's case, though he acknowledges that discrimination goes on (and provides examples), he is absolutely opposed to any positive action strategies in favour of women. In H's case, while he articulates a sympathy for positive action, his insistence that there would be insufficient support for it to have any chance of being adopted as university policy has similar implications. Positive action, possibly the most 'radical' of the equal opportunities policies available, is used ritually by the two men as a signifier for *marking the boundaries* of equal opportunity policy-making. In this they reveal, it seems to us, their vested interests as male and white, in colluding with the status quo to keep women and other under-represented groups out of the academy.

Concluding remarks

In this chapter we have attempted to build upon recent emphasis on the complexities of gender relations and their intersection with other forms of inequality and subordination. In working towards an understanding of institutional equal opportunities policies and practices, we employed a variety of micro-political, post-structural and standpoint frameworks for the analysis of project data.

If the case studies reported earlier in this volume have been produced in a primarily narrative form in order to 'hold the data together', in this chapter we have used the research moment to 'prise the data apart'. In so doing, we think we have exposed some of the reasons why policy implementation, particularly in the area of equal opportunities, appears to have relatively unstable, unpredictable and sometimes disappointing outcomes.

We can, of course, point out what we think 'good practice' might look like (see Chapter 9 for a discussion of this) but we cannot 'predict' (and this is where science might be said to have failed us) which practices will take root best in which institutions. Our suggestion is that institutions, themselves, will need to engage in a continual cycle of policy review involving, perhaps, some of the forms of research used for the equity and staffing project. Even if they are able to share their experiences with others in similar work contexts, they will need to do the 'spade work' in their own institutions if they genuinely want to see their equal opportunities policies working in practice – which, of course, will inevitably (and ironically) bring new threats and challenges to the power bases of the policy-makers themselves.

6

Codifying Policy and Practice

Introduction

Throughout the period of the research, the researchers were provided with a large pile of documents from the case study institutions, all of which related to each institution's equal opportunities policies and practices. In addition, colleagues with an interest in the research passed on to us a variety of documents from other institutions which they felt might be relevant.

The documents were of two types. First, there were specific equal opportunities policy documents, in which the institutions aimed to codify existing policy for staff. Second, there was an extensive range of other documents: staff training materials, newsletters, student prospectuses, recruitment literature etc. For example, in an institution which emphasized in its equal opportunities policy document that all staff would have equal opportunities in relation to promotion procedures, one might expect that documents dealing with promotion procedures would contain details of precisely how equality of opportunity was to be achieved.

Both types of document were clearly relevant to the research, though in different ways. The policy documents themselves were of particular value in the early stages of the project, when we were seeking to establish each institution's interpretation of the concept of equal opportunities. We were interested in establishing whether such documents were essentially similar in nature, given that the goals set by such policies were likely to be the same or similar; or whether they differed markedly and, if so, why this was the case (see McPake, 1992, for a more detailed discussion of this).

Subsequently, we looked at other types of documents which we had gathered in the course of the research. We realized that there were two aspects of these documents which were likely to be of most interest. First, they could be seen as additional sources of information about practice and policy at work in the institutions, along with our interview and observation data. Second, such documents might be perceived as a more durable record of an institution's stance on equal opportunities: they represent a more carefully thought out, long-term position on, for example, recruitment than does a single example of a job interview. Such documents should therefore, to some extent at least, represent the codification of an institution's *practice*.

A particular problem emerged, however, when we came to look carefully at such documents. While the use of interview and observation data has become standard in qualitative research, document analysis is a less commonly practised research method, and we had no appropriate model for analysis. Developing a method of analysis turned out to be a time-consuming task, and consequently, at the end of the project, we found we had more to say about the development of the method than about the documents themselves. Only recruitment 'packages' (the collection of papers, normally including job descriptions, application forms and literature about the institution in general, which is sent out to prospective job applicants) were analysed in detail. The final section of this chapter deals with our approach to other types of documents gathered in the course of the case studies, and is principally a description of the method used.

Policy documents

We first studied the nature of formal policy statements. We began by drawing up lists of the sorts of stipulations made in each document, and comparing these with those of other documents to see the extent to which they either resembled each other or differed. The underlying hypothesis was that documents would, in the main, be very similar, but might reveal significant differences in certain key points. Surprisingly, it emerged that the documents were, in fact, different from each other: even in appearance, they ranged from brief one-page accessible statements designed to encapsulate the principles of the policy to long, rambling documents in draft form with all the implications of the policy and implementation procedures spelt out. The tone of documents also varied: from highly formal 'institutionalese' to overt political commitment and a semblance of 'plain English'. There were also considerable differences in content: some policy documents were limited to specific areas of equal opportunities or certain areas of application; others aimed for global reference.

This diversity is, in itself, an interesting finding. What was more problematic was the difficulty of making sense of these differences. In the case of the three institutions involved in the project, we were able to answer a number of these questions with reference to what we already knew about them from our research. We knew, for example, that responsibility for equal opportunities at Metropolitan University had been assumed by the personnel department – and this, in part, explained the policy document's employment-oriented focus. Town University, on the other hand, had a comparatively long history of senior management commitment to equal opportunities which enabled us to understand its 'umbrella-like' document – with a central policy statement closely bound up with the mission statement, and more specific policy areas, each with its own mini-statement and list of recommended actions. Clearly, policy documents were closely tied up with the practice of the institution. Thus it was decided to restrict the study of policy documents to those of the three case study institutions themselves.

Contextual factors influencing the development of policy documents

The Metropolitan University Equal Opportunities Policy (MEOP) was in the final committee stages before formal adoption by the university. The version we studied was the second draft of a policy originally drawn up in 1990, before the Committee of Vice Chancellors and Principals (CVCP) published guidelines on equal opportunities policies at the end of 1991. If adopted (as subsequently occurred), MEOP would be the first equal opportunities policy document Metropolitan University had produced, though non-sexist language guidelines were already in existence.

The main focus of the first draft of MEOP was equal opportunities in employment. It was a short document – a page in length – consisting of a boxed policy statement followed by a list of more detailed principles on which implementation was to be based. The language of the document was formal, identical to that of other university administrative and policy documents. The addition of policies relating to sexual and racial harassment to the second draft increased the number of pages from one to four, with the harassment policies being considerably more detailed than the rest of the document.

Town University had a number of policy documents dating back to about 1985 but was also in the process of redrafting them, in response to various issues which had emerged over the years. The university's intention was to produce a policy booklet which would contain the various interconnected policies: the Town University Equal Opportunities Policy (TEOP) is thus the umbrella which shelters policies on equal opportunities in academic affairs, harassment and language. The final draft of the proposed booklet was being circulated to staff at the time when the case study came to an end. The language of TEOP was also formal, and similar in style to that of many other documents produced by the university.

Borough College's policy documents date from the mid-1980s, originally developed with the Inner London Education Authority. These policies were also in the process of being revised at the time we studied them. The intention was both to reflect the changed status of the college and to respond to developments in equal opportunities thinking. The college did not have one overarching equal opportunities policy but a series of policies on anti-sexism, anti-racism and special needs. An anti-heterosexism policy was also being discussed, as well as the possibility of the development of a set of common procedures relating to all policy areas. We selected the Borough College Anti-sexism Policy (BASP) for the study as it was furthest ahead in terms of redrafting.

We identified the following key contextual factors as having a bearing on the way in which each institution's policies evolved.

- *Impetus*: both the initial push to get equal opportunities on the agenda and the maintenance of interest and commitment determine the principal focus of the policy document.
- *Knowledge of equal opportunities*: both the accumulation of specialist knowledge by key individuals and general awareness of the principles among staff influence the assumptions made in the document.
- *Experience of the implementation of equal opportunities policy*: for the first-time policy, specific events may have triggered awareness of the need for a policy to guide practice; for longer-term policy-making, the impact of policy may lead to amendments of documents.
- *Authorship*: policy documents, though appearing anonymous and institutional, are written by individuals or groups whose perspectives will have an important influence.
- *Audience*: a hostile, indifferent or well-informed and committed audience will make a difference to the tone of the document and its contents.
- *Responsibility for implementation*: the assumption of responsibility for the implementation of policy by particular individuals or groups will affect the nature of what is to be implemented.
- *Power of institutional documents*: formal documents differ in importance as they interact with the day-to-day life of institutions.

One important difference in the contexts of implementation is that while Metropolitan University was in the process of adopting its first equal opportunities policy, Town University and Borough College were redrafting policies which had been in existence for a number of years. This had an important bearing on the authorship of the policy documents: at Borough and Town, there were many more people in a position to be involved in the redrafting of the document, and a more knowledgeable audience. Metropolitan University clearly was in a different position. As a member of staff involved in the development of the policy at Metropolitan noted: 'Once we get into implementing the policies and people see how it is impacting on them and upon the procedures of the university, then I think we'll hear some noises being made. At the moment, people think it's a very nice idea.'

Thus, the adoption of a policy cannot be seen as a 'once and for all' act, though certainly the appearance and tone of formal policy documents give them an air of permanence. In reality, there is a constant process of redefining in the light of developing knowledge and experience. Policies are the product of the contexts in which they develop but they in turn influence those contexts. Thus a cyclical motion is evolved – of drafting, adoption, operation and redrafting.

Issues emerging from the policy documents

Our initial analysis of the documents suggested that the most important questions to ask of a policy were the following.

- Who is expected to benefit from the policy?
- What, specifically, does the policy consist of?
- What explanation for the existence of the policy is given?
- Who is responsible for implementing the policy?
- How is the policy to be implemented?

The Appendix at the end of this chapter summarizes the answers to each of these questions provided by the policies of each of the case study institutions. We can see that there are some similarities between the three documents but also a great number of differences.

Definitions of equal opportunities

How did each institution define equal opportunities? Metropolitan University chose to focus on equal opportunities in employment and harassment, and the policy document spells out in some detail what this entails. Borough College focused on opposition to sexism, going into considerable detail and listing the various steps to be taken to counter it. Town University had perhaps the most comprehensive definition.

Why do the three documents differ so widely from each other on this question of definition? Our understanding of the contexts in which the policies were developed offers some explanation. We know, for example, that the history of the policy at Metropolitan University was likely to emphasize employment issues: the original spark was the publication of The Metropolitan Report, which was critical of the university's employment practices towards women. For this reason, the issue was taken up by the personnel department. Another factor was the appearance of the CVCP guidelines recommending the inclusion of sexual and racial harassment policies, at the time the university was discussing the form of the policy document. Consequently these were added to the document which was eventually adopted.

At Borough College, current policies have derived from those of the former ILEA. Traditionally, in the ILEA single-issue policies (e.g. anti-sexism, anti-racism, anti-heterosexism) were regarded as preferable to more inclusive policies, such as equal opportunities or multi-culturalism; and it may be that the original policy created a more 'radical' ethos which the college now seeks to maintain. Adopting an *anti-sexist* rather than an *equal opportunities* policy may also be the key to BASP being more explicit in its definition of sexism, and how it may be challenged.

Why has Town University arrived at a more comprehensive definition? Perhaps it is because the original policy was put in place by senior management, and the mechanisms developed for implementation have involved staff in both academic and personnel fields.

Language of the documents

Difference in tone is another aspect of documentation uncovered in the research. For example, MEOP is often extremely tentative: '*Wherever possible* all posts will be advertised *as widely as possible* and be designed to encourage applications from *relevant* groups' (MEOP; emphasis added). But BASP is determined: 'Sexual harassment *will not* be tolerated' (BASP; emphasis added).

Explanation of these differences may lie with the audiences to whom the policies are directed. For adoption, MEOP had to pass through a number of consultative committees, members of which may not have had an interest in, or commitment to, equal opportunities, and might have tried to block the document's path. BASP, on the other hand, was aimed at an audience that is likely to have developed some knowledge of equal opportunities and experience of the practical implications, as a result of the previous policy. For them, debates about the necessity of policy are a thing of the past; what is important is that the message should be clear, unequivocal and lead to action. Thus 'This policy is intended to instigate action in all aspects of college life' (BASP).

Equal opportunities policy as a dynamic concept

Perhaps one of the major differences between TEOP and BASP on the one hand, and MEOP on the other, is related to the interrelationship between context and policy – and, in particular, to MEOP representing the first equal opportunities policy document for the university. MEOP has a somewhat passive view of equal opportunities, no doubt because the process of awareness will only begin after the policy is in place. Clues are apparent in the verbs used to describe how the policy will operate: 'individuals . . . *are treated* on their relative merits and abilities and *are given* equal opportunities within the University' (MEOP; emphasis added).

In contrast, TEOP and BASP seem to see equal opportunities in the form of action rather than as a state. For example, TEOP asserts: '*Pursuit* of equal opportunities means that all forms of unfair discrimination will be *challenged*' (TEOP; emphasis added). BASP contains an explicit call to action:

Borough College is opposed to sexism in all its forms and *will not accept passivity in the fight against it*... *We* are committed to *taking positive action* to *identify and eradicate* sexism and to *develop* equality for women throughout the college.

(BASP; emphasis added)

The use of 'we' and the number of active verbs in such passages indicate both commitment and a sense that things will happen. This dynamic view of policy implementation is further illustrated, confirmed in the following BASP statement: 'It is essential that this policy is enriched and developed through democratic debate throughout the college (by students, teaching and support staff).'

Thus the notion of policy as a cycle of development, which has been the *experience* of the two institutions with policies in place, is now incorporated into the policy document itself, and has become *part of the policy* – confirming the close developmental links between context and policy documentation.

Other institutional documents

The second focus of the project study of documents was on documents other than those relating explicitly to equal opportunities policy. The aim was to investigate the extent to which equal opportunities were reflected in wider institutional documentation. First, however, we needed to find a method of analysing such documents. This was more difficult than we had anticipated, as document analysis is a relatively uncommon research method in qualitative studies. This section considers how the method of analysis evolved, and includes a brief discussion of the differences between equal opportunities policy documents and other institutional documents.

Developing a method of analysis

We collected a wide range of documents from the case study and other institutions, including newsletters, institutional calendars, institutional histories and staff appraisal guidelines. These were classified according to whether they were intended primarily for an internal readership or an outside audience. Examples included:

Internal audience	*External audience*
Academic review documents	Prospectus
Staff training material	Annual report
Minutes of meetings	Job advertisement
Staff newsletter	Recruitment literature
Policy documents	Press release

It was decided to concentrate, in particular, on recruitment literature: job descriptions, application forms and various other documents customarily sent to those who enquire about posts advertised externally. One reason for this decision was that, because recruitment literature is designed for an external audience, knowing the context would be less important as the audience would be expected to have little background knowledge of the institution. Such material could therefore be presumed to contrast in a number of ways with the case study policy documents we had previously studied.

We gathered together a collection of recruitment documents in the first three months of 1993, using as a source advertisements in the *Education Guardian* and in the education section of *The Scotsman*. The aim was to collect sample sets of documents covering as wide a range of jobs – from research assistants to vice chancellors – in as many different institutions as possible. No institution was contacted more than once, though clearly recruitment packages might vary according to the job available. The posts we responded to (as though we were applicants) were mainly academic, although we were able to include some administrative and support staff posts. In all, 20 sets of recruitment documents were collected.

When starting the analysis, we had no recourse to a systematic method for analysing their 'meaning' in terms of equal opportunities practices. What we did was to read through them fairly rapidly and note anything which seemed relevant. The kinds of observations generated by this very impressionistic approach included lists of types of documents in a 'recruitment package', quotations of sections referring explicitly to equal opportunities, notes of favourable or unfavourable impressions etc.

We attempted to categorize our notes and consider other issues which we might have omitted. From this, the rudiments of an analytical method began to emerge in the form of two main questions:

1. What do the documents say explicitly about equal opportunities and related issues in the institution (e.g. childcare provision, job-sharing, wheelchair access)?
2. What is missing from the documents?

We returned to the documents and started asking these two questions more systematically. We were able to identify more specifically what kinds of information our questions could provide, and also the implications of asking these questions.

What do the documents say explicitly about equal opportunities in the institution?
As we became familiar with the kinds of references to equal opportunities which were most likely to be included in recruitment packages, we began to look for:

- a statement relating to the institution's position on equal opportunities;
- a monitoring of forms, an explanation of its purpose and assurances that the information provided would be used only for the monitoring exercise;
- a copy of the institution's equal opportunities policy;
- references to the potential post holder's responsibilities in relation to equal opportunities (usually in the job description or the person specification);
- references to provision made by the institution of practical commitment to equal opportunities (e.g. maternity leave provision, existence of support group for Black staff, hearing loops);
- use of non-discriminatory language;
- images of the institution which avoid stereotyping and indicate diversity.

What do the documents appear to miss out?
On one level, this simply involved noting down all the elements listed above which were *not* included in the package. However, there were also absences which emerged from comparison with other elements in the package. Internal imbalances were difficult to identify, and perhaps potentially more subjective in nature. For example, one of the institutions whose recruitment package placed considerable emphasis on its extensive and up-to-date sports facilities made no mention of a workplace nursery. Are these comparable items? Might an emphasis on sport suggest, subtly, that the institution's image of its staff is young, energetic and predominantly male? Or does this reading reveal the researchers' own stereotypical views?

Another problem concerns features that appear to be absent from *all* documents we have examined, such as mention of support groups for Black staff (or indeed other groups of staff). Because we were aware of the existence of the ABACAS support group at Borough College (see Chapter 2), we expected other institutions to have such groups. However, they were not mentioned in any of the packages we studied. Why? Is it because mention of such groups is thought inappropriate in recruitment packages, or because it is assumed that few candidates would be interested in this information?

Refining the method

Over time, documentary analysis became more complex, as we began to look not only at the content but also at the language used in the document and the ways in which documents were presented. Gradually, we were able to refine our methods of study according to 'content', 'language' and 'presentation', as we explain below.

Content
This covers everything the documents tell us about the nature and extent of the institution's equal opportunities policy, including:

- information about the institution's equal opportunities policy;
- information about the implementation of policy (for example, on monitoring);
- information aimed specifically at encouraging applications from traditionally under-represented groups (e.g. crèche provision, wheelchair access);
- indications of the extent to which equal opportunities permeates institutional culture.

Language

We noted two linguistic areas which had relevance to equal opportunities: 'politically correct' and 'authoritarian/empowering' language.

'Politically correct' or anti-discriminatory language, despite the negative connotations, are terms we have come to use for a linguistic practice which represents attempts to avoid labelling people in ways which are perceived as negative, stereotypical or abusive; particularly those who come from groups which are disadvantaged in some way. Instead, terms which have more positive connotations are adopted, and their use often acts as a political marker in discourse, indicating sympathy with members of the group and awareness of their circumstances.

There is now a wide range of examples of such shifts in terminology. Examples relevant to recruitment documents include references to: 'people with disabilities' (rather than 'handicapped' or 'disabled' people); 'people from minority ethnic backgrounds' (rather than 'immigrants', 'ethnics', 'ethnic minorities'); 'parents' or 'carers' (in most circumstances preferable to 'mothers'); and avoidance of the generic use of 'he' (as referring to both male and female) by using 's/he' or 'he or she', or by recasting sentences in the plural.

The issue of 'authoritarian' or, in contrast, 'empowering' language emerged where we observed that some documents used stark imperatives or other formulations implying obligation ('must', 'should', 'are required to' etc.) in order to instruct applicants in completion of forms, while others explained the purpose of the various sections, appearing to encourage completion in ways which allowed applicants to demonstrate the qualities they could bring to the job.

Examples of 'authoritarian' formats include:

- 'Applicants must complete this form in black ink.'
- 'Do not telephone the department. No applicant will be informed of decisions relating to short-listing by telephone.'
- 'References should be sent to the personnel department.'

Examples of 'empowering' formats include:

- Softening commands with 'please' and 'thank you', or 'if you wish to . . .'

- Explanations of requirements, such as: 'We ask you to complete the equal opportunities form in order for us to be able to monitor applications and, if necessary, to help us improve our recruitment procedures in order to encourage applications from under-represented groups on the university's staff.'
- Encouraging applicants to demonstrate their abilities, as in the request for a supporting statement, which should 'explain how your knowledge, skills and experience make you a suitable candidate for this particular post and should specifically address all the selection criteria stated in the person specification. Wherever possible give practical examples rather than making vague, general statements.'

Our own response to 'authoritarian' language was that this format constructed the applicant as someone who should obey instructions and fit in with the structures for applications determined by the institution. 'Empowering' language, in contrast, appeared to encourage applicants to collaborate with the institution in producing the best application possible.

In addition, the lack of explanation in 'authoritarian' packages was likely to favour people with experience in filling in application forms, and in presenting CVs and supporting statements, and to disadvantage those with less experience of the unstated conventions of qualifications, skills and abilities. 'Empowering' packages explained what was expected of the applicants and gave suggestions (e.g. 'Where possible, give practical examples rather than making vague general statements') which would go some way to helping inexperienced applicants.

We hypothesized that 'authoritarian' language was more likely to dominate in the recruitment packages of institutions which did not have a very obvious commitment to equal opportunities (as far as we could determine from other evidence in the documents) and that 'empowering' language would predominate in those with a greater commitment. However, it is important to emphasize that our interpretation of such linguistic differences is not shared by all. Some have described the 'empowering' styles as patronizing, and some have felt 'safer' with documents written in more traditional ways because 'you know exactly what you have to do'.

Presentation
This seemed the most difficult aspect of the recruitment packages to analyse, possibly because we were less familiar with issues relating to visual presentation than we were with those relating to language. We focused on two points: *visual elements* (such as paper quality, quality and style of printing, use of logos and other symbols, and use of pictures); and *quantity of information*.

Although the use of pictures in documents prepared for an external audience could be revealing, in fact it was rare for pictures to be used in recruitment packages. Moreover, the quantity of information varied considerably, ranging from half a sheet of typed paper to packages in glossy

Name of institution Post advertised		
	What is explicit?	What is missing?
Content		
Language		
Presentation		

Figure 2 A miniature version of the analysis grid

folders containing not only job description, application form and general information about the institution, but also financial statements, annual reports and so on. Not surprisingly, quantity tended to vary according to the status of the post advertised; those applying for senior posts such as that of deputy principal, for example, were perceived as needing more information about the institution.

Analysis grids
In developing this line of analysis, we were able to construct a grid which set out appropriately the elements of the recruitment packages on which we had focused. Figure 2 shows a version of the grid which we used to analyse some of the recruitment packages in our collection.

Validating the method

We had begun the analysis with little specific guidance. It was only in examining the documents that the various dimensions to the analysis emerged. This process was ongoing: as we gained more experience of scrutinizing documents, we returned to the analysis grids to refine categories and definitions. The more we refined the method, the more confident we became that it was valid. Presentation and discussion of some of our ideas at two conferences further aided our deliberations. One aspect of the development of the method was the ways in which we attempted to validate (or challenge) our own perceptions by testing the method on other people.

It was noted, for example, that impressions of an institution's equal opportunities commitment could be coloured by the way any gaps were identified. Conference participants' reading of documents appeared quite similar to our own; but perhaps this is not surprising in that those who attended the conferences also clearly had an interest in equal opportunities issues. However, additional practical points were raised by participants whose work involved the promotion of equal opportunities for people with disabilities; for example, the use of heavy grey paper for institutional documentation. We were made aware that grey or blue tinted paper is very difficult to read for people with certain types of visual impairments. This point does suggest that other issues relating to the visual style of documents should be considered from the perspective of people with visual impairments (size of font, overprinting text on faint images which provide a 'background' on the paper). There may be a range of such problems which require wider dissemination.

It is clear that these discussions brought us valuable insights as well as contrasting views to our own. An important element in the development of the analytic method was therefore the testing of our own readings against those of other people.

The findings

We noted at the beginning of this section that the development of a method to analyse documents designed for an audience beyond the institution had produced contrasting points compared with internal policy documents. These contrasts relate, we suggest, to the different nature of the audiences. We note the principal differences in Table 6.1.

We suggest that the development of a standard format of analysis with institutional variations is helpful in these circumstances because comprehension and effectiveness are the key criteria. The aim of the packages is that applicants make an appropriate and informed application which will enable the institution's selectors to short-list (correctly) the most suitable candidates for the job. Variation in the standard format relates principally to the area of work concerned (different job descriptions for lecturers in different departments, or for teaching as opposed to administrative posts) and to the status of the post (quantity of information provided, we have seen, increases in relation to the post's place in the institutional hierarchy). Innovative formats (for example, the development of the 'empowering' linguistic style) may not be very well received by applicants who have developed certain expectations of the appropriate standard format, which, as we have seen, can create insecurity.

In contrast, a policy document is produced for an audience with inside knowledge of the context in which the policy developed and who can be expected to refer to the policy on a number of occasions as a means of clarifying, justifying or condemning practice. The intention is to raise awareness, stimulate debate about equal opportunities in practice and provide a basis for action. Thus the process becomes a dynamic spiral, whereby policy influences practice and is in turn affected by practice. Thus, policy documents can be, and indeed frequently are, highly idiosyncratic, but at the same time the 'right' policy for a particular institution at a particular time. An innovative or challenging style may be an appropriate method to stimulate debate, and conversely a policy which reads like a 'standard format' equal opportunities policy may inhibit it.

Table 6.1 Contrasting elements emerging from the analysis of policy documents and recruitment packages

Policy documents	*Recruitment packages*
Policy documents emerge from the particular history of equal opportunities in an institution and reflect the interests of the individuals or groups who have been most closely involved in policy development.	Recruitment packages also have their own histories, of course, and no doubt reflect the particular emphases which the personnel departments devising them wish to give them. However, it is also clear that there is a 'standard format' on which most packages are based; and it is probably the case that the standard format is more important in determining the nature of the package than the individual concerns of the various personnel departments.
It is not realistic to think that 'one [perfect] policy fits all'.	Thus it is more likely that a 'perfect' standard format – in relation to equal opportunities – could be devised.
The publication of an equal opportunities policy document in an institution does not mark the end of the process but the beginning of a new cycle of awareness-raising and critical response to the policy, eventually leading to policy review, and ultimately the revision, refocusing of expansion of the original policy.	We have no knowledge of the frequency with which recruitment packages are updated. We would argue that it would be appropriate for an institution to review its recruitment package every time the equal opportunities policy is revised. (Our current estimate is that equal opportunities policies go through a revision cycle lasting approximately ten years.) We do not know whether this is a realistic expectation.
Policy documents should be seen as a stage in a cyclical – or more accurately *spiral* – process of developing equal opportunities policies and practices in an institution.	We do not think that recruitment packages are likely to provoke the same kind of spiral dynamic as equal opportunities policies (because their principal impact is on an external audience) unless there were serious concern in the institution over aspects of the recruitment process, or it were decided to make recruitment the central focus of an equal opportunities initiative.

What does document analysis tell us that other methods do not about an institution?

The last issue we raise is a more general point about the value of document analysis. Particularly in case study research, document analysis is less

Table 6.2   Differences in types of information provided about an institution by interviews and document analysis

Interviews	Documents
'The insider view' – personal experience of policy and practice, or 'what it is like' to be inside the organization at a particular time.	A 'message' about how the institution perceives itself, and also about how the institution would like to be perceived.
Clearly an individual and personal perspective.	Documents are usually anonymous and therefore have the appearance of being 'neutral' or 'objective'. They appear to represent an 'official' perspective.
The position of the interviewee within the organization may give his or her perspective considerable weight; but often status may not be an important factor for the researcher. Other relevant factors may be the department to which the interviewee belongs, the social contacts he or she has etc.	The weight given to a document can be determined both by its author (senior registrar, anonymous member of personnel department), and by the nature of its audience (members of the senior management committee, new staff, parents of third-year pupils) and the extent of the audience (all staff, a particular group of staff, the public in general).
An interviewee's opinions on a particular occasion may be influenced by a wide range of external events, of which the researcher may or may not be aware.	Documents for an internal audience in particular need to be examined in the context of institutional practice generally; but as fixed statements, usually developed by more than one person and intended to hold good over time, they are less likely to contain idiosyncrasies.

frequently used than interviewing or observation, and consequently has received less critical attention (though see Webb, 1966; Holsti, 1968). In some ways, this seems unfortunate, because many institutional documents are freely available to researchers, and an analysis of such documents is a relatively economical approach. We identified a number of ways in which documents differ from interviews, in particular, in what they can tell the researcher about an institution. Table 6.2 summarizes these differences.

We also realized that there are a number of similarities in issues affecting the analysis of interviews and documents. In the first place, it is usually the researcher who determines what is significant in the analysis of either interviews or documents. The problem of subjectivity in interview analysis has been well aired, and various solutions sought (see Measor, 1985). We have referred to some of our own concerns about subjectivity and attempts at resolution as they applied to our analysis of recruitment packages.

We suggest that document analysis should not merely be viewed as a counting exercise; say, of the number of times the words 'equal opportunities' appear, or a checklist of various 'ingredients' present. It should rather attempt to emulate a 'considering attentiveness' which re-creates, to some degree, the process by which documents were devised and the kinds of issues the documents aim to raise and/or resolve. Successful analysis should result in greater insight into the way in which equal opportunities policies and practices are, or can be, encoded in documents.

Appendix: An analysis of the enqual opportunities policy documents from the three case study institutions

BASP	TEOP	MEOP

Who is expected to benefit from the policy?

BASP	TEOP	MEOP
Male and female students. Women staff. Black and white women. Community groups, including parents with small children.	Staff and students generally. People affected by issues of • disability • race • colour • ethnic/national origin • sexuality • gender • marital status. Equitable gender balance to be achieved. Appropriate representation of • minority ethnic groups • people with disabilities to be achieved.	Those who are not to receive less favourable treatment on the grounds of • race • colour • nationality • ethnic or national origins • gender or marital status • disability • religion • political belief • socio-economic status • parental status • sexual orientation • age (subject to normal retirement conventions) • trade union membership. Individuals who are • selected • trained • appraised • promoted • otherwise treated on the basis of their relative merits and abilities. Employes both present and future.

BASP	TEOP	MEOP
		Any members of staff who believe themselves to have been the subject of discrimination or harassment.

What, specifically, does the policy consist of?

BASP	TEOP	MEOP

Sexism is a process of discrimination based on supposed gender differences. It reflects a power relationship which is based upon and perpetuates the notion of male superiority. Sexism affects both sexes but women and girls suffer most.
 	
Institutional sexism is a form of sexism whereby the formal structure and social and frinancial priorities of the institution reinforce the power relationship which perpetuates the notion of male superiority.
 	
Borough College is opposed to sexism in all its forms and will not accept passivity in the fight against it.
 	
We are committed to taking positive action to identify and eradicate sexism and to develop equality for women throughout the college.
	Pursuit of equality of opportunity means that all forms of unfair discrimination will be challenged in whatever way they arise. The university is committed to the view that unfair discimination can arise across the whole spectrum of its activities, in
	• staff recruitment
	• selection
	• promotion
	• dismissal
	• rewards
	• resources
	• curriculum
	• hidden curriculum.
	  Equality of opportunity can be threatened by the use of language, gesture and other forms of symbolic behaviour.
		Metropolitan University confirms its commitment to equal opportunities in employment, in which individuals are
		• selected
		• trained
		• appraised
		• promoted
		and otherwise treated on the basis of their relative merits and given equal opportunities within the university.
		  The law requires that no job applicant or employee will receive less favourable treatment on the grounds of race, colour, nationality, ethnic or national origins, gender or marital status. Where the law does not prescribe, every effort will be made to avoid discrimination on the grounds of disability, religion, political belief, socio-economic background, parental status, sexual orientation, age (subject to normal retirement conventions) and trade union membership.

BASP	TEOP	MEOP

This policy is part of the college's overall anti-discriminatory and equality strategies ... This policy is intended to instigate action in all aspects of college life.

What explanation for the existence of the policy is given?

We are committed to taking positive action to identify and eradicate sexism and to develop equality for women throughout the college.

Borough College is opposed to sexism in all its forms and will not accept passivity in the fight against it.

A detailed rationale covers the following points:
- sex-stereotyping of subject areas
- male ethos of certain subject areas
- sex discrimination on work experience placements
- under-representation of women staff at management level
- and also on decision-making bodies
- lack of childcare facilities
- sexual harassment.

The university believes that the pursuit of equality of opportunity is fundamental to the achievement of the mission statement, being central to the provision of an environment in which those who work or study at the university can achieve their full potential.

The university wishes to ensure that an environment is created in which individual potential can be fostered and encouraged, that staff and students can act with confidence and competence with open critical minds.

The university believes that a properly implemented and monitored equal opportunities policy is in the best interests of the university and its employees both present and future.

BASP	*TEOP*	*MEOP*

Each of these points becomes the heading for separate sections of the policy, where the rationale is elaborated.

Who is responsible for implementing the policy?

Students, teaching and support staff.

Borough College is opposed to sexism in all its forms and will not accept passivity in the fight against it.

All employees and students of the university will be responsible for ensuring that their actions are carried out in the spirit of the policy and, under the provisions of the law, may be personally accountable should any complaint arise.

All line managers. All those involved in the selection of staff and students. All those involved in curriculum development and review. Visitors or contractors not employed by the university but affected by its activities.

The vice chancellor.

Staff involved in
• selection
• management
• supervision of other staff
have a duty to ensure that no discrimination occurs in the administration of the university's procedure or the application of agreed terms of employment.

All employees have a personal responsibility to adhere to and apply this policy in their dealings with others both internal and external to the university.

The university.

How is the policy to be implemented?

It is essential that [the policy] is enriched and developed through democratic debate throughout the college (by students, teaching and support staff). . . . Over the years this policy should continue to develop. . . . Sexual harassment will not be tolerated.

By pursuing not only the letter but also the spirit of the law.
  By ensuring that actions are to be carried out in the spirit of the policy and everyone is to be 'personally accountable'.
  By ensuring the integrity of management decisions.
  Specific measures include the following:
• appropriate EO training courses for those involved in recruitment;

The university is committed to a programme of action to ensure that this policy be fully effective.
  The following is a summary of the procedures listed:
• ensuring that employment practices are not discriminatory;
• encouraging 'relevant' groups to apply for jobs;
• providing guidance and training 'for those staff involved in the selection,

BASP	TEOP	MEOP
There follows a long list of recommendations, of which the following are the main points: • women only courses; • staff development programme; • course review; • college-wide monitoring; • examination of publicity and recruitment procedures; • establishment of women's unit, with bases, resource centres and rest rooms on each college site; • development of sexual harassment procedure and provision of counselling; • crèche; • welcoming ethos.	• addressing EO issues in curriculum development, delivery and review; • reflecting EO policy in all publications; • maintaining excellent processes for the promotion, planning, management and monitoring of EO; • monitoring race, gender and disability in relation to staff and student profiles; • taking positive action where necessary to ensure an equitable gender balance and appropriate representation of minority ethnic groups and people with disability; • reporting grievances to the vice chancellor; • enforcing disciplinary action for failure to comply with the policy.	management or supervision of other staff' in the application of the policy; • dealing with discrimination, harassment or victimization through disciplinary procedures; • publicizing the policy both within the university and to prospective employees; • monitoring and evaluating the effectiveness of the policy and developing the appropriate methods for doing this; • consulting 'relevant specialist bodies'.

7

Contrasting Contexts

Introduction

When the project began, a question we were frequently asked was how we had chosen the three institutions which were to take part in the case studies. Behind this question, there was often an assumption that 'good practice' in terms of equal opportunities was something relatively easy to define and to identify. The reality, as the research team discovered when they began to investigate what was meant by equal opportunities in each institution, was rather different. Although the institutions were selected on the basis of their good reputation for equal opportunities developments, this did not mean that they approached the issue in similar ways or had developed similar strategies to promote equality of opportunity for staff. We realized early on in the study that there were no 'correct answers', and no policies or practices which could be translated unchanged from one institution to another. Equal opportunities in each of the institutions had developed in very different directions, because of the differences in the nature of the institutions and in their histories and experiences of issues relating to equal opportunities.

Understanding the context in which policies and practices had evolved in each institution thus became an important area for the researchers, and our findings have already been discussed in some detail in the case study chapters. The aim of this chapter is to explore in more general terms the influence of context on the development of policy and practice, by comparing and contrasting a number of factors across the three institutions.

It is important to be clear that this exercise does not imply a ranking system by which one or other of the institutions may score more highly than the other two on particular aspects of its approach to equal opportunities. Indeed the effect of exploring the influence of context is rather the reverse: emphasizing the uniqueness of each institution and the impossibility of measuring one against the others. The value of exploring the influence of context has been in clarifying the reasons for particular emphases or developments in each institution. For readers whose institutions are similarly engaged in developing equal opportunities policies and practices, the value may lie in helping to identify influential factors which have already had a part to play in the particular policies, practices and structures adopted, or which are likely to determine directions of development in the future.

To aid our reflections on the influence of context, the research team drew up a table of the factors we found to be most relevant (such as the location or the history of the institution). This is included as an Appendix, see pps 138–46, to which the reader is referred, both for an overview of the issues to be discussed in this chapter and, more generally, as a summary of the principal points discussed in the case study chapters. This chapter takes most of the contextual factors listed in the table in turn, and considers the issues raised by each, in relation to our case study institutions.

Location

Location is the first factor that the team considered, particularly as one of the criteria for selection of the institutions was that they should be geographically quite distinct from each other, in terms of both distance and local setting. Thus we chose one institution (Borough College) in the south of England, one in the north (Town University) and one in Scotland (Metropolitan University). Borough College is located in an 'inner-city' area, Town University in a county town and Metropolitan University in a city centre. There are marked differences in terms of the ethnic mix of the areas in which the three institutions are situated: the local population in the area where Metropolitan University is located is predominantly white; a significant section of the population comes from minority ethnic backgrounds in the area served by Town University; and Borough College is located in an area where approximately 50 per cent of the local population is Black or from minority ethnic backgrounds.

These differences have affected the development of equal opportunities in a number of ways in each institution. In particular, the different emphases on 'race' issues (marked at Borough College, moderate at Town University and slight at Metropolitan University) may well be attributable to the ethnic mix of the local populations (and consequently the pool of people from which the majority of students and staff in an institution are likely to be drawn). This is both because an institution in an area with a comparatively large Black or minority ethnic origin population is likely to be more aware of 'race' issues generally, and because there will consequently be a larger number of people putting pressure on the institution to address these issues. Conversely, institutions in areas where the population is predominantly white are less likely to be aware of such issues or to feel them to be relevant.

However, though such differences in emphasis may appear to be both pragmatic and unremarkable, the assumption that 'race' is unlikely to be an important focus for equal opportunities work in predominantly white areas needs to be challenged. First, the point of identifying minority groups is precisely that they are minorities and more vulnerable in terms of the opportunities available because their experiences, their needs and their abilities may differ in significant ways from those of the majority. Second, it is important to consider to what extent an educational institution can think of its staff and student pool exclusively in terms of the local population. While this may be a reasonable assumption for a further education college in terms of its student population (less so, perhaps, for staff), universities have conventionally advertised nationally for staff and also expect a substantial number of students to come from outside the local area. Consequently, they will need to think of their profile among Black and minority ethnic groups, even where the local population and staff and students in the institution are predominantly white, in order to ensure that they are reaching the widest possible audience of potential students and members of staff.

History

One feature which the three case study institutions shared in relation to their general histories was that the origins of each lay in technical and vocational provision, aimed principally at working-class students. Possibly this early emphasis on what might be seen as 'non-traditional' students in the higher education sector has had an influence on the ethos of the three institutions, encouraging a commitment to access and support for students from a wide variety of backgrounds, interests, needs and abilities. The institutions' strong local reputations for this may also have affected staffing practices, though we have to be tentative in drawing these conclusions as we have no example of a long-established 'traditional' university with which to compare our case study institutions.

More recently, as we have seen, all three institutions have experienced considerable change and upheaval as a result of changes in status and mergers with other institutions. The specific details of the effects of these changes on the individual institutions are described in Chapters 2, 3 and 4. However, the fact that all three institutions were going through substantial changes at the time the research was carried out had implications for the direction of the research as a whole. The study therefore does not represent a picture of equal opportunities policy and practice in a period of stability but rather reveals the potential fragility of what might appear to be well-established policies, structures and practices in a period of change and transition. Important points to emerge from this aspect of the study include the fact that, each time a merger occurred, policies and practices needed to be renegotiated, producing gains or losses, or changes in emphasis, the consequences of which then needed to be evaluated. On a more pragmatic level, staff contracts and job descriptions also changed, and where these changes were perceived as less favourable than previously, staff perceived this as failure to adhere to the principles of equal opportunities, leading to a loss of confidence in the institution's commitment.

In addition, changes in institutional status of polytechnics and further education colleges during the project, motivated by a political desire to see market forces at work in the education sector, had a marked effect on the role and status of equal opportunities work in the two institutions affected. The impact was perhaps most noticeable at Borough College, where the restructuring exercise, designed to reflect changing emphases in the further education 'market', involved the dismantling of the Staff Development and Equality Unit and the relocation of the gender and 'race' coordinators in the Quality and Equality Assurance Unit. This represented a clear shift in perception of the role of equal opportunities in the college (as is discussed in Chapter 2). At Town University too, changes in corporate status were interpreted as placing considerably greater personal responsibility for the consequences of management decisions on the chief executive (the vice chancellor), with a corresponding loss of decision-making power for committees such as the equal opportunities committee. Elsewhere (see Chapter 3) we discuss the implications of this shift in power. What is important to note here, in our examination of the influences of contextual factors and practices, is that however committed institutions may be on an individual basis to the principles of equal opportunities, they cannot remain aloof from the influence of political developments on a national scale.

Current provision

The kinds of provision institutions make for their students, and the student groups they aim to attract, are likely to have some effect on staffing patterns. For example, Metropolitan University, with its traditional emphasis on science and technology, has, because of the male bias in these subject areas, few female academic staff in these faculties in particular; and clearly this is one reason why the overall number of female staff in the academic sector of the university is substantially lower than the national average. This in turn has affected the proportion of women in senior posts, and ultimately perceptions of women's abilities to perform well at this level. Women staff at Metropolitan University talked of the absence of role models for those women with ambitions to reach the top, and of mentors to support their progress, while men at Metropolitan University were, on occasion, unsure whether women really aspire to such positions. Such tensions have led to an emphasis on gender issues in relation to staffing. The absence of a noticeable Black or minority ethnic student body and of staff from these groups has, conversely, meant that little attention has been paid to 'race' issues at Metropolitan University.

At Town University, the fact that a noticeable proportion of the student body comes from minority ethnic backgrounds (and that the university would like to attract more students from such groups, in keeping with the local population mix) has led to specific provision being made to represent the needs and interests of these students. This appears to have had somewhat contradictory effects on staffing policies. On the one hand, Black staff and staff from minority ethnic backgrounds have benefited to a certain extent from the emphasis on 'race' issues, which has included consideration of methods to attract more staff from these groups (in part in order to provide appropriate role models for students) and training in issues relating to their recruitment and appointment. On the other hand, it is also the case that 'race' issues tend to be seen predominantly as student-related at Town University and that less attention has been paid to Black staff and staff from minority ethnic backgrounds than has been paid to female staff.

At Borough College, where approximately 50 per cent of students are female and 50 per cent are Black, and also where substantial numbers of students are from white minority ethnic groups, equality of access and provision was the foremost consideration in terms of course construction and student support. While structural support for the three main identified areas of inequality – 'race', gender and disability – appeared equally distributed in terms of posts etc., the main emphasis in the college was on 'race' issues, particularly because of racist attacks on Black students (see Chapter 2) and other similar incidents.

Staff profiles

The composition of the staff body is similarly likely to influence the ways in which equal opportunities issues are perceived and developed in an institution. We have already commented on the different profiles of 'race' issues at Borough College, where there are a substantial number of Black staff and staff from minority ethnic backgrounds, and at Metropolitan University, where there are very few members of staff in this category.

Another significant factor is likely to be the kind of work which men and women, Black and white, able-bodied staff or staff with disabilities, do in an institution. For example, if clerical workers are predominantly female and technicians predominantly male, then, despite the fact that there may be roughly equal numbers of men and women in the institution as a whole, it is likely that stereotypical views of the kinds of work appropriate for men and women may prevail. In addition, it is important to consider the profile of part-time, temporary and contracted out staff in relation to the staff body as a whole: frequently, people from traditionally disadvantaged groups predominate in these sectors, where prospects for good salaries, promotion and job security are less positive.

While it is possible that significant levels of dissatisfaction with work conditions among such groups might put pressure on the institutions to improve equality of opportunity for staff in particular sectors, this had not happened in the case study institutions. Particularly at Metropolitan and Town Universities, the original impetus for action arose as a result of a perception of staffing inequalities in the academic sector, and the focus of discussion continues to be primarily among staff in academic and academic-related sectors. At Town University, this has also contributed to the greater focus on gender rather than 'race' issues, since the largest concentration of Black staff and staff from minority ethnic backgrounds is in campus services. An important issue for institutions to consider is, therefore, the access to equal opportunities committees and meetings for staff in sectors other than academic and academic-related areas.

Stimuli leading to institutional involvement in equal opportunities

We have seen how the general history of the institutions affected the way in which equal opportunities developed. However, in each institution, specific events in the past with a bearing on equal opportunities provided the initial impetus to looking seriously at equity in relation to staff, and to subsequent developments.

At Town University, the appointment in the early 1980s of a vice chancellor with a history of strong commitment set in motion a series of events which have determined the particular emphases of equal opportunities work in the university. The former vice chancellor requested a report on the status of women in the polytechnic (as was), which pointed to the relatively disadvantaged position of women in the institution and made a number of recommendations, most of which have, over time, been implemented. Similar research in the mid-1980s on 'race' issues led to the setting up of the Race Equality Unit, former members of which now serve as equal opportunities officers in each of the university's five faculties. Although the actions of the former vice chancellor can be seen as having had long-term effects on the development of 'race'- and gender-related policies and practices, it is also true that the fact that the structures set up in the first instance to promote initiatives in this area were unconnected to each other has produced certain imbalances in the way 'race' and gender issues are currently managed, and ultimately to a degree of fragmentation of effort.

At Metropolitan University, concern in the early 1980s among women academics about the low numbers of women staff and their lack of opportunities led both to the establishment of a pressure group promoting women's interests (which continues to campaign on behalf of women staff) and to research on the position of women in the university. As at Town University, the research report revealed women academics to be disadvantaged in a number of ways and made a series of recommendations, several of which have subsequently been implemented. In the absence of similar groups or research into issues relating to 'race' and disability in the university, the same attention has not been paid to these areas of equal opportunities.

Borough College has a somewhat different history: until its abolition in the late 1980s, the Inner London Education Authority was responsible for the college, and, in keeping with its political and educational philosophies, initiated a series of policies and practices designed to combat sexism and racism in all its educational establishments. All schools and colleges within ILEA were required to adopt the authority's policies, though in addition they were encouraged to develop their own institution-specific policies and practices, as happened at Borough College. Though there were activists associated with gender and 'race' issues in the college throughout the 1980s, the principal stimulus to become involved can be seen to have been the strong commitment of the local education authority and the encouragement given to individual institutions to focus on them. In addition, the fact that ILEA organized staff training courses on equal opportunities meant that staff were able, at a relatively early stage in the history of equal opportunities initiatives generally in education, to develop an understanding and expertise in this field. This factor has been particularly important at Borough College, in creating both a well informed staff group and expectations that equality of opportunity for all staff is achievable. The long history of awareness raising and staff participation in the initiation and development of equal opportunities policies and practices at Borough College is one of the principal factors underlying the more advanced attitudes among staff, compared with staff at Metropolitan University with no such history.

Institutional definitions of equal opportunities

From the contextual factors already considered, the reasons why the three institutions have developed somewhat different definitions of equal opportunities become clear. For example, at Borough College the emphasis in policy terms is on anti-sexism and anti-racism, with the strong feeling among staff that these issues should remain separate, rather than come under a more general 'equal opportunities' aegis. Additionally, the forceful tone of the policy documents clearly dates back to the college's earlier association with ILEA, which similarly took a 'separatist' line (see Chapter 8 for a discussion of 'separatist' and 'integralist' positions) and couched its policies in what might be seen as a combative style.

At Metropolitan University, a very specific element in the history of the development of policy has come to be particularly influential in formal policy document definitions. As a result of the 1985 research report on the position of women in the university, which made a number of recommendations relating to ways of improving women's employment conditions, the personnel department became involved in the implementation of the recommendations and continued as a key player in moves to have a formal equal opportunities policy adopted by the university. Indeed, it was staff in the personnel department who drafted the policy; and consequently it is not surprising that the main emphasis in the original draft document was on employment rights. (Harassment policies were added to the second draft, as a result of recommendations made, at the time the policy was being debated in the university, by the CVCP.) More generally, throughout the university, equal opportunities tends to be interpreted primarily in terms of gender issues; for historical reasons, as we have seen, gender has had a higher profile than 'race' or disability.

At Town University, early work concerning 'race' and gender developed in somewhat different directions, in part because of the view that 'race' issues were primarily a student concern, and in part because the research instigated by the former vice chancellor indicated different courses of action for each. More recently, however, there has been a deliberate attempt to create a more unified approach to equal opportunities, reflected in the new policy documents which present a particularly comprehensive definition of discriminatory practices and strategies to combat these. Informally, however, it is probable that many staff at Town University think primarily in terms of gender when discussing equal opportunities for staff, as traditionally this has had a higher profile:

> 'Race' issues I find difficult because I don't know enough about them. It's as simple as that . . . We work hard at it but we don't know as much about 'race' as we do about sex. We don't know as much about racial harassment as we do about sexual harassment. We don't really know as much about racial discrimination as we do about sexual discrimination. We are under-represented in terms of minority groups on the staff. So I suppose institutionally we just don't know as much. We've got a long way to go.
>
> (Senior manager, Town University)

Institutional support for equal opportunities: policy, structures and practices

Clearly, the kinds of support for equal opportunities which institutions develop are closely related both to the general context from which interest has arisen, and to the definitions, formal and informal, which institutions have consequently adopted. The point to be made here is that whatever forms of support an institution adopts, these then become part of the context influencing the ways in which attitudes towards equal opportunities and related initiatives continue to develop over time.

To take one example of an initiative which developed from the particular context of the institution, we can see that at Town University the combination of a vice chancellor in the early 1980s with a history of committed involvement to equal opportunities, and a predominantly white staff body of whom a significant proportion were women, has meant that the university has a long history of debate around the issues relating to gender, including two substantial pieces of research into the position of female staff in the university. As a consequence, posts concerned with gender issues (such as the women's and sex harassment officers) have had a high profile and an institution-wide remit.

Similarly, at Metropolitan University, the specific focus on equal opportunities developed by the personnel department produced a policy document with an emphasis on employment issues, and the subsequent appointment of an equal opportunities officer *within* the personnel department, whose job will be to implement and monitor the policy. At Borough College, the influence of ILEA policy has also had far-reaching effects, in terms both of maintaining the 'separatist' focus of gender-, race- and disability-related initiatives, and of creating a well informed staff group with high expectations of what is achievable in these fields.

Support and resistance among staff

An important factor affecting the ongoing context in which institutions develop policies and practices is staff responses to equal opportunities. Such attitudes are both a powerful influence and the product of a particular context. For example, at Metropolitan University, women staff often found themselves in a minority (especially in the academic sector). It is therefore not surprising that many of the women academics we spoke to, or made contact with through the questionnaire, conveyed strong views on the importance of promoting equal opportunities, combined with a powerful sense that on a number of occasions discriminatory practices were preventing women from reaching their true potential. In contrast, their male peers, while mostly giving a generalized expression of goodwill in relation to equal opportunities (providing nothing controversial was proposed), appeared fundamentally uninterested. The indifference of the majority group (white men), which was also the group from which most of those in positions of power in the university were drawn, constituted a formidable barrier for those seeking to promote equality. This is possibly one reason why it has taken so long to agree initiatives and to implement them.

At Borough College, in contrast, the particularly high proportion of Black staff and students and staff and students from minority ethnic backgrounds, has meant that there has long been pressure on the college to take 'race' issues seriously. Indeed, the college cannot assume that white male perspectives are 'the norm' against which other approaches are to be judged, in a way that may be possible in other institutions where Black and/or female staff are fewer in number. In addition, as we have seen, part of the legacy of ILEA's (and, subsequently, the borough education authority's) early focus on staff training has been to create a well-informed staff body with clear expectations that equality of opportunity will be delivered. These expectations are found not only among Black and/or female staff, but also among white male members of staff who are similarly concerned about their rights within the college. Hence, policy decisions have been widely debated by staff generally and are seen as having profound effects on the development of the institution.

At Town University, staff expectations are similarly high, though at the same time there has been a degree of confusion about the roles of the various groups with a specific brief to promote equal opportunities issues. Both our own research and the ethics and values audit carried out in the same period in the university (see Chapter 3) indicate that staff perceive contradictions between the dominant role adopted by management in the decision-making process and the notion that policy decisions, particularly those relating to equal opportunities, should be more democratically determined. However, as a result of these findings, managers at Town University have begun to consider ways of delegating parts of the process, without jeopardizing the position of the chief executive who has legal responsibility for all decisions taken in the institution. It is clear that staff responsiveness to initiatives is likely to be influenced by whether or not they feel that such initiatives are the product of consultation with staff and staff participation in the decision-making process, or imposed from above.

Conclusions

Contextual factors have a key role to play in determining the way in which institutions develop their equal opportunities policies and practices. This is one reason why 'good practice' cannot easily be defined, and why strategies and solutions developed by one institution cannot be applied unaltered to others. By understanding the contextual influences likely to have a bearing on the development of equal opportunities policy and practice, however, institutions can come to identify the areas of greatest need and relevance in their own particular circumstances. We suggest, therefore, whether they are devising policies for the first time or in the process of reviewing progress, that an important step for institutions is to take explicit account of the context in which their work is evolving and of the influence of their own experiences.

However, contextual factors should not become an excuse for inertia or neglect. Our argument is not a deterministic one, and it is important to note that, having become aware of the less positive effects of certain circumstances and experiences, an institution can take steps to counter these. In the discussion above, a number of examples of this approach have been described, most notably in the case of Town University, which has made a determined attempt to counter the fragmentation of effort caused, originally, by the very different approaches to 'race' and gender issues which developed from their different histories and profiles in the university. More recently, Town University has also begun to address the issue of management control over the decision-making process, enhanced by recent changes in institutional status, as a consequence of staff disquiet at the increased centralization of power. While the policies, structures and strategies developed by an institution have a momentum of their own which helps to determine future developments, in our view it is important to be alert to external factors which similarly have a major part to play in influencing success or failure and the direction in which policies are likely to evolve.

Appendix: Contextual factors influencing development of equitable staffing policies in the three case study institutions

	Metropolitan University	Town University	Borough College
Location	'Campus' style university in the centre of a large industrial city currently undergoing substantial urban renewal. City minority ethnic population approx. 5%; negligible in surrounding area.	Multi-site university in the centre of busy county town. City minority ethnic population approx. 10%; approx. 4% in county as a whole.	Multi-site further education college in London. About 24% of the borough's residents are from Black or minority ethnic backgrounds. In addition, the borough has a substantial refugee population. Many residents are bi- or multi-lingual.
History	Dates back to nineteenth-century technological college with a history of commitment to education for working-class men and women. Became a university in 1960s, with	Originally a polytechnic formed from a number of smaller technical and vocational institutions, became a university in 1992. Has recently merged with college of midwifery.	A further education college under the Inner London Education Authority and subsequently the borough education authority. Merged

	Metropolitan University	Town University	Borough College
	marked science and technology focus. Has recently merged with a college of education.		with local sixth form centre in 1992 and became incorporated in 1993. Recently merged with local adult education institute.
Current provision	Caters for some 13 000[a] undergraduate and postgraduate students, in five faculties: arts and social sciences, business, education, engineering and science. Approx. 47% of the students are female.	Approx. 15 000 students in five faculties: business, health, social sciences and law, design and technology, and science. Approx. 50% of the students are female. Approx. 7% of the students are from minority ethnic backgrounds. Approx. 250 students have recognized special needs.	Caters for about 9000 students, mostly from local community. Wide range of academic, pre-vocational and vocational courses. Access and franchised degree programmes. Special programmes for students with learning difficulties and for those with hearing impairments. Approx. 50% are female. Approx. 50% of the student population is Black, and substantial numbers are from Black and white minority ethnic groups.
Percentage of female staff	Academic year 1991–2: full-time 34% part-time 97% overall 46%	On 4 February 1993: overall 47%	December 1993: lecturers 50% 1991: support staff 71%

Note: [a] This number represents the total number of full-time students and the full-time equivalent (FTE) number of part-time students, from home and overseas.

	Metropolitan University	Town University	Borough College
Percentage of staff from minority ethnic backgrounds	Figures not kept, but believed to be low.	On 4 February 1993: 　overall 3%	December 1993: 　lecturers 15% March 1992: 　support staff 25%
Project team's definition of institution's EO position	An institution in the early stages of developing EO policies and practices.	A recognized leader in the field of EO: innovative and dynamic practice.	Sophisticated understanding of EO issues throughout organization. Little overt debate but assumptions that EO will underpin all practice.
Stimuli leading to institution's involvement in EO issues	Early 1980s Women's pressure group formed by female academics concerned about low numbers of women in university and perceived lack of opportunity for women academics in particular. Mid-1980s Research carried out under auspices of sole female professor in this period revealed: • sex-segregated patterns of work across the university as a whole; • weak promotion prospects for women; • lack of support (such as flexible work arrange-ments, job-share	Early 1980s Previous vice chancellor requested report on women. Also a women's pres-sure group formed around this time. EO committee set up to deal with employment policy, language and sexual harassment. Mid-1980s Based on internal unpublished research initiated by previous vice chancellor, Race Equality Unit estab-lished from Section 11 funding – con-centrated mainly on student affairs. External researcher invited to examine sex equality policy progress. Commented at length on relatively	Cultural diversity of locality. Long involvement with EO initiated by ILEA. Many college staff attended EO courses organized by ILEA (and more recently by college). Activists within the college associated with both gender and race equality. Reports produced by ILEA, FEU and internal college reports, providing critiques of existing practices.

	Metropolitan University	Town University	Borough College
	opportunities or childcare provision) for women workers; • the average wage for women in the university represented 60% of the average male wage. Report calls for detailed monitoring of pay and promotion data in order to establish extent of discrimination experienced by women, and for the university to draw up a code of conduct in relation to EO. To date, there has been little interest in the university in aspects of EO relating to race or disability.	disadvantaged position of women staff and made key recommendations: • need for women's centre to be set up (established 1992); • need for detailed monitoring statistics representing an 'imaginative' range of indicators of women's position in the institution (produced from 1989 onwards); • need to ensure that all responsible, whether they agree with positive action for sex equality or not, know what the rules of the organization are and act on them; • need to ensure that sex equality is *not* considered in isolation from racial equality.	
Institutional definitions of EO	Principal focus is on equality in employment rights, though a formal commitment to combating sexual and racial harassment is also contained in EO policy document. Moves towards anti-discriminatory policy and practice are	All forms of unfair discrimination will be challenged. Unfair discrimination can arise in staff recruitment, selection and promotion, dismissal, rewards, resources, as well as the curriculum and hidden curriculum.	Important to maintain separate focus of three principal areas connected to EO: gender, race and disability. Emphasis in gender and race policies on combating discrimination in all areas of the

	Metropolitan University	*Town University*	*Borough College*
	resisted, on the basis that the university appoints and promotes on merit alone.	EO can be threatened by use of language, gesture and other symbolic behaviour.	college's work and on bringing about fundamental changes in attitudes and assumptions.
			Disability takes a somewhat different approach, in trying to strike a balance between the desirable and the feasible.
			Greater emphasis on student issues in relation to disability, while staff issues have high profile in relation to gender and race.
Institutional support for EO: policy	Policies on EO in employment, and on sexual and racial harassment adopted in 1992. Guidelines on gender-free language issued in 1991.	Mission statement adopted in 1986. EO statement revised 1992. EO language policy statement and codes of practice agreed 1992. Sex harassment policy and complaints procedure in operation since 1990. Harassment policy and complaints procedures (covering harassment on grounds of sex, race and disability) agreed 1993.	EO policies for gender and race since mid 1980s; updated 1993–4. Disability policy 1992–3. Harassment policy since 1990, covering all instances of violence, abuse and harassment. Language policy well established and implemented. Clear policies and procedures for recruiting and appointing staff.

	Metropolitan University	Town University	Borough College
		Employment policies (job share, flexi-hours, career break).	
		EO in academic affairs policy drafted 1992, covering curriculum and student issues.	
Institutional support for EO: structures	Vice principal has formal responsibility for EO issues. Personnel department has in practice taken on much of the work of drafting policy and securing its adoption, as well as subsequently arguing for the appointment of an EO officer to oversee policy implementation. EO officer (within personnel department) appointed 1994. No EO committee.	A range of posts fitting into different management structures and line management responsibilities. Five EO advisors based in Faculties and responsible to respective deans. Sexual harassment (now harassment) officer reports directly to senior management. Institution-wide responsibility. Centre for Racial Equality: one post accountable to head of programmes. Responsibility mainly for student issues. Women's unit with two women's officers (job share) accountable to dean with responsibility for women's issues. Responsibility for staff only. EO committee and three advisory EO groups: disability, race and gender.	Deputy principal has executive responsibility for all EO. Three EO senior lecturers: anti-racism, anti-sexism and disability. All working within the Staff Development and Equality Unit (since 1992), with timetabled remission (0.5). Disability post primarily for students but other posts cover staff and students. Small budget available for each post holder. Anti-sexism, anti-racism and disability committees: all three committees responsible to academic board, via deputy principal. Black staff group set up as principal's working group:

	Metropolitan University	Town University	Borough College
		Equality staff working group formed to reassess EO in 1993; brings together all EO workers with aim of determining future progress for EO in institution. Reports to senior management.	one meeting per term timetabled for Black staff. Childcare facilities: a crèche and two nurseries on different sites. Responsibility for ensuring equal opportunities located at faculty level (since March 1994).
Institutional support for EO: practices	Policy had yet to be implemented at end of research period. Existing practices held by university management to promote EO in that merit is the sole criteria for appointments or promotion. Research team observed appointments and promotions procedures and found no evidence of overt discrimination. The low numbers of women, particularly in the academic sector (10% against a national average of 22%) and the low proportion of women reaching the highest grades in all sectors raise unanswered questions about the efficacy of the merit	All members of selection panels have attended equality issues and interview process courses. Review of application form informed by recommendations from key EO sources. In-house staff development programme, generously resourced and staffed. Innovative employment policies, widely advertised and implemented. Practical support for those with disabilities.	All policies have implementation plans and annual targets have now been established. Briefing packs prepared for lecturing and support staff provide information and advice about EO policies and practices, and guidance on use of language. Recruitment, appointment and promotion procedures pay careful attention to EO and there is representative from Black staff on interviewing panels. Panels trained in 'good' EO practice. Staff development programme includes courses to support staff

	Metropolitan University	Town University	Borough College
	principle in promoting EO.		under-represented in higher grades.
			Expectation that *all* staff – academic and support – will put policy into practice.
Staff support for EO	Women's pressure group in existence since early 1980s campaigns on a number of issues relating to the image of women in the university and to women's conditions of employment.	On the whole, there is much positive support for EO among staff. Staff have high expectations that EO should be adhered to and that it should have a high profile in the university.	Very high awareness of EO issues, which are no longer debated but assumed.
	Separate group has campaigned for adequate childcare provision for staff.	Women's gender issues have a higher profile than those relating to minority ethnic groups.	Core of experienced EO activists in gender and race.
	General goodwill towards EO principles among university staff, providing issues are non-controversial.	Sex harassment policy and procedures have had some impact on behaviour.	Generally very good support for policies and practices, although all groups think not enough is being done for their own group – including white males.
		Management claims significant impact of language policy.	Race policy currently has higher profile than others – a source of some comment.
			Staff generally have high expectations of EO from college.
Staff resistance to EO	A wide range of other issues are seen as having higher priority than EO.	This has been manifested in the course of the research around the implementation of sex harassment procedures. Trade	Little overt antagonism to EO – this would not be tolerated by the college.
	Some staff hostile to EO issues, particularly to		Some resentment among

	Metropolitan University	Town University	Borough College
	perceived 'threat' to introduce 'positive discrimination'. Widespread lack of interest and awareness in EO issues.	union resistance and criticism from harassment victims of poor follow-up to investigations. But dynamic nature of EO in university means that these problems have now been resolved.	'beleaguered' white males. Some impatience that there are still perceived inequalities of opportunity for staff.
Issues and debates in the course of the project	Adoption of EO policy. Childcare provision. Appointment of EO officer.	Establishment of harassment policy and procedures using framework of existing sex harassment policy. Large-scale restructuring of departments and staff groups. Moves to have various grievances dealt with under the EO policy. Positive reappraisal of university application package in light of revised EO statement. Ethics and values audit carried out: 'soft focus' EO?	Restructuring proposals included dispersal of staff development and equality unit and withdrawal of time from post holders. Final agreement to reinstate post holders but locate race and gender in quality assurance unit and disability in student affairs. Major racial abuse incident on one site with wide media coverage led to site meetings of staff and students and review of college and borough situations. Beginning of anti-heterosexist policy.

8

Shared Themes

Introduction

It is in the nature of policy case study research to focus on the particular circumstances of a policy, and to emphasize the unique rather than the generalizable. This feature of case study research is both its strength and its weakness. While other chapters in this volume have explored the particular contexts of the three institutions which have produced very different approaches to the promotion of equal opportunities for staff, the aim of this chapter is to examine aspects which they have in common. The following shared themes occurred time and time again across the case studies.

- *Developing definitions of 'equal opportunities'.* Debates within the institutions focused on whether 'equal opportunities' can be better interpreted as an umbrella term, or as one or more of a number of distinctive 'areas' (typically 'race', gender and disability).
- *Proliferation of policy and the achievement of policy cohesion.* Particularly in the institutions with experience of equal opportunities policy-making over a number of years, increased awareness of the complexities of the process appear to lead to the continual reviewing and rewriting of existing policies and, in the process, the extension of their scope. While such developments reflect the greater sophistication of the institutions in dealing with equal opportunities issues, new problems are also created in terms of the accessibility of policy for staff generally, and, potentially, of conflicts between different policies.
- *Fragmentation or cohesion of support structures.* As equal opportunities policies multiply and diversify over time, the structures designed to support the implementation of policy show similar tendencies to proliferate and mutate. Without strategies to develop a cohesive overall structure, however, there appears to be a danger of fragmentation, with the consequent possibilities of either duplication of effort or conflict of initiatives.

- *Fragility or embeddedness of support structures.* However long-standing they are, it emerged that apparently deep-rooted structures can easily be removed. A number of factors, both internal and external, can come into play in changing political and institutional perceptions of the importance of equal opportunities, and in the resulting structural alterations.
- *Management styles: managerialism and 'democracy'.* The commitment of management to supporting equal opportunities policies was crucial in all three institutions. Management styles differed markedly, however, and the adoption of either 'managerialist' or 'democratic' methods of decision-making had considerable implications for the development of policies generally. The power and influence of senior managers hence need to be considered alongside other structures.
- *Power relationships.* Ultimately, the themes raised above led to discussions about the location of power within an institution, the implications of power relationships for genuine equality of opportunity, and the perspectives adopted by staff at different levels in the institution.

Each of these themes is now considered in some detail.

Developing definitions of 'equal opportunities'

One of the most fundamental issues raised in the course of our research was how 'equal opportunities' itself is to be defined. The researchers were frequently asked how we ourselves defined 'equal opportunities'. Our reply – that it was not our own definition, but that of the staff in the institution which would inform the research – was often seen by participants as disconcerting. It would have been both convenient and reassuring to have opted for a standard definition of 'equal opportunities', but, as our case studies show quite clearly, not only does each institution differ in its operational interpretation of the concept, but individual members of staff also disagreed, sometimes quite markedly, on what it could and did mean within their own organization.

Broadly speaking, we identified two somewhat contradictory trends in the interpretation of 'equal opportunities': the separation of the principal areas subsumed under the heading of 'equal opportunities' (i.e. principally gender, 'race' and disability, though class and sexual orientation also featured on occasion) and stressing common ground in moves towards equality of opportunity (though drawing attention to the complexity of power relationships). These two positions are referred to, for convenience, as the 'separatist' and the 'integralist' definitions in the discussion which follows. However, it is important to recognize that these are not stark alternatives: aspects of both perspectives emerged in all three institutions, and each has advantages and disadvantages.

As we have already noted, definitions of 'equal opportunities' at Metropolitan University were at a relatively early stage of development, both in the institution as a whole and among members of staff. Embryonic 'integralist' and 'separatist' positions can both be identified from formal and informal sources: for example, the university's equal opportunities in employment policy incorporates a comprehensive list of groups which might, theoretically, suffer discrimination:

> The law requires that no job applicant or employee will receive less favourable treatment on the grounds of 'race', colour, nationality, ethnic or national origins, gender or marital status . . . every effort will be made to avoid discrimination on the grounds of disability, religion, political belief, socio-economic background, parental status, sexual orientation, age (subject to normal retirement conventions) and trade union membership.

It also has a general statement on equality of opportunity for all:

> Metropolitan University confirms its commitment to a policy of equal opportunities in employment in which individuals are selected, trained, appraised, promoted and otherwise treated on the basis of their relative merits and abilities and are given equal opportunities within the university.

In practice, for the historical reasons which we examined in Chapter 4, the emphasis at Metropolitan University has tended to be on gender issues, and most of the staff whose views we gathered through interview or questionnaire thought principally in terms of gender when we discussed equal opportunities. This can be seen not only from the kinds of issues which were raised, but also from the nature of the 'backlash' against what some saw as excessive emphasis on such issues. 'Race' and disability had a much lower profile.

Senior managers, however, tended to adopt the 'integralist' approach, though some staff identified flaws in this perspective, seeing a blanket commitment to equality of opportunity as a way of avoiding issues of discrimination or devising strategies to deal with them:

> My definition of equal opportunities involves positive discrimination as the 'playing field' is unequal in a number of ways, and it is necessary to counteract the effects of bias which are built into the structures of educational institutions. I am aware that my definition is not the same as that of the university, which I see as a negative definition – an assurance that aspects of people which are not relevant to a job are not taken into account. Effectively it is a declaration that prejudice does not operate – but the issue has not been thought through.
>
> (Senior academic)

The longer history of involvement in equal opportunities issues at both Town University and Borough College provides evidence of how separatist and integralist interpretations can develop over time. In both institutions, concern about 'race' and gender issues and the consequent policies developed separately in the first instance. In both cases, disability was an area of equal opportunities which emerged later and with a somewhat different emphasis. The initial stimulus which provokes an institution to address equal opportunities can be provided by individual activists and pressure groups, and consequently it is not surprising that there are uneven emphases on the different areas of equal opportunities.

In both Borough College and Town University, a range of initiatives has developed over recent years to make the treatment of the different areas relating to equal opportunities more even-handed. At Borough College, parallel structures to support the different areas were created such that each of the coordinators (for 'race', gender and disability) reported through the deputy principal to the academic board, there was a committee to support each area and the coordinators attended all three committees to avoid any duplication of work. Similarly, there has been a move to ensure that policies relating to the different areas reflect common goals; for example, an aim of each policy is that 'all staff and all students feel safe, welcome and fully able to participate in College life'.

Stylistically, policies at Borough College have also developed a common approach to changes in practice, such as stressing action, specifying behaviours which will be opposed, and emphasizing precise targets in annual reviews. Nevertheless, staff involved in equal opportunities have rejected suggestions that the separate areas should be combined under an equal opportunities umbrella, arguing that one committee would have less impact on the work of the college than the present three.

At Town University, the fact that those with day-to-day responsibility for promoting 'race' and gender issues have different remits and different relationships with the university hierarchy reflects the different histories of the two areas (e.g. the equal opportunities officers working in the faculties, the Centre for Racial Equality workers, the women's officers with responsibility for staff issues across the university and the harassment officer). More recently, the establishment of the advisory groups for the separate areas, reporting to a central equal opportunities committee, and the extension of the sexual harassment officer's role to harassment officer, indicate the university's intention to balance the areas and to focus on aspects of equal opportunities which the various areas have in common. As we have seen, this attempt at harmonization has been problematic in some ways, and has not necessarily avoided duplication of work. Moreover, the fact that there is frequently considerable disagreement among the representatives of the different areas about common initiatives (for example, about the role and remit of the harassment officer) suggests either that there is resistance to the integralist approach among those with interests in specific areas or that there are genuine difficulties in attempting to harmonize provision for groups affected by different types of disadvantage.

A more fundamental move towards the integralist position at Town

University has been the development of the ethics and values audit, and the establishment of the Centre for Professional Ethics. As was noted in Chapter 3, the recommendations of the audit involved

> an attempt to encourage a University management style and culture in which recognition of and respect for all members of its community is the paramount value and where a climate of genuine trust, participation in decision making and collaboration is fostered. The assumption then is that good and fair ethical practice will naturally evolve and become the norm.
>
> (Town University Ethics and Values Audit Project, 1992)

The implications of this are that all members of an institution may potentially suffer discrimination, whether on the grounds of historic social prejudices – against minority ethnic groups, against women, against those with disabilities etc. – or for less tangible reasons relating, for example, to the personality of the individual. Similarly, all those in positions of power are seen as having the opportunity to abuse their positions. The principal strategy to deal with this appears to be educative in that when all staff are imbued with a sense of trust, participation and collaboration, institutional practices will 'naturally' become equitable.

In a number of ways, this perspective contrasts with the more long-standing approaches to equal opportunities. It appears to involve a more complex view of power relationships than the notion that power accrues 'naturally' to white middle-class men without disabilities. Particularly in institutions with a long history of activity, such a move may be a logical development as awareness of the intricacies of power relationships increases. On the other hand, it also seems naive to imply that an innate sense of fairness in men will automatically lead to the eradication of these practices. Twenty-five years of feminist struggle has revealed this not to be the case. More disturbing, perhaps, is the seemingly apolitical nature of the ethics and values approach, ignoring the social and historical causes of disadvantage for certain well-defined groups. In some ways, the perspective is not greatly different from that of the senior managers at Metropolitan University, criticized by staff there for an apparent refusal to accept that there is no 'level playing field' and that some form of positive discrimination is necessary to counter decades – indeed centuries – of prejudice. However, the development of an ethics and values 'culture' is in the very early stages at Town University and it is not possible to say at this stage what the long-term effects of such an initiative may be. While potentially dangerous in an institution with little or no experience of working towards equal opportunities, in one such as Town University, with a long and distinguished record in this field, it may result in a more sophisticated and ultimately more effective way of promoting equal opportunities.

Table 8.1 summarizes the advantages and disadvantages of the two approaches to defining 'equal opportunities'.

Table 8.1   Advantages and disadvantages of separatist and integralist approaches

	Advantages	Disadvantages
Separatist approaches	• Maintain sharp focus on particular causes of disadvantage. • Avoid blanket solutions which may not be appropriate for all groups. • May have greater impact on the institution as a whole.	• Different areas can be played off against each other. • One area can emerge as dominant, at the expense of the others. • Potential for conflict among various areas. • Danger of reinventing the wheel, or of spending excessive amounts of time discussing similar issues in different committees. • Non-parallel structures to support each area can cause confusion and hamper effective implementation of policy.
Integralist approaches	• Concerted effort may lead to greater impact on institution, and specifically to more effective implementation of policy. • Focus on common ground in various areas avoids unnecessary duplication of work. • Promotion of a more sophisticated understanding of power relationships.	• Attempt to unite areas which have very different priorities may lead to prolonged arguments and failure to implement policy. • Failure to recognize differences between areas can lead to marginalization of certain area-specific issues. • Depoliticization of historic patterns of disadvantage and oppression.

Proliferation of policy and the achievement of policy cohesion

Our research suggests that while institutions at an early stage of equal opportunities policy development are likely to condense the policy into a single policy document, those with a longer history may develop a series of policies which relate to specific aspects of equal opportunities. This feature implies a tendency of equality initiatives to 'snowball' over time, as well as an increasing sophistication of understanding of the implications of equal opportunities principles. At the same time, however, the scope of equal opportunities policies can also lead to fragmentation and, in some cases, to conflicts between different policy areas. A cohesive overall view of all policy initiatives thus becomes an important goal for institutions whose policies have 'branched out' into a number of different areas.

At the beginning of the research period, Metropolitan University was in the early stages of developing and implementing its first equal opportunities policy. Initially, the policy document was particularly succinct, consisting of a boxed policy statement focusing on equal opportunities in relation to employment rights, and a series of more detailed principles on which implementation was to be based. The focus on employment rights arose from campaigns by women in the university to improve employment conditions for women, and from the subsequent acceptance of responsibility by the personnel department. However, early in the project, the Committee of Vice Chancellors and Principals issued guidelines recommending that universities should incorporate sexual and racial harassment policies into their general equal opportunities policies. Metropolitan University's original policy document was therefore expanded from one to four pages in order to include policy and procedures relating to these aspects of equal opportunities.

The two policies (on employment and harassment) embody quite different approaches to the encoding of policy in policy documents. The employment policy is a particularly succinct document, stating general principles but leaving open the ways in which these principles are to be interpreted. It is only when specific cases are brought for adjudication that the precise meanings of phrases can be established. For example, '*Wherever possible* all posts will be advertised *as widely as possible* and be designed to encourage applications from *relevant* groups' (Metropolitan University equal opportunities policy; emphasis added). In addition, the policy omits specific recommendations relating to implementation. There are advantages and disadvantages to this form of policy writing. On the one hand, it is difficult to see how the policy will bring about changes within the institution, leaving the way open to accusations of 'lip-service'. Was the university primarily interested in creating a progressive image for the institution? On the other hand, a longer and more detailed document might have discouraged staff from reading or thinking about the issues dealt with in the policy. Until then, few people apart from those actively involved in promoting equal opportunities issues had shown interest or enthusiasm, and a more detailed document might have provoked opposition. A deliberately general policy had the advantage of being acceptable to most, freeing those more likely to be engaged in the implementation of the policy to devise appropriate interpretations of the principles once the policy came into force.

The sexual and racial harassment policy, on the other hand, though stylistically similar to the employment policy, is considerably more detailed. It begins with a boxed policy statement, followed by a list of more specific definitions of actions likely to be considered as harassment, guidelines for victims of harassment and a list of procedures to be followed when complaints of harassment are made. The addition of the guidelines and procedures expands the document from just over one page to three, thereby simultaneously providing a much more specific picture of the university's response to harassment and potentially limiting the readership of the document. As a consequence, implementation of the harassment policy was likely to develop more rapidly than implementation of the employment policy, where it seemed likely that little practical implementation might ensue unless members of staff complained about specific instances in which they believed the policy had been breached. In fact, information which reached the team after the research had come to an end suggested that the newly appointed equal opportunities officer had decided to focus first on the implementation of the harassment policy.

In the case of Metropolitan University, it was possible to argue that the harassment policy could be linked to the policy on employment rights by the notion that the university was committed to ensuring a working environment free from intimidation and discrimination for its staff (and students). Borough College, on the other hand, was in the middle of a major revision of its policy documents, which, at least temporarily, appeared to create considerable confusion about the exact nature of the college policies that had developed over the preceding ten years. In theory, the college had adopted a number of policies relating to equal opportunities. These included:

- anti-sexist (now sex equality) policy (dating back to the mid-1980s);
- multi-ethnic (subsequently anti-racist) policy (dating back to the mid-1980s);
- disability policy (developed in 1992–3);
- harassment policy (developed in 1990);
- language policy (date of original development unknown).

In addition, an anti-heterosexism policy was in the course of being developed at the time of the research. In practice, it was difficult to obtain copies of any of these policies because the older ones were under review and the newer ones were in the course of development.

This resulted in a certain lack of coherence in the approach to equal opportunities overall. For example, the early anti-sexist and multi-ethnic policies reflect the deliberately confrontational approach to these issues adopted by ILEA, under the auspices of which the college had originally developed the policies. The language used in these policies is similarly unequivocal: the anti-sexist policy, for example, states that 'We are *committed* to taking *positive action* to identify and *eradicate* sexism and to develop equality for women throughout the College' (Borough College anti-sexism policy; emphasis added). Both policies aim to raise awareness of issues and to promote specific measures designed to combat racism and sexism. The disability policy, on the other hand, perhaps as the product of a different period in the college's history, is a less 'political' document. Rather than attacking unwanted behaviour, it aims to encourage and support individuals and groups.

The increase in policies related to equal opportunities at Borough College and the lack of an overall guiding principle to link them created the risk of different policies conflicting with each other. Moreover, the apparent fragmentation of policy could have led to a dilution of effort in relation to equal opportunities generally within the college. However, this was not the case. We attribute the deep-rooted commitment to equal opportunities among the staff in the college to a number of compensating factors. In the first place, management commitment to equal opportunities was strong, and enabled the deputy principal to devote time to the development and promotion of a range of equality-related initiatives. The deputy principal thus constituted a unifying factor which overcame the potential problem of fragmentation and dilution of concerted effort. Second, practices promoting equal opportunities were well established in the college and most members of staff were aware of the particular aspects which impinged on their own work. There was perhaps less need to appeal to policy for support or guidance.

A third factor is connected to the impetus which has led to the diversification of policy: as we have seen, initial policy development is likely to produce documentation without specific detail of policy targets and strategies. Once staff gain experience of the implications and practical workings of the policy, it is probable that this will lead to moves for the policy to be changed in various ways. Such changes may involve alterations to aspects of the policy and moves to specify in greater detail what is meant by general statements of intent. As awareness of equality-related initiatives increases, this will lead to an extension into areas which were not previously covered. This seemed to be the position at Borough College at the time of the research. The state of flux of the policies during this period can therefore be seen to be a necessary stage of the policy development process.

Ultimately, what emerged from the lengthy review process was not so much a change to the policies; rather there was a change in presentation, with the formulation of specific targets to be achieved. Thus, though the specific issues raised in each area remain separate, there was more coherence in the presentation of policy and in the strategies adopted.

As we have seen, Town University also had a wide range of policies relating, including among others:

- equal opportunities statement;
- equal opportunities language statement;
- harassment policy and complaints procedures;
- employment policies (including policies on job-sharing, flexi-hours and career breaks);
- equal opportunities in academic affairs.

As at Borough College, Town University had developed a wide range of policies representing an increasingly sophisticated understanding of the implications of equal opportunities principles. The university had similarly gone through a process of reviewing and developing policies, which in some cases dated back to the mid-1980s. These similarities between Borough College and Town University appeared to confirm the view that policy review and proliferation may be a particular stage in the life of an institution as policies and practices begin to become established features of an institution's way of working.

However, Town University seemed to be one stage further on in that the university was in the process of harmonizing various policies. This harmonization was reflected in what we termed the 'umbrella' policy structure: the 'umbrella' equal opportunities statement was poised above various specific policies. The statement articulated the essential principles of equal opportunities and other policies represented more detailed workings out of these principles in various selected areas.

In addition, the university's planning and development department had rewritten the policies relating to equal opportunities and a range of other policies in order to produce a more uniform style of policy documentation as follows:

> When we had a mission statement first of all, we did a trawl of all the documentation, all the academic board minutes . . . we documented them and tried to systematize them, to see where there were gaps and also to raise questions about what was a policy. It became very clear to us that people were mixing up what was a policy and what was a procedure . . . Now we're in the process of revamping all our policies . . . So we're trying to get very clear, one-side statements of the principles of the policy, why we've got it and what we want from it – what we want to see happen. We're going to try to do that for all the policies that we've got.
>
> (Member of planning and development department)

Response to this development was mixed. On the one hand, some staff felt that the policies had been 'taken away' from those who had been responsible for devising them in the first place, and then rewritten to alter the emphasis intended by the committees or working parties involved. '[The document] had been completely rewritten in the corporate style of polytechnic policy – and it's different – a completely new format' (Member of equal opportunities committee). On the other hand, a cohesive policy structure was clearly an important aim. It is not clear that the 'umbrella' policy structure will avoid such situations occurring in future, because the project ended before the implications of 'cohesion' had been fully understood. Nevertheless, such developments represented important steps towards the development of a cohesive policy structure which simultaneously covers the wide range of institutional areas on which equal opportunities impinge.

Fragmentation or cohesion of support structures

As people in an institution become more aware of equality issues, and more committed to the principles, supporting structures tend to multiply and diversify. This is not surprising given that increasing the number of people with an active role to play in equality issues will inevitably enhance the speed of change. However, unless there is a unifying overall structure, it is possible for individuals or groups to work in ignorance of what the others are doing.

Metropolitan University, as we have seen, was in the process of developing a basic structure for its equal opportunities policy. At the same time it had been decided to allocate overall responsibility for equal opportunities at Metropolitan University to the vice principal. In the absence of an overall strategy or effective monitoring, pressure groups, such as the Programme for Opportunities for Women and the childcare group, which had campaigned on particular issues, had found it difficult to make their voices heard in the committees in which decisions were taken. Members of the childcare group, for example, were aware that they were unlikely to succeed in their campaign without a 'champion' who could argue their case for them. Once it had been decided that the vice principal was to take formal responsibility for equality issues at the university, the pressure groups found it much easier to gain access to the key planning and resource committees.

A second development over this period was the decision to appoint an equal opportunities officer. The appointee, in fact, took up her post after the research had come to an end and it was not possible for us to investigate how the officer would coordinate and take forward the various initiatives. However, it seems clear that the university was beginning to develop the kind of support structures which were also in evidence, though at more advanced stages, at Borough College and Town University. Metropolitan University did not have a specific committee devoted to equal opportunities during the research period, though it might consider such a support structure useful in the future.

The role of committees has been complex. Development of policy structures at Town University makes clear both the tendency of support structures to multiply and mutate over time, and the kinds of problems which this can create. Table 8.2 shows the complexity of the structures which have developed to support equal opportunities at Town University. It shows three types of structure: designated posts, advisory committees and a set of 'overarching' structures which cut across equal opportunities categories.

It will already be clear from the Town University case study that the way in which these structures developed was somewhat haphazard and uneven. Table 8.2 also reveals imbalances in the structural pattern; for example, there are no designated posts for disability issues and the role of the

Table 8.2 Structures supporting equal opportunities at Town University

Designated EO posts

Race			Gender		
Name	*Remit*	*Report to*	*Name*	*Remit*	*Report to*
Race Equality Unit (1985–90)	Mainly students	Vice chancellor (?)			
Five EO officers (1990 on)	Individual faculties; remit determined by each faculty	Individually to faculty deans	Women's officers (1992 on)	All staff: recruitment; monitoring; academic affairs; curriculum	Dean with responsibility for women's affairs
Centre for Racial Equality (1990 on)	Mainly students	Head of department (head of programmes)	Sexual harassment officer (1990–3)	Counter sexual harassment across university	Vice chancellor

Advisory groups

Race			Gender			Disability		
Name	*Remit*	*Report to*	*Name*	*Remit*	*Report to*	*Name*	*Remit*	*Report to*
Race advisory group	Discuss race issues	Recommendations to equal opportunities committee	Gender advisory group	Discuss gender issues	Recommendations to equal opportunities committee	Disability advisory group	Discuss disability issues	Recommendations to equal opportunities committee

Overarching structures

Name	Remit	Report to
Harassment officer (1993 onwards)	Counter all forms of harassment across the university	Dean
Equal opportunities committee (original EOC dates back to 1983; committee exists in current form since 1992)	To develop policy on the basis of recommendations made by advisory groups; to advise vice chancellor	Vice chancellor
Equalities staff working group (1993 on)	To review university's position in relation to equal opportunities and determine course of future progress for the institution	Management team
Management team	Strategic planning group, dealing with policy matters	Vice chancellor
Executive team	To provide support for boards and carry out executive decisions	Vice chancellor

gender post holders is rather different from that of the 'race' post holders. Certain historical factors come into play here; for example, the development of the Race Equality Unit (REQU) in the mid-1980s occurred because there was Section 11 money available for such initiatives, but no comparable funding for gender. The 'built-in obsolescence' of the unit, which relates to the nature of Section 11 funding, was also influential in the decision to disperse the original REQU members to the faculties. Initially, these equal opportunities officers tended to be seen as 'race experts' but have gradually come to be accepted as having a wider role. At the same time, 'race' has tended to be seen predominantly as a student-related issue rather than a staff issue at Town University. Both REQU and its successor, the Centre for Racial Equality (CRE) have focused mainly on student issues: student access, the development of curricula more in tune with a multi-cultural student body and student resources. The faculties too have dealt primarily with issues affecting students.

The development of the gender-related posts has been different. Though there were no specific posts in existence before 1990, such posts have a higher profile across the university than the race-related posts appear to have or to have had in the past. The post of women's officer (currently filled by two people in a job-share) has a university-wide remit and relates exclusively to staff. Among other responsibilities, the women's officer has a specific obligation to look at recruitment and other employment issues, whereas 'race' advisors have, it appears, been discouraged from addressing these issues in the past. The sexual harassment officer similarly had a specific brief to counter sexual harassment, and it emerged that most cases involved members of staff harassing other members of staff. In contrast, the university CRE appears to have dealt principally with cases of racial harassment of students. Since the harassment officer's brief has widened to include all types of harassment within the university, it will be interesting to discover whether racial harassment is predominantly a student issue.

One aspect of the higher profile accorded to gender issues is how the women's officer and the (sexual) harassment officer are managed. The latter reports directly to the vice chancellor, while the women's officer reports to the dean with responsibility for women's affairs. Thus both gain access to the key committees such as the executive team and the management team, where university policy and financial support for developments and new initiatives are determined. In contrast, the head of the CRE does not have direct access to these committees. The ex-REQU equal opportunities officers, like the women's officers, report directly to their faculty deans, but their position can be seen to be disadvantageous in two respects. First, they have teaching commitments and therefore are not able to devote as much time to their equal opportunities responsibilities as the women's officers. Second, the equal opportunities officers' roles are limited to their own faculties. They have not been able to develop common strategies or goals as a group; nor have there been any specific posts to deal with issues relating to Black staff or those from minority ethnic groups in other sectors of the university.

The contrasting position of the equal opportunities officers and the women's officers illustrates the advantages and disadvantages of each model. The strength of the equal opportunities officers lies in the fact that they have a direct influence on the work and the development of their own faculties, and have continued to develop initiatives initially undertaken by REQU, such as ensuring increased access for Black students, monitoring the degree of access afforded to Black students on part-time courses and raising awareness among lecturers generally of teaching and learning styles which take greater account of the interests and experiences of Black students. Their weakness is that they have not been in a position to develop university-wide strategies. In contrast, the women's officers are relatively well positioned to develop university-wide strategies, both because this specifically constitutes their remit and because they have greater access to management. However, the women's officers do not have any direct impact on the work of any one area of the university, and it is clear that they can on occasion find their position somewhat isolated from the rest of the university.

> We seem to be outside the main structures of the university: everything else comes under the faculties or services but we are in a structure of our own . . . It would be better to be consulted about things beforehand, so that we can be proactive. For example, the restructuring exercise carried out recently: it has particular implications for women in the University, affecting the ways in which they progress; it may be creating a particular kind of glass ceiling. If we had been consulted, we would have been able to put forward the women's point of view . . . We are not seen as important enough and often no one thinks to include the women's perspective, or that if there is a woman involved in discussions, that in itself is enough.
>
> (Women's officer, Town University)

The second tier of structures supporting equal opportunities at Town University comprises the three advisory groups for 'race', gender and disability. Each of these groups is composed of co-opted equal opportunities 'activists' and each includes both staff and students. Each group is chaired by a dean, and though the groups formally report to the equal opportunities committee (EOC), the presence of the deans also means that issues raised in the advisory groups can inform the work of the executive and management teams. In some ways these advisory groups are perhaps the most effective and cohesive structures supporting equal opportunities in the university, as the membership of each group includes designated post holders, equal opportunities activists and those in senior positions with the power to promote the recommendations made by each group. However, the complex relationship between the advisory groups and the EOC means that these groups are less effective than they might first appear. On their own, they have no power to take decisions. They can only make recommendations; and they seem often to operate in ignorance of what the other groups are doing.

In theory, the EOC should be in a position to bring together the recommendations of each of the advisory groups as university policy. However, a number of factors appear to prevent this from occurring. First, designated as advisory to the vice chancellor, the committee can only pass on the recommendations of the advisory groups, for the vice chancellor to make the final decision. This seems to have led the committee to spend much of its time debating issues rather than taking decisions. Representatives of the advisory groups who also sit on the EOC find this process particularly irritating, though, as we have seen, others criticized its excessively 'procedural' approach, partly because of the duplication of discussions which have already taken place at advisory group level, and partly because these joint debates seem to focus on areas of differences rather than building on common ground.

Ultimately the dilemma which the role of the EOC poses, in relation to both the advisory groups and the vice chancellor, is a product of the 'managerial' structure of Town University. It has led to the establishment of a separate 'overarching' group (the Equality Staff Working Group) to review the current position and determine the future progress of equal opportunities at Town University. Figure 3 shows the complex hierarchies and interrelationships among the various groups supporting equal opportunities at Town University. The Equality Staff Working Group may be an important first step in coordinating the highly fragmented equal opportunities structures at Town University, though we were unable to evaluate its effectiveness.

At first glance, Borough College appears to have developed a similar support structure to that at Town University: there is a similar three-tier system, comprising post holders, committees and overarching structures. As at Town University, the historical development of the 'race', gender and disability structures has not been parallel. However, it does appear that Borough College had achieved a structure which balances the three areas relatively evenly, as can be seen by comparing the structures supporting each sector in Table 8.3.

At Borough College, focus on gender and 'race' has a longer history than that on disability: 'race' and gender posts were created in the mid-1980s. In contrast the disability post was created only in 1992. The origin of each post seems also to have been rather different: the gender post was originally created within the pre-vocational preparation department, while the 'race' post had a college-wide brief from the outset. The late appearance of disability as an issue can be explained by the fact that much of the support for students with disabilities was carried out by the special needs department. Thus the remit of the disability post holder is seen principally as related to student rather than staff needs. The 'race' and gender post holders have also interpreted their remits somewhat differently from each

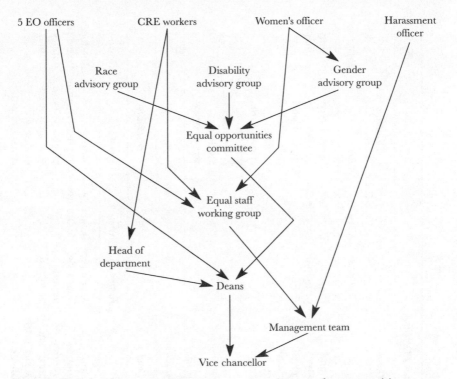

Figure 3 Relationships among structures supporting equal opportunities at Town University

other: the 'race' post holder addresses issues involving not only students and staff but also the community served by the college, while the gender coordinator concentrates principally on issues affecting staff and students.

The positioning of the coordinators within the college structure was, until recently, parallel: each coordinator was located in the staff development unit and reported to the deputy principal. Thus Borough College avoided the implication that any one equal opportunities area was more important than another. However, the most recent restructuring exercise, which began in 1993, contained proposals which moved the 'race' and gender coordinators to the quality and equality division and reduced the amount of time they were able to devote to equal opportunities work. The disability coordinator, on the other hand, was relocated in client services, still full-time but focusing principally on student needs. Simultaneously, it was proposed that the 'race' and gender coordinators would no longer sit on the academic board.

The second tier of support structures at Borough College was also parallel for all three areas. There were three committees, for 'race', gender and disability, each involving the deputy principal, the three coordinators and representatives from the faculties and from various staff groups. As can be

Table 8.3 Structures supporting equal opportunities at Borough College

Designated EO posts

	Race			Gender			Disability	
Name	Remit	Report to	Name	Remit	Report to	Name	Remit	Report to
Race coordinator	Staff, relations with community, curriculum, appointments, training	Deputy principal	Gender coordinator	Staff and student concerns in relation to gender issues	Deputy principal	Disability coordinator	Special Needs courses; student and staff disability, facilities, curriculum, student recruitment. Students are priority	Deputy principal

Committees

	Race			Gender			Disability	
Name	Remit	Report to	Name	Remit	Report to	Name	Remit	Report to
Race committee	Review/update college race equality policy and promote its implementation; propose and	Academic board via deputy principal	Gender committee	Develop/ monitor EO gender provision and anti-sexist work in college;	Academic board via deputy principal	Disability committee	Monitor implementation of policy; raise staff awareness of disability issues affecting	Academic board via deputy principal

Name	Remit	Report to
	monitor race equality targets; support race coordinator; make recommendations to academic board; act as channel of communication across college	
	develop anti-heterosexism policy; support implementation of anti-sexist and anti-heterosexist policies; support gender coordinator	
	both staff and students; increase number of staff with disabilities; promote increased accessibility, welcoming environment, greater sensitivity to people's needs	
ABACAS	Voluntary support and pressure group (set up as principal's working group) for all Black staff	Deputy principal

Overarching structures

Name	Remit	Report to
Staff Development and Equality Unit (until December 1993)	Facilitate coherent approach to equality within staff recruitment and development activities	Deputy principal
Academic board	?	Principal?
Deputy principal	?	Principal?

seen from Table 8.3, the role of these committees was primarily to monitor and assist the implementation of equal opportunities, and to support and advise the coordinators. There seemed to be little conflict between the committees and the senior management of the college, though decisions taken by the committees would subsequently be discussed at faculty level and ratified by the academic board. Moreover, although the possibility of merging the three committees into one had been discussed, it had been decided that three committees were likely to have a more forceful impact on the college as a whole. Members of the committees were, however, in a position to coordinate initiatives. Another common link was that each committee reported to the deputy principal, as did the post holders themselves.

A key difference in this tier, between 'race' on the one hand and gender and disability on the other, has arisen from the presence of ABACAS (Association of Black, African, Caribbean and Asian Staff), which has provided support for staff members and acted as a pressure group in the college. There has been no comparable group for female staff or for staff with disabilities. The existence of ABACAS provided an additional voice for Black staff and staff from minority ethnic backgrounds in the college; furthermore, its meetings are timetabled, and thus included in workload planning. Significantly, representatives of the group also sit on the academic board and participate in all job interviews. Undoubtedly, therefore, ABACAS has been influential in bringing about a number of changes in the way the college has been run, and its existence has been one of the factors which has secured prominence for 'race' issues at the college.

Understanding of the function of the third tier of structures supporting equal opportunities has been complicated by the fact that the staff development and equality unit, one of the key elements of this tier, was disbanded towards the end of the project. Until its disappearance, this unit was responsible for coordinating equality initiatives specifically relating to staffing issues (notably recruitment, appointments, training and promotion). For the gender and 'race' coordinators, staffing issues were always a particular focus of their work and consequently the role of the unit, in which the three coordinators were located, was of considerable significance. The remaining policy coordinating structures at the college (the deputy principal and the academic board) clearly had other responsibilities not directly connected to equality issues, and it was less easy to determine their effectiveness in coordinating initiatives, particularly in a time of transition. However, as has already been noted, a substantial amount of the deputy principal's time was allocated to equality issues, and this feature of the support structure had been one of the particular strengths of Borough College.

The cohesion of the structures supporting equal opportunities in the college is shown in Figure 4. Evidence of the effectiveness of the equal opportunities structures at Borough College can be seen in the way in which a major racist incident (described in Chapter 2) was handled. The

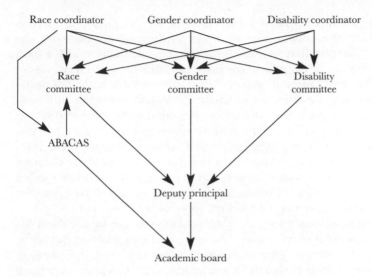

Figure 4 Interrelationships among structures supporting equal opportunities at Borough College

college responded to the incident according to the strategy previously determined by the 'race' coordinator, the deputy principal, the principal and officers of the borough council, designed to be responsive to local situations and potential conflict.

The experience of the case study institutions reveals the importance of effective structures to support policy implementation, monitoring and evaluation. Where individuals and groups with designated responsibilities are missing, it is likely that policy development and evaluation will be haphazard.

Fragility or embeddedness of support structures

Undertaken at a time of considerable upheaval and change in the further and higher education sectors, our study suggests that seemingly solid structures can, in fact, be easily uprooted, as new priorities emerge and crowd out longer-established concerns. All three case study institutions underwent structural changes in the course of the research period, some of which were in response to changing priorities in the wider institutional scene, others relating to external pressures, such as the introduction of new funding systems. However, the fragility of structures was most clearly demonstrated at Borough College, where it was suddenly proposed effectively to downgrade the status of the gender and 'race' coordinators, who were to have less time to devote to their respective areas of responsibility and who would no longer sit on the academic board.

These changes were explained by reference to the changing circumstances in which the college was working. The rapid extension of the college's overall responsibilities (which included amalgamation with a sixth form centre and an adult education institute, and incorporation under the new FE Funding Council) meant that the institution had undergone radical restructuring designed to enhance flexibility, efficiency and cost-effectiveness. Of necessity, the coordinators needed to be relocated within the new college structure, when the staff development unit ceased to exist. Relocation was not, however, straightforward; as we have seen, the gender and 'race' coordinators were moved to the quality and equality division, while the disability coordinator went to client services. These moves failed to retain the evenly balanced relationships among the three coordinators which the previous structure had begun to achieve.

Moreover, these changes suggested an implicit change in priorities for the college following incorporation. The increased emphasis on quality in many further and higher education institutions reflected the growing influence of the market economy in education, with the perceived need both to provide value for money and to become more flexible in response to the changing demands of employers. Thus the change in emphasis from staff development to quality represented a move away from a focus on the needs and abilities of individual staff members to prioritizing those aspects of the college's provision most relevant to the competitive market place. The effect of this change of emphasis on the equality post holders was not at all clear.

The removal of the 'race' and gender coordinators from the academic board was explained by the fact that, following the amalgamations, space on the board needed to be made for representatives of the sixth form centre and the adult education institute. However, we were unable to discover why the 'race' and gender coordinators, rather than other members of the academic board, were specifically targeted for removal. Another option might have been to increase the number of representatives on the academic board to reflect the wider range of educational provision of the college. Indeed, it was difficult to find out from where the decision to remove the coordinators from the academic board had come!

These developments were all the more unexpected as Borough College was clearly a college in which equality issues had enjoyed, for many years, a high priority. The rationale given by the college management was that the remit of the coordinators, though valuable in the past in terms of raising awareness of issues and of developing appropriate strategies, had begun to hamper further progress. It was now more necessary to embed responsibility throughout the institution, and therefore, in the course of restructuring, the job descriptions of the heads of faculty were rewritten to include specific responsibility for promoting equal opportunities. Additional support roles were also proposed in the restructuring; for example, issues relating to equality in recruitment and appointments were to be dealt with by a senior personnel officer, and monitoring of progress in relation to equal opportunities within each faculty would be the responsibility of designated heads of school. However, as these proposals had not been finalized by the time the project finished, it was not possible for us to establish whether such changes would work as planned.

A separate issue was raised through the project questionnaire survey of Borough College staff. It was implied that the coordinators were ineffective, both because they were seen as marginal to the college hierarchy and because particular coordinators had been in post too long (for 'race' from 1987, for gender from 1985). Though the disability coordinator had a long history of work with students with special educational needs, his was a more recent appointment. Perhaps, then, one of the reasons for downgrading the coordinators' role was a perception that they were ineffective.

These points raise the issue of the position of such coordinators generally, and of career structures for those working in this field. At both Town University and Borough College, there was a degree of marginalization of those occupying equal opportunities posts, who were not part of the management team, nor fitted easily within other categories of cross-institutional work. It seems likely that such marginalization is inevitable where such work requires a critical stance that questions the extent of discrimination and inequality. One of the women's officers at Town University recognized the problematic nature of their role within the institution:

> I feel that management sees us as part of the institutional framework – that our existence is evidence that women's issues are taken seriously. Moreover, the fact that the institution has women's officers should raise the external profile of the university in a positive way. However, we are not expected to challenge policy at all: our role is to smooth the path of management and not to rock the boat. Even if they are aware that there are policies which cause anxiety, management does not want to know about them. We can instigate change, but only if it follows the management line.
> (Women's officer, Town University)

How long is it feasible to expect individual post holders to remain in this contradictory role? Why should ambitious staff be attracted to such work if they are seen both as marginal to the core work of the institution, and without any clear career development route? None of our case study institutions addressed these questions. We suggest that the failure to consider the long-term position of such post holders is one factor contributing to the fragility of potentially well-established support structures.

Management styles: managerialism and 'democracy'

The commitment of the senior management to supporting and promoting equal opportunities emerged as one of the key factors in each of the case studies, both in initiating equal opportunities policies and in main-taining the momentum of any initiatives. Yet in each institution, the role adopted by management was quite distinct, and, in certain ways, the prin-ciples by which each management body implemented equal opportunities contrasted to the principles in the other institutions.

Metropolitan University described its management style as 'democratic'. Principally, this referred to the relatively devolved decision-making processes adopted by the university; for example, there was greater scope for those at departmental level to become involved in decision-making. Thus, the university could be said to be 'democratic' in that decisions about policy and administration were spread among a large number of people.

One of the effects of the 'democratic' decision-making process was that change tended to be slow, as a large number of committees needed to be consulted before any new policy was agreed. Hence the process of adopting the equal opportunities policy took several years; and the same was true of the decision to provide crèche facilities for staff. In parallel, the committee system aimed for consensus: a large number of amendments to any proposition would require a return to the start of the committee process again, and consequently further delays. Indeed, the length of time it took for the equal opportunities policy to pass through was, in part, the consequence of the amendments to the original draft policy following the publication of the CVCP report on harassment. The additional section on harassment, as well as minor amendments from the first round of committee discussion, needed to be approved by the original spread of committees, which required a further nine months before the policy could be adopted.

The 'democratic' devolution of the management process from senior management to a wide-ranging sweep of committees had a number of implications. First, though the slow pace seemed inevitable as a conse-quence of the way the system operated, it was suggested to us that other, higher, priorities moved much more quickly through the system; for ex-ample, that on quality assurance. There were other disadvantages and advantages to this cautious approach to decision-making. A weakness was that those actively involved in promoting an issue sometimes found it deeply frustrating that it took so long for decisions to be made, and that delays occurred between making decisions and implementation. There is a possibility of momentum being lost and cynicism setting in; and, in the context of the equal opportunities policy, it was argued that while the university debated the policy and appropriate implementation measures, there was a risk of losing female staff and members of staff from minority groups who were dissatisfied with their working conditions or with the ethos of the institution. An advantage of the approach, however, is that controversy was kept to a minimum and rash decisions were unlikely. In an institution the size of Metropolitan University, where awareness of equal opportunities issues was low, there seems to be a greater chance of the policy being successfully implemented which seeks both to avoid alienating particular groups and to obtain general agreement to the policy. What is gained and what is lost by this approach needs to be carefully judged.

Town University had developed yet another decision-making model. As chief executive, the vice chancellor of the university was actively involved at all levels of decision-making and maintained a high level of control over decisions taken. For example, in the case of the equal opportunities committee at Town University, it was made clear that the committee was *advisory*: the committee could make recommendations to the vice chancellor, but could not take any decisions. The vice chancellor took a very close interest in the issues raised in the committee and the ensuing discussion. He was also the chair of the committee, and he and the three deans who, also by virtue of their position, chaired the gender, 'race' and disability advisory groups were the most active participants in the committee's discussions.

As a consequence, the powerful position of the vice chancellor in the decision-making process at Town University had somewhat paradoxical effects on the development and implementation of equality initiatives. On the one hand, the hamstringing of the equal opportunities committee was felt by participants to be particularly frustrating: 'We were moving to a vote, but it was clear that the chair wanted it retained. He stated, "This committee is advisory to me. Therefore I will make the decisions," and no vote was taken. We thought – why bother with discussions?' (EOC member). It was also felt that the role the vice chancellor had adopted was antithetical to the principles of equal opportunities, according to which the voices of all members of staff, regardless of their position in the institution, should be given equal weight. The vice chancellor, however, countered this more idealized version of equal opportunities by pointing out that legally it was he who was responsible for decisions taken in the university, and that consequently it was essential that he should have the last word. 'We would seek views generally through the EOC, but at the end of the day a decision about the organization and the management of the institution under our articles of government has to be mine' (Vice chancellor of Town University).

Significantly, the fact that the vice chancellor was personally highly committed to equality issues meant that decisions could be taken quickly, when necessary; and, in general, it would appear that initiatives proceeded more quickly and were more thoroughly rooted in the institution because of the vice chancellor's wide-ranging involvement in decision-making processes. For example, despite the fact that the vice chancellor's close involvement in the development of sexual harassment policy and procedures attracted considerable criticism from staff with different views on the form these should take, it is doubtful whether the university would have made such rapid progress without his high level of support and commitment.

Borough College had a management strategy which might be seen as a modified version of the managerialist approach of Town University. It was recognized that a high level of commitment to equal opportunities from senior members of staff was necessary to ensure that the policy continued to be effective and that new initiatives developed throughout the institution. Without this, it was unlikely that anyone would have a sufficiently broad overview of college developments generally or the degree of 'clout' necessary to ensure that initiatives and developments in this field received an appropriate share of resourcing: 'An important criterion (in college support for equal opportunities) is access to resources and access to a power base' (Member of the college project advisory group). In Borough College this supportive role was largely associated with the deputy principal, who clearly had considerable personal commitment to equality issues and devoted much of her time to supporting work relating to this area.

As with the vice chancellor at Town University, this meant that initiatives were expedited which might otherwise have taken much longer. However, events at Borough College also showed how identification of overall responsibility for equal opportunities with one person might render the area more vulnerable if resources are scarce. For example, during the project, the deputy principal was also responsible for implementing the two mergers (with the sixth form college and the adult education institute) and the consequent changes in job descriptions, as well as the college restructuring. All these tasks raised difficult issues in relation to equal opportunities. There seemed also to be tensions for senior management in maintaining a smooth-running institution and finding time to devote to equal opportunities. It was clear that at Borough College the staff believed that the future progress of equality initiatives in the college was secure in the hands of the principal and the deputy principal for the time being; but that there was no guarantee that eventual successors would continue as before.

In adopting a modified version of the 'managerial' approach, Borough College benefited from the fact that the deputy principal's style of management was not generally interpreted as confrontational. She was therefore able to take responsibility for decision-making on issues relating to equal opportunities without incurring widespread antagonism from staff who might feel excluded from the decision-making process. Some elements of policy-making and of the dissemination and implementation of policy were also devolved to various committees and working parties. The size of the institution (considerably smaller than Town and Metropolitan Universities) is also likely to have been a factor in ensuring that most members of staff felt themselves to be relatively well informed and to have had the opportunity to participate in the various initiatives under way. Even so, there was some criticism within the college that only a small group of staff members was actively involved in the discussion and formulation of policy, and also that the committees had no direct access to the academic board.

Nevertheless, it was clear that the work of the committees had a genuine impact on the way in which the college worked and that this was owing as much to the commitment of committee members (in debating issues, coming to conclusions and making recommendations) as it was to the deputy principal's willingness to act on recommendations and ensure that they were put into place.

Power relationships

Several of the themes which we have identified as recurring across the three case study institutions ultimately raise questions about the nature of institutional power relationships, questions which reveal a central paradox in the understanding of how policies promoting equal opportunities are supported and implemented. As we have stated, the support of an institution's senior management seemed crucial to the success of equality initiatives. Yet, in accepting that the power to bring about effective change lay with the most senior staff, we were nevertheless aware of a contradiction between institutional reality and what might be seen as a more idealistic view: that equality of opportunity should mean a greater levelling of distinctions, active participation of staff in the decision-making process and the recognition that those who are disadvantaged for historical and social reasons are best placed to understand what constitutes inequality and how it can be countered.

In each institution, we were aware of tensions between activists and senior managers, which ultimately related to who had the power to bring about change. At Metropolitan University, activists (such as the childcare group) found that without a 'champion' at senior management level it was difficult even to raise the issue of childcare provision for staff, let alone to secure agreement that such provision would be made. The power to ensure the development of equal opportunities policy and effective monitoring of implementation lay entirely with the university's senior management. Thus it is probable that the absence of a nominated person or group with responsibility for policy monitoring and implementation was one reason for the slow pace of change at Metropolitan University. A Catch 22 situation ensued in that, because of its 'democratic' management style, no senior manager could be allocated sufficient time to shape an equal opportunities policy – until the policy was approved. However, it seemed likely that the eventual appointment of an equal opportunities officer at Metropolitan University, plus the incorporation into the university of a more female-oriented education faculty, would speed up the development of future equal opportunities policies.

How, then, can an institution ensure that there are formal support structures which aid the implementation of equal opportunities policies and monitor progress, and which, more crucially perhaps, can counterbalance the power of senior management. Grass roots movements alone are unlikely to be able to achieve this without the support of senior management. At Metropolitan University, the appointment of the equal opportunities officer took a year of vigorous lobbying, and was achieved as a result of pressure not (directly) from lobby groups but from the personnel department and ultimately the director of personnel, himself a senior manager. At both Town University and Borough College, the initial decision to establish such bodies posts, committees and so on was also taken at a high level – by the previous vice chancellor in the case of Town University, and by the education authority in the case of Borough College. Clearly, activists can raise issues and bring pressure to bear on senior management, but they cannot bring about structural changes independently of management. At both Town University and Borough College, neither post holders nor committees had a free hand to bring about changes; and just as senior management support is needed to create structures, they can as easily be dismantled when other issues appear to be more pressing.

Nevertheless, activists and grass roots campaigns have had a major part to play in raising awareness of issues and ensuring that the importance of resolving certain inequalities is recognized by senior managers. This has been the case with issue-specific campaigns, such as the childcare group at Metropolitan University, and with more general awareness raising exercises, such as the reports on the position of women staff at Metropolitan University and Town University, and on Black female perspectives at Borough College. Moreover, there can be a 'snowball' effect leading to greater awareness and interest in equality issues by staff more generally. Conversely, for staff who are not themselves actively involved in campaigning for particular changes or developments but who have certain equal opportunities expectations, failure on the part of senior management to be seen to be promoting equal opportunities can lead to considerable frustration. Often this relates to the fact that receivers of policy are unaware of the institutional mechanisms at work and/or lack the relevant information to make sense of decisions. Whether justified or not, dissatisfaction at this level can breed cynicism and have a destabilizing effect on what has so far been achieved.

Activists thus seem to have a dual function: on the one hand, they can raise awareness generally about equality issues and ensure that more members of staff participate actively in debates relating to inequalities and the solutions proposed; on the other, they can lobby decision-makers, emphasizing that any institutional goals (say, those involving currently populist terminology such as 'quality' and 'standards') cannot properly be achieved without genuine commitment to equality of opportunity for both staff and students.

9

Munro Bagging: Towards Better Practices

In the introduction to this book, we noted that there was a growing interest in equal opportunities in further and higher education and a nascent literature documenting institutional policies and practices, yet little evidence as yet of the effectiveness of these endeavours. 'Where are the success stories?', we asked. The findings from this project indicate various levels of activity and sophistication. This chapter summarizes the project findings and then considers difficulties and contradictions in establishing the case for success despite the existence of some evidently good and innovative practice. We end on a hopeful note – with a discussion of possibilities for the future.

Main research findings

The findings of the project largely echo the themes from the literature as outlined in Chapter 1. The specific aim of the research project on which this book is based was to show through the detailed reporting of three case studies the distinct nature of adherence or resistance to equal opportunities policy-making for staff and how each policy is shaped by institutional history, specific individual context and policy structure. The findings are grouped into four sections: emergent patterns, policy implementation, monitoring and development, and research issues.

Emergent patterns

A wide variety of equal opportunity policies have been successfully developed concerning staff. These include what might be regarded as 'core' equal opportunities policies, i.e. on recruitment and conditions of service (appointments and promotions procedures) and on language usage, which are the most widely implemented of the staff policies. In Borough College and Town

University, however, there were far wider ranges of equal opportunity policies and structures. For instance, at Town University these included:

- mission statement;
- equal opportunities policy;
- policies for language and academic affairs;
- employment policies;
- sex harassment/harassment policy and procedures;
- Women's Unit and women's officers;
- Centre for Women in Technology, Design and Manufacture;
- Centre for Racial Equality;
- Centre for Professional Ethics;
- charter for management;
- equal opportunities committee structure;
- committed senior management team;
- in-house expertise for staff training.

Each institution has set its own priorities, selecting different aspects of equal opportunities as most important. In Borough College, 'race' and ethnicity predominated at the time of the case study, though other forms of inequality were taken into account, while at both universities gender issues were foregrounded. For example, in Borough College the anti-racist targets for the academic year 1993–4 related to: extension of ethnic minority monitoring; review of community liaison strategy with particular reference to racial equality and Black/minority ethnic groups; continued development of strategy of racial equality at the site where there had been racist incidents; and recommendations for a network to promote racial equality initiatives in different areas of the college linked to the community. There were similar targets for anti-sexism and disability. In the two other case study institutions staff policy on 'race' issues tended to be confined to the language and recruitment, though Town University had a longer history of addressing 'race' issues. In all three institutions policies on disability were of relatively lower priority and only Borough College included sexual orientation in its policy framework.

Different institutional histories and cultures have had a substantial impact on equal opportunities policy development. While all three institutions have had a decade or more of equality 'activism' of one kind or another, key policy initiatives at Borough College (by the local authority) and Town University (by the previous and present vice chancellors) have led to more advanced forms of policy-making in the 1990s.

Institutional principles and structures which promote democracy and/or meritocracy can create barriers to the development of equal opportunities policies and practices. Thus, at Metropolitan University, progress towards creating an equal opportunities policy has been relatively slow.

The length of time which it takes for decisions to be made, and the delay between making a decision and implementing it can be deeply

frustrating for those actively promoting a particular issue. There is a
risk of momentum being lost and cynicism setting in, and it is important also to take into account the likelihood, for example, of losing
female staff or staff from minority groups if conditions of work and
the ethos of the institution are felt to be unfavourable, and the likelihood of change seems remote.

(Metropolitan University case study report)

Significantly, other policy initiatives, such as that of quality assurance, have
had speedier institutional trajectories, as one staff member at Metropolitan University implied: 'a comparison between the speed with which the
equal opportunities policy was being implemented . . . and the university's
policy on quality assurance would be instructive.'

The case study institutions showed conventional patterns of staff employment.
There was a preponderance of white males in senior hierarchies, and
these patterns seemed highly resistant to any attempts at change, despite
the obvious contribution that equal opportunities policies had made to
greater equality in the workplace and in creating a more comfortable
work ethos. Although there had been long-standing concern about un-
fairness in staffing patterns at Town University, in 1993 only 3.5 per cent
of total teaching staff came from minority ethnic groups, with campus
services the department with the highest concentration (6 per cent) of
minority ethnic staff. While women represented 47 per cent of the total
staff at the university, over half (51 per cent) the female workers were
employed in 'traditional' female occupations as cleaners, catering staff,
library staff, clerks, typists and administrative assistants. Indeed, categories
of staff such as clerical assistant, clerk, typist, receptionist, administrative
assistant and personal assistant were all *exclusively* female. At the other end
of the spectrum, Town University had 14 female heads or directors out of
a total of 64, and a senior management team comprising seven women
from a total of 21. Despite their still minority status in relation to their
male colleagues, the relatively high profile of women managers at such
senior levels in the university is probably unique in higher education
institutions in the UK.

Borough College, in contrast, had rather more Black and women staff
at senior management levels and on the staff generally, with the senior
management team comprising a male principal, female deputy, five male
and seven female managers (all white) and one Black male manager.

Policy implementation

*The manner in which equal opportunity policy is first introduced emerged as crucially
important to any future success.* 'First time round' policy necessitates carefully
drafting and sensitive negotiation over a period of time. At Metropolitan
University, there was a clear need for circumspection in drafting a policy

in an institution where awareness of equal opportunities and a commitment to the principles were not particularly high. As a consequence, 'the policy document itself . . . became an awareness raising tool' (Metropolitan University case study report). The length of time taken for the preliminary phases of implementation, while disappointing to the institution's 'activists', demonstrated the amount of time which equal opportunities initiatives can take in a large organization with diverse interests where 'the securing of funds for potentially controversial projects requires both patience and tactical skill.'

A coherent policy structure in which different policies are integrated is more likely to lead to successful implementation, thus preventing fragmentation, policy overload and alienation. At Borough College, three distinct policies (on 'race', gender and disability) were negotiated and approved within a single agreed framework of presentation and implementation. However, at Town University, one of the tensions between the policy as it is written and how it then becomes embedded in the practice has been the fragmentation in the development of the various policies addressing equality. For example, there was

> evidence of different equality groups acting independently of each other; for example, with its office situated centrally in the Rectorate, the harassment policy operates from a significantly stronger power base than any other equality initiative.
>
> (Town University case study report)

Particular contradictions have emerged in the role of senior management as policy-makers in the area of equal opportunities. On the one hand, strong policy directives seemed to emphasize the importance of equal opportunities to staff; on the other, the very silencing of dissent that this approach encourages seemed also to militate against the empowerment that lies at the heart of the policy.

The process of equal opportunities policy-making and articulation can be simultaneously 'enabling' and 'disabling'. At Town University, the power and influence of senior management has certainly enabled policy to be transformed into visible changes in practice (as in the case of university harassment procedures). But the responsibility of senior management for the administration of the university overall has also been seen by some staff as disabling staff lower down in the hierarchy from taking action at grass roots level. At Borough College, enabling features seemed to be institutional history, strong staff support for equality and support from the senior management team. Disabling features included lack of systematic staff monitoring and of formal power of equality committees, and a staff profile which continues to reflect conventional patterns of inequality (although it is still more representative than most other colleges or universities).

Acceptance and implementation of equal opportunities policy-making by individuals and groups of staff depended, to a large extent, on their position in the institutional hierarchy and/or their involvement in the policy process. Invariably, the 'receivers' of policy showed less understanding than those higher up in the organization about the details of any particular policy or why it has been thought necessary. Knowledge of policy, support of, resistance to, identification with and criticism of policy were all closely related to each individual's immediate professional and personal contexts.

Thus, within the almost exclusively white staff of Metropolitan University, women staff's perception of the policy and its actual (or potential) impact depended on their immediate circumstances; whether they were, for example, professors or research assistants. Women's differences – in terms of age, status, job security etc. – as much as their shared experiences of sexism, helped to shape their perspectives on the effectiveness of the policy. Male staff, in contrast, showed more hostility to the policy, particularly any attempts at 'positive action' in favour of women, and were more likely to distance themselves from the policy as 'not for them'.

Monitoring and development

The necessity for a coordinated and well-resourced structure of policy development and monitoring emerged as crucially important in checking whether a policy is working, and what improvements might be made. Baseline and continual systematic auditing of staff (and students) were seen as important features of the equal opportunities policies, though the quality of the monitoring varied between project institutions.

Constant vigilance seems to be necessary in order to prevent policy slippage and to maintain interest and commitment among staff and policy-makers more generally, because of an apparent inevitable reversion to the norm of sexist and racist practices. In the case of Borough College, 'the existence of structures at one time is no guarantee for the future; structures . . . can be amended fairly quickly.' Here, on one occasion, equal opportunities post holders were excluded from an important policy committee without warning. The question posed by Borough College case study report was: 'How can staff ensure that their organization does not move backwards?'

The policy process can never be perceived as complete or finished: each new horizon and equality agenda item will inevitably lead to a fresh policy process. As the final paragraph of the Town University case study report testifies,

> Inevitably, 'work[ing] towards equality' will always make demands for further change. We shall let the Rector have the last word. 'Once you have reached a situation you realize you can still do better . . . For when you reach the horizon you thought you wanted . . . you find there is a new horizon.'

There were also findings which helped us reflect on the chosen research methodology and its strengths and weaknesses (see Appendix for greater detail).

Research issues

The chosen research approach, the policy case study, proved to be as rich and flexible as anticipated. It enabled the research team to focus on specific equal opportunity policies within an institutional framework, at the same time enabling access to a multiplicity of perspectives. It also allowed for attention to the complexities of institutional policy-making and the development of patterns of analysis which incorporated themes from organizational, policy, feminist and social justice theory (Weiner, 1994).

Significantly, problems emerged in the research as a consequence of the increasingly marketized and competitive culture of British education in the 1990s. The most serious were as follows.

The project was frequently used by institutions as part of their agenda-setting and public relations objectives. Thus, some senior managers attempted to shape final drafts of the case study report according to their particular institutional interests. The securing of agreement to the final case study report proved difficult to negotiate because of fear that any critical comments might hit the local press and/or affect recruitment and funding.

Some interviewees were so anxious about being labelled as trouble-makers in their institution that they eradicated all perceived contentious statements from the written accounts of their interviews (despite frequent assurances of confidentiality). On several occasions, important sections (e.g. on gay staff) were deleted, and one Black senior manager withdrew her entire interview because she believed she was too easily identifiable.

Difficulties also occurred in evaluating practice associated with equal opportunities when each case study institution was simultaneously going through structural disruption, including incorporation, amalgamations and restructuring, in a period of continual institutional change. This made it problematic to estimate the impact of equal opportunities as a discrete policy area.

Establishing the case for success

Much of the discussion about developing appropriate policies and implementing practices, in this book as elsewhere, may be read as implying that these are desirable ends in themselves. But if, at the end of the day, institutions retain conventional staffing patterns, might their equal opportunities policies and practices be viewed merely as window dressing. Throughout the project, the view was put forward that the case study institutions were interested primarily in projecting positive and progressive images of themselves, rather than in bringing about substantive changes which would genuinely enhance the employment opportunities of staff. There is clearly a risk that much apparent activity could be viewed as a smoke-screen behind which the status quo remains largely unaffected.

While disadvantaged – or disaffected – members of staff may have provided a particularly negative view of their institutions' efforts, those closely involved in the development of policies and practices also found it difficult to point to concrete gains made as a result of their work. One of the principal reasons for this must be the changing political and economic context of further and higher education in recent years, the influence of which has been discussed at some length in earlier chapters. Several factors have required institutions to make extensive changes both to the place of equal opportunities on the institutional agenda and to particular orientations of policy; for example, changes in the funding of further and higher education, with a concomitant emphasis on quality assurance as a key management strategy, as well as the spate of mergers and internal restructuring exercises provoked by these changes. In these circumstances – of constantly shifting goalposts at both national and institutional levels – it is clear that any evaluation of the effects of individual policy initiatives undertaken in this period was likely to be excessively complex. At the same time, gains made as a result of earlier initiatives tended to vanish or become submerged.

The complexities in attempting to interpret recruitment and promotion statistics from our case study institutions provide a specific example of the difficulties of assessing the impact of policy and practice in a period of rapid change. Mergers with other institutions, for example, could fundamentally alter the proportions of female or Black staff without this being in any way attributable to equal opportunities initiatives. Contracting out of certain groups of staff similarly made it difficult to track developments over time. Internal factors, such as moves to streamline management and personnel structures which resulted in changed job designations and grading systems, also complicated the construction of a historical equal opportunities narrative. Even an increased awareness of equality issues could, paradoxically, interfere with evaluation of successes to date; for example, a more sophisticated gender and 'race' monitoring system might disrupt previous patterns of statistical data collection and make interpretation of change even more complex. As a result, it proved impossible to show definitive improvement in any of the case study institutions in, for example, the proportions of women to men or ethnic staff ratios (though all three institutions indicated favourable trends).

In the long term, institutions will need to be able to provide evidence of such changes in order to justify the amount of work devoted to promoting equality issues. This will involve having clear overall plans for how equality of opportunity is to be achieved, and a specific timetable noting dates by which shorter-term goals are to be met. Such planning would provide the basis for monitoring progress and evaluating achievements. As none of the case study institutions had such plans, we can only speculate on the possibility that vulnerable initiatives might have proved more difficult to downgrade or abandon had the policies been tied to specific predetermined targets.

In the context of wide-ranging change within and around the institutions, and in the consequent absence of clear-cut evidence from monitoring or evaluation of progress, identifying success stories has been particularly difficult. Nevertheless, in each institution we were able to point to certain concrete gains over the research period, which might be said to constitute *de facto* goals in a longer-term programme (albeit an unarticulated one). At Metropolitan University, the decision to appoint an equal opportunities officer indicated that the university's newly adopted policy was aimed at raising awareness of the need to coordinate equal opportunities initiatives and to develop systematic structures and practices. Similarly, the achievement of a commitment to childcare provision for university staff demonstrated that locating the responsibility for equal opportunities at a senior level was an effective way of ensuring that what had hitherto been considered marginal concerns could be addressed. The resilience of Borough College's equal opportunities policies was demonstrated in how a series of racist incidents affecting both students and staff was dealt with. Both Borough College and Town University had harassment policies and procedures that were operating smoothly without incurring the flood of trivial complaints which might have been feared. There were also well tried and tested appointments and promotions procedures deliberately designed to promote equality of opportunity for staff at Borough College (and at Town University) – which had produced higher proportions of Black and female staff than previously.

Factors enhancing equal opportunities for staff

What are the factors in institutional practice which are likely to lead to success in enhancing equality of opportunities for staff? As we have seen, our research reaffirms the necessity for clear and public formulations of long-term aims, plans for their achievement, the setting of shorter-term goals and the specification of the timescale by which each is to be met. A wider ownership of policy and careful consultation and discussion prior to implementation are also critical. The following factors, therefore, appear to have been particularly influential in developing and promoting good practice:

- established location of responsibility and accountability for the achievement of equal opportunities;
- structures which facilitate initiatives;
- staff participation in developments;
- appropriate funding and resources;
- user-friendly procedures;
- monitoring and evaluation which are not too labour-intensive yet lead to action;
- pervasive equal opportunities ethos.

Each of these factors is now discussed in more detail:

Responsibility and accountability

Equal opportunities needs to be a key to institutional policy-making and part of the long-term view of what is to be achieved. At all levels of education, organizations produce mission statements and development plans; and institutions committed to greater equality of opportunity will also need to ensure that there are specific and appropriate targets for the institution as a whole as well as for individual faculties and departments. Only if these are formally agreed as part of an institution's legitimate business will strategies and targets be effectively implemented and monitored.

Additionally, it may be appropriate to pursue a whole-institutional responsibility for the achievement of fair practice, though there is always then the danger that little is being done at individual level. In the longer term, effective equal opportunities policies and their concomitant practices require the dedication of at least one member of senior management; someone who has the 'clout' and the resources to lead developments and to ensure implementation of agreed policy.

Facilitating structures

It is difficult to put policy aims into practice if the necessary organizational structures are absent or inconsistent. The most obvious example might be an advertisement claiming that an institution is an equal opportunities employer when there is no agreed method for establishing or measuring levels of equality; for example, in employment matters such as appointments and promotions procedures. In our view, policies and intentions are of little avail without structures to provide support for their development, implementation and review. For equal opportunities to be effective, committees, posts of responsibility and methods of reporting and accountability should be comparable with other areas of institutional activity. The research found that most progress was made where there were clearly designated posts of responsibility, associated committees and a requirement to report to the executive or to an academic board. What is crucial is that the mechanisms for dealing with equal opportunities policies form a coherent strategy which is consistent with other aspects of institutional policy.

Staff participation

In each of the case study institutions, the initial motivation for specific policy initiatives came from a few highly committed individuals. 'Activists', as well as 'champions' (senior staff whose commitment can facilitate institutional adoption of initiatives) have a key role in raising awareness of inequalities and in suggesting ways of combating them. However, institutions also need to seek the involvement of other staff in the development of policy and practice, in order to combat apathy or hostility. At the same time, it is important to set realistic limits to such participation: never-ending consultations can mean that policy documents remain forever in draft form and that initiatives are continually debated but never acted upon. Such practices ultimately result in an abdication of responsibility to bring about change, though in our view it is enormously difficult for institutions to achieve a proper balance – though they must, of course, endeavour to do so.

Appropriate funding and resources

The suggestions made in the preceding paragraphs have financial implications. For example, time allocation for senior staff and equal opportunity post holders represents an institutional commitment. Developments are likely to be exceedingly slow when individual initiatives are confined to what can be done in the margins of work time. Induction and staff development also need to be planned for, as successful policy-making inevitably increases staff expectation of support. Other less expensive but nevertheless important investments in resources include well-publicized policy documents and guidelines on, for instance, what to do when confronted with discriminatory behaviour. Being an equal opportunities employer certainly doesn't come cheap!

User-friendly procedures

Policies will be doomed to failure if procedures for their implementation are unavailable or inaccessible. Ideally, copies of key documents should be made easily available in libraries, staff handbooks, departments and faculties. Accessibility also covers language and style of presentation. We found excellent examples of easily obtainable and readable documents in which procedures were clearly signposted and written in such a way that any complaints or grievances that were taken up were likely to be dealt with speedily and with due process.

Monitoring and evaluation

Data collection proved enormously important in evaluating the impact of policies. There is thus a need to collate evidence on existing inequalities and on where gains have been made. Development plans can offer a framework as well as an incentive, and figures kept over several years can provide a series of snapshots of, for example, the number of women in senior positions, the distribution of part-time staff in different faculties or the ethnic composition of staff overall. The most effective form of data enables a fairly sophisticated analysis of employment patterns, providing sufficient information for institutions to review policies and practices and take appropriate remedial action.

Pervasive equal opportunities ethos

One of the most effective, yet least tangible, factors is the degree to which equality concerns permeate the institution. An equal opportunities ethos is likely to be present where staff are aware both of their rights and their responsibilities, where initiatives are widely debated and where the equal opportunities 'angle' is always considered, even in apparently unrelated policy areas. Such an ethos is characterized by an openness to debate and to criticism – even negative criticism – and awareness that good equal opportunities practice requires a recognition that previous or existing practices have been unsatisfactory and need to be changed. The road to genuine equality, if it is ever attainable, is likely to be difficult and controversial; it is therefore important to recognize that, inevitably, mistakes will be made and decisions challenged.

Some institutions may find this easier to acknowledge than others. For example, smaller organizations such as further education colleges, rather than larger ones such as universities, are in a better position to develop effective equal opportunities policies and practices (Powney and Weiner, 1992). Though there are likely to be various reasons for this, one important difference between further and higher education lies in the 'pool' from which students are selected. Universities tend to compete at national level for 'high calibre' students (however calibre is defined); further education colleges have conventionally catered for a wide range of aptitudes and abilities among local students. Ever increasing and ever more intense competition among universities makes it difficult for such institutions to countenance publicly the notion that certain features may be in need of reform, or that certain initiatives need to be rethought. This was reflected in the research by concerns expressed about how the case studies were to be written up and/or how anonymity could be preserved. Further education colleges, at least for the moment, seem less compelled to maintain such a high profile and cleaner-than-clean public image, and therefore appear more willing to assess policy successes and failures.

Conclusions

Genuine equality of opportunity for staff (and students) often appears to be a combination of a chimera and the holy grail: *unimaginable* because there are so many different views of what it might consist of, and *unattainable* because of widely differing opinions about how it might be achieved. As the vice chancellor of Town University said, 'When you reach the horizon you thought you wanted . . . you find there is a new horizon.'

The Scottish-based members of the research team preferred the local, and more positive, image of 'Munro bagging': the long-term pursuit of climbing all 277 Scottish mountains of 3000 feet and above. A lifetime's ambition for most (though the record is 66 days), it certainly represents a challenging task, seeming almost insuperable at the outset and frequently daunting, if only because after each successful ascent the 'bagger' has to contemplate (literally or in the imagination) the foot of the next mountain to be attempted. (The Munro, traditionally left till last on the list, is termed the 'Inaccessible Pinnacle'.) At the same time, however, the bagger experiences the exhilaration of the climb and the view from the peak (or, in our case, the contemplation of a policy successfully launched), and the satisfaction of progress towards the ultimate goal.

Institutions pursuing the long-term aim of achieving equality of opportunity for staff (and for students), as we have stressed, must always be aware of how much more remains to be done. At the same time, it is important for those involved in this often daunting task to recognize the value of what has already been accomplished. For us as researchers, it is also appropriate to conclude by acknowledging the extent of the commitment of those actively engaged in promoting equal opportunities in the case study institutions and their many achievements to date.

Appendix: Research Methodology

This appendix reports on the research and methodological aspects of the project – which might or might not be of much interest to policy-makers or lay readers, but will be of some interest to other educational researchers and academics. It is divided into a number of sections: project introduction and description, policy case study method, project organization, research process, gaining access, the politics of researching organizations, presenting findings and the ethics in reporting research.

Introduction to the project

The project, the full title of which was 'Case Studies in the Development of Equitable Staff Policies in Further and Higher Education', was funded by the Economic and Social Research Council (ESRC) to run from 1991 to 1994. Although funding was relatively modest (approximately £40 000 in all) it provided the opportunity to explore, in some detail, three institutions which had developed a reputation as pioneers in the area of equal opportunities. The aims of the project were four-fold:

1. To develop understanding of staffing policies and practices in further and higher education which enhance the recruitment, promotion and work conditions of under-represented groups (in particular female and Black and minority ethnic staff).
2. To encourage wider implementation and evaluation of such policies and practices.
3. To develop understanding of processes of change by drawing together theoretical and empirical work in the fields of equal opportunities, policy studies and the study of organizations.
4. To contribute to an understanding and utilization of evaluative policy case study methodologies.

The project had the determinedly *social justice* brief of promoting greater equity for staff in colleges and universities. It involved detailed and longitudinal (two-year) case studies of three educational institutions, one each from the further education (Borough College), new university (Town University) and traditional university (Metropolitan University) sectors – the aim being to see what happens to equal opportunities staff policies *after* they have been created.

The policy case study

The project's chosen methodology was that of the policy case study because of its institutional and policy focus, its multi-method and interactive character and its potential for description and illumination.

Stake (1994) puts forward the proposition that *case study* is not really a methodology, rather it is a choice of object to be studied: 'We choose to study the case. We could study it in many ways' (Stake, 1994: 236). Our object of study was equal opportunities policy-making in three settings and, because the focus was on policy – in conceptualization, implementation and evaluation – we drew on the following characteristics of the *policy case study*:

- focus on a specific policy or policies within an institutional framework;
- documentation of the process of decision-making and its embeddedness in policy;
- focus upon individuals and/or groups, their perceptions and accounts and happenings;
- careful contextualization and offering of a multiplicity of perspectives;
- evaluation of past and present policy, as a resource for future policy-making;
- rich and vivid description(s) of events within the case, invoking a 'reasonable measure of normality or realism';
- particular mode of presentation that captures the parameters of the case, such as chronological narrative or description of events within and leading up to that case.
- integral involvement of the researcher of the case;
- internal debate between the description of events and the analysis of events. (Adapted from Bridges, 1989: 142–4; Hitchcock and Hughes, 1989: 214.)

While we aimed to investigate the institutional structures supporting equal opportunities, we also viewed equal opportunities policy as a specific discourse. On the one hand, it is linked to dominant institutional values in the location of problems and the identification of remedies; on the other, it produces sets of practices involving compliance and resistance. As Bowe *et al.* (1992: 13) point out, policies need to be seen 'as a set of claims about how the world should and might be, a matter of "authoritative allocation of values"'. If the policy being advocated aims to transfer power to hitherto disenfranchised groups or disrupt existing sets of power relations, as is the overt aim of most equal opportunities policies, then the micropolitics of such policies are likely to be particularly complex.

The policy case study format provided the research team with a framework which legitimated our study of just three, though they are relatively large, educational institutions, enabling us to track through the history of equal opportunities policy-making in each of the institutions in order to understand the priorities and practices of current policies. In choosing institutions with a high profile in the area of equal opportunities, we were searching for examples of good or effective practice, though we were conscious of the fact that 'good practice' can rarely be transported intact from one context to another.

The policy case study also allowed for the multiplicity of perspectives of policy that was bound to occur in such large organizations, which was particularly crucial if, like Bowe *et al.*, we were going to identify any subterranean resistances to the policies.

> In part this [the study of policy] involves the identification of resistance, accommodation, subterfuge and conformity within and between arenas of practice and the plotting of clashes and mismatches between contending discourses at work in these arenas e.g. professionalism vs conformity, autonomy vs constraint, specification vs latitude, the managerial vs the educational.
>
> (Bowe *et al.*, 1992: 13)

We were able to concentrate specifically on equal opportunities policy-making, though, inevitably, we were made aware of numerous other aspects of organizational policy and practice as they impinged on and interacted with those with which we were immediately concerned. As Stake points out, we had to make strategic decisions within the boundary limits of our resources:

> The case study researcher faces a strategic choice in deciding how much and how long the complexities of a case should be studied. Not everything about the case can be understood – how much needs to be? Each researcher will make up his or her mind.
>
> (Stake, 1994: 238)

Within the project team we constantly revisited and re-examined the events of each institution as we saw them, continually trying to identify how they might contribute to a more generally focused analysis of equal opportunities policy and practice. The narrative format, which we used both for the case study report to each institution and for this book, helped us to render to the institutions involved an account of our research activities in an accessible form, and simultaneously to 'stitch together' and 'pull apart' the various institutional policies in order to understand them more thoroughly. Thus, through the policy case study, we were able to portray the complexity of the equal opportunities policy process – what Powney (1992: 5) referred to as 'the inevitable messiness of institutional policies' – in, we hoped, a coherent and accessible fashion.

The original plan of the research team had been to spend five days per term over two years in each institution. However, for various administrative reasons, the actual fieldwork period was truncated to 18 months, and the number of days of fieldwork redistributed throughout the shorter period. Overall, a minimum of 30 days of fieldwork was undertaken for each case study (though additional time was spent outside the institutions on, for example, document analysis) with each utilizing a similar research approach but with variations according to the specific policy context of each institution. The intention was to understand the different policy contexts and applications of equal opportunities policies rather than to make comparisons between institutions with very different histories, cultures and practices.

We decided on a variety of methods for collecting evidence, including: *interviews*, with policy-makers and academic and support staff, in groups or with individuals; *observation*, of formal meetings, staff development training, induction etc.; *document analysis*, of the range of institutional policy documentation; *questionnaire surveys*, to samples of staff; *work shadowing*, of senior management. We also received written comments in response to invitations to do so in institutional newsletters and circulars etc.

In an early project paper, two of the project team justified the adoption of a multi-theory, multi-method approach to the project, drawing on 'grounded theory', 'case study', 'organizational theory' and 'feminist epistemology' (Farish and Weiner, 1992). The policy case study appeared to offer this, enabling us to draw on feminist epistemological frameworks which allowed for both the promotion of greater equality and the recognition of difference (Nicholson, 1990; Walkerdine, 1990).

Project organization

Concern in the research team about the principles of ethical practice led us to focus on a number of different issues: in particular, composition of the project team, the relationship between the project and individual case study researchers, project organization, the research process and analysis and presentation of findings.

The research team comprised four white women from various ethnic backgrounds, at different levels in academia and of different ages and stages in their lives and careers. Two of us worked at South Bank University in London and two at the Scottish Council for Research in Education in Edinburgh. None of us was full-time as the project was relatively low-funded, but the fact that the project work was spread across the four of us meant that we felt able to share perspectives, interests, decisions and responsibilities, and also to provide support and 'cover' for other project members where necessary. Importantly, we all had previous experience of working on equal opportunities issues and of working collaboratively.

The principles of feminist research were seen by us as applicable to forms of humanist research relating to groups other than women. Thus, by adopting a 'feminist standpoint' for the project which recognizes difference between women (see Harding, 1986), we were provided with the framework for the recognition of difference within and between other social groupings. As Cockburn (1989: 10) notes:

> Men tell us 'women cannot claim to be equal if they are different from men. You have to choose'. We now have a reply. If we say, as women, we can be both the same as you *and* different from you, at various times and in various ways. We can also be the same and different from each other. What we are seeking is not in fact *equality* but *equivalence*, not *sameness* for individual women and men but *parity* for women as a sex, or for groups of women in their specificity.

We were conscious, however, that as white women the research team represented one main segment of under-representation (owing to the unintended exclusion of Black researchers from the project team because of what might be seen as the structural racism of the contract research process). We aimed to redress this imbalance by having a more representative project advisory group and also by being particularly alert to issues of 'race' and ethnicity and other forms of inequality in our research practice. However, we were also conscious of the significance of the absence of a Black feminist standpoint (Hill Collins, 1990) from our research.

The structure of the project was designed to be relatively flat and non-hierarchical, though, inevitably, status differences between project members could not entirely be eradicated. As the project director, Gaby Weiner took main responsibility for general administration, including organizing project meetings, writing and distributing minutes and taking any necessary follow-up action. She was also responsible for the overall smooth running of the project, filling any pressing 'gaps' in the fieldwork. Each of the other researchers (Maureen Farish, Joanna McPake and Janet Powney) had the main responsibility for one of the case studies and also played a 'minor' role in a second case study, taking a share of the fieldwork and having some familiarity with the specific institutional context. Most importantly, this web of responsibility enabled at least one member of the project team to be present at any 'significant' event within any one case study.

Research process

Initially, access to the case study institutions was negotiated by the project director and the principal case study researcher through a member of the senior management, approved by the governing body, who granted approvals for access to committees etc. The research team were conscious of the pitfalls (and advantages) of such a top-down research entry. Some degree of 'protection' for both researchers and staff from the case study institutions was gained, however, through agreement to ethical guidelines involving access to information, opportunities to respond and amend research accounts and guaranteed anonymity, where possible. Thus, all research accounts were returned to appropriate staff members for checking for meaning and accuracy.

As with much institution-based research, it was clear that the organizations involved wished to benefit from, rather than be disadvantaged by, participation in the project. Some interviewees and respondents revealed their anxiety and feelings of vulnerability concerning their own institutional positioning by the manner in which they scrutinized the research accounts, eradicating any perceived contentious statements. Certainly, in one case, statements about the difficulties for gay members of staff were eliminated from an interview account, generating much discussion in the research team about who had ultimate control over the research data. We questioned, for instance, whether it is ethical *in all instances* for an interviewee to retain control over the research account. Moreover, when we presented each case study institution with early drafts of the final report, inevitably, perhaps, senior managers made great attempts to shape final drafts according to their own 'world view'.

Different research approaches were replicated across institutions, though not every institution was researched identically. These included tracking a senior manager, following through the staff recruitment process and distributing a questionnaire eliciting the response of the main body of staff to equal opportunities policy-making. The intention was not to compare policies and practices between institutions which have very different histories and cultures, but rather to seek understanding through the prism of difference.

Gaining access

First, it is important to put on the record that this project could not have had more freedom in how we conducted the research. We were able to approach any member of staff in the case study institutions, and any member of staff had the right to refuse to cooperate. This is an important aspect of what has in the past been proudly recognized as academic freedom. The politics of this project are the politics of institutions in an environment becoming increasingly competitive and entrepreneurial, and having to be concerned with marketability. We were aware of this from our first contacts, although at that point we had not appreciated the subtleties of each organization; that came later.

Negotiating access seems to be a question of getting in to key parts of an organization's work without compromising likely outcomes. Experienced researchers are possibly more aware than staff within organizations of what the resulting report of a wide-ranging study might be – put negatively, the kinds of controversies, 'home truths' and misconceptions which, when published, threaten individuals and groups, undermine structures, even show up ineffectual policies and people. In order to avoid misunderstandings, we discussed terms of collaboration with senior managers. As a team, we had prepared a summary of the evidence we would be drawing on, our proposed methods, the ethical guidelines we were using in our work and the likely elements of research reports.

Our main principle was that power was not to be held by any one party. Gaining collaborative agreement not only ensured the limits of what we might do but also indicated what we needed to complete in the study. In that sense it provided the public framework for the evidence base from the beginning. Any members of staff in the institutions who considered that the proposed conduct of the research was too biased or narrow could make their views known and, where such dissent was expressed, any problem could be quickly addressed. Such collaboration agreements clarify the rights of all participants in the research – not just those of the researchers.

What happened in practice was that no one proposed any changes to the suggested collaboration. We kept as far as possible to our side of the bargain and were unaware of any lapse in protocols, although the interpretations varied slightly according to the context of the institution. Individual informants returned our accounts of interviews and meetings, with comments on the accuracy and fairness of what was written; sometimes they added further illuminative points or suggested other people who could provide interesting insights for the research. Few totally rejected a record or refused permission to use a quotation (except where an individual felt clearly identifiable), although one interviewee withdrew her whole interview and several eradicated portions of the record – more from fear of identification than because of inaccuracy or misrepresentation.

Dealing with accounts of meetings was more problematic. To whom should the account be returned? In principle, every participant had the right to see it but this we rejected as too unwieldy unless there were relatively few people involved. For example, one meeting at Borough College was attended by over 200 people, including substantial numbers of students and staff and a few individuals from outside the college. There was no record of those attending. In this instance, the account of the meeting was sent only to the deputy principal, who had also made her own minute of the meeting, which became part of the research evidence. Similarly, we were able to use the minutes of large committees to corroborate our own observations.

Having access to key individuals (especially to senior staff) could have pitfalls, in particular if they tried to manipulate the account in order to represent the management perspective or to defend the institution's reputation. For policy researchers, there seems to be a constant need to balance honest reportage with tact in placing potentially compromising information in the public domain.

Our initial contacts were all with male senior managers with whom we felt an extra need to display research competence as well as skills of tact and discretion. Our research experience was primarily related to education although we each had experience of other disciplines. In each case, the project director and the main case study researcher attended the preliminary meeting with the institutional representative. Neither party was known to each other so the 'selling points' had to include the trustworthiness of the researchers as well as the potential benefits to the institution of being involved in the project.

There is no doubt that being funded by the ESRC gave the project respectability and prestige, particularly with the two universities. The case study methodology had been recognized as appropriate by the ESRC and we had a clear statement about the basis of collaboration for discussion and agreement. There were additional safeguards for the institutions in terms of representation on the project advisory committee and on individual advisory committees established for each case study. Nevertheless, we were, to some extent, gambling on the potential of each institution as suggested by its reputation for equal opportunities nationally. The project's main aim was to evaluate the effectiveness of equal opportunities policies in educational institutions. At the same time, we had to assure the case study institutions that they had good practices which it would be in their interests for us to investigate and describe. However, our anxiety was that, perhaps, there was very little good practice to report. Perhaps institutional reputations had been based on insubstantial evidence. We were confident that our choices would prove appropriate but at the point of preliminary negotiations there was a core of uncertainty which we chose not to reveal.

The institutions needed to be approached separately and, in the case of committee attendance, approval had to be sought beforehand. Sometimes this was done on our behalf, especially for the more formal committees such as governors or promotions boards. The degree of access therefore often depended on the negotiating skills of institutional representatives. In other instances, we introduced ourselves by phone, through an individual letter or by the project information leaflet.

The politics of researching organizations

Evaluations necessarily change the nature of the institution or feature being evaluated. While we were not evaluators, our descriptions were often very detailed, making staff aware of, for example, inconsistencies between policy and practice or between departments. It could be argued that the mere existence of a project on institutional policy and practice is likely to affect staff behaviour, especially a project concerned with the sensitive areas around equal opportunities. This did not seem to be the case. Despite the publication of project information in newsletters on more than one occasion, we commonly found that informants were unaware of our presence.

Nevertheless, there were two factors which indicated that the project acted as a change agent. The first was on those being observed, shadowed or interviewed, or having an opportunity to write to us about their views under the auspices of the project. Making opinions explicit can provide confirmation and make them a stronger part of an individual's belief system. Being interviewed about their views on staffing policies seemed to make some individuals more self-reflective, with increased insights into personal standpoints, behaviours and inconsistencies.

However, self-reflection can also reinforce existing prejudices. A strong theme which emerged from interviews at Metropolitan University was that 'the kinds of practices most likely to be affected by the [new equal opportunities] policy were already egalitarian and that, in effect, the policy simply codified what was already practised.' This echoed the views of a Black woman lecturer, in an earlier study, about the self-image of the male professorial hierarchy:

[The view of them] as fair minded people has proved a real problem to get over in the universities. You are working against the grain of people who feel they have been fair all their lives and couldn't possibly . . . they don't have the understanding of things like indirect discrimination. It's not a concept they acknowledge.

(Powney and Weiner, 1992)

The second factor was the extent to which, if at all, the existence of the project changed institutional practices and activities. Did equal opportunities committees meet more or less frequently because researchers wanted to attend meetings? We found no evidence to suggest they did. On the other hand, were equal opportunities issues normally discussed at so many meetings attended by a senior manager whom we observed as part of a three-day shadowing exercise? We thought not and that there was a danger of observing 'manufactured' rather than usual behaviour. If equality issues were deliberately introduced into conversations because we were present, might this not invalidate what was said? In our view, it meant that we needed to be cautious in our analyses and interpretations of data.

Unpleasant contemporary events at Borough College provided valuable information about the resilience of equal opportunities policies when tested against racist incidents. This was certainly not staged for the benefit of the project, which was, after all, largely peripheral to the complex business of college and university life. In summary, we were able to take advantage of circumstances as they occurred. Our presence caused few special events – other than advisory committees. However, our very presence, with us clearly labelled as researchers of equal opportunities, probably had an effect (if minor) on institutional agendas and on individual people. Occasionally we were invited to contribute to the discussion at meetings we attended but more often we took notes which were sent back for confirmation.

Elsewhere we have referred to problems of institutional changes during the life of the project. As outsiders, we were in privileged positions: managers, academic and support staff and other key personnel provided information, access to events, opinions and information which were often inaccessible to other colleagues. Shadowing senior staff enabled us to share the otherwise unique experiences of their working day. We then had the opportunity to talk frankly to their colleagues, thus gaining multiple perspectives on, for example, the same event or policy initiative. In each of the case studies, we provided the appropriate advisory group with an interim report at the end of the first year of the case study. There were also the accounts of conversations and meetings returned to informants. Both of these could have affected the future thinking of individuals and contributed to future discussions.

Presentation of findings

There were a number of stages through which the findings of the project passed in order to enter the public domain: accounts were written up, sent back to those involved to check for accuracy and meaning, incorporated into regular reports back to the case study institutions and to various advisory groups and incorporated into academic papers and the final report. Overall the project aimed to reach some sort of 'truth' about the policy-making process and to enhance the effectiveness of those attempting to promote greater equality. So, clearly, the manner in which we framed the reports back was important, and indeed was carefully discussed beforehand. For example, were we going to be challenging or congratulatory, critical or sympathetic? Were we going to play the naive researcher or the seasoned academic? Most of all, what we sought from the institutions involved in the study was to win them over to a more highly prioritized commitment to equality and, through the research data provided on their institution, to help them explore how they could best move forward.

It should be noted here that our initial intention had been to research each institution and present a report on how equal opportunities was working. Subsequently, and perhaps inevitably, as we became more involved in the case studies we saw our role as expanding to support and improve the various policies we were scrutinizing.

A difficulty raised by the final case study reports to each institution at the end of the project was that frequently we were commenting on events and problems that were deemed to have long since passed. As we have said, fieldwork for the project took place at various points over an 18-month period and therefore scrutiny of equal opportunities could not be continuous. Moreover, we framed our reports back to the case study institutions as narratives within which various accounts needed to be understood as 'snapshots' of events and practices. Critical issues which had been apparent at the beginning of the study were not necessarily present towards the end of the research period – particularly as each of the institutions had been involved in at least one extensive reorganization. In some instances, by alerting the college or university to particular difficulties in policy-making and implementation, the very presence of the project speeded up the change process. Our dilemma was that we found it less easy to emphasize the positive than to identify omissions and blocks to policy. Significantly, senior managers seemed particularly sensitive to any perceived criticism because, in the increasingly marketized culture of further and higher education, any criticism by the project might catch the eye of the local or national press and thus affect recruitment and funding. In such instances, securing anonymity for those involved in each case study proved an important consideration. Thus, while every effort was made in case study reports to reflect accurately the chronology of events and to accommodate the multiple perspectives of all involved, inevitably, at times, the perspective of the project differed from those managing the institutions.

Ethics in reporting

What happens after evidence has been collected, analysed and written up is partly the result of the initial negotiation. A project team can try to ensure that the report will be made public but who is going to have the last say? For the project, individuals controlled their own feedback in approving the text of interviews and meetings. Moreover, managers tried to safeguard what they saw as the interests of the institution. For example, no educational establishment would want its public image to convey an *un*equal opportunities message.

It is true that we were seeking examples of good practice in policies for staff. However, in attempting to identify specific examples of practice, we were also sieving through a number of activities, documents, people's views and experiences. Inevitably, perhaps, we came across some practices which contradicted the espoused aims of institutional policy-makers. Our reporting them was likely to be perceived as subversive and irresponsible: after all, we were outside researchers with no long-term commitment to the organization. In fact, we did not find any dreadful skeletons in academic cupboards but we did attempt to present information in ways which were not unnecessarily provocative.

In our view, this did not lead to a lowered research rigour or quality; rather it meant that our writing and communication skills had greater demands made on them. It seemed to us that we needed to respect the complexities of institutions which had rendered themselves more vulnerable by allowing us in. External evaluators and researchers can only gain glimpses of institutional life. These glimpses are necessarily partial, constrained by the timing and duration of visits, as compared with the views of permanent members of staff who have a fuller, 'insider' picture. However, staff likewise will have a partial perspective, depending on their function and status; on the other hand, external researchers may have greater flexibility in taking up a specific issue at different organizational levels. The instances of shadowing in the case studies illustrate the broad range of people that senior managers make contact with on a daily basis and also the limitations of those contacts, which are necessarily constrained by status and relationships of power. We saw staff in different settings: with and without managers, with and without immediate colleagues.

The responsibilities of researchers are also considerable. Individuals' rights to confidentiality and anonymity are part and parcel of their informal or formal contract with researchers. The account of one interview and parts of others were withdrawn precisely because there was a fear of identification if the full accounts were used and published. It is a little trickier to consider how group vulnerabilities might be exposed in the reporting of institutional research. For example, reporting on meetings of lobby groups, governors, planning teams or senior managers is likely to expose their methods of working, priorities and strategies to those outside the groups.

Institutional policy research thus goes beyond description and analysis, beyond looking at match and mismatch of policy and practice. It involves researchers in complex issues of judgement, fairness and integrity. In our view the aim should be to attempt to provide a realistic portrayal of 'things as they are' in all their complexity rather than to target individuals or groups for criticism.

Bibliography

Adler, S., Laney, J. and Packer, M. (1993) *Managing Women.* Buckingham, Open University Press.

Alban Metcalfe, B. N. and Nicholson, N. (1984) *The Career Development of British Managers.* London, British Institute of Management Foundation.

Al Khalifa, E. (1989) Management by halves: women teachers and school management, in Migniuolo, F. and De Lyon, H. (eds) *Women Teachers: Issues and Evidence.* Milton Keynes, Open University Press.

Anand, P. (1992) Equality faces an unknown hurdle, *Times Higher Education Supplement*, 27 November.

Ball, S. J. (1987) *The Micro-politics of Schools: towards a Theory of School Organisations.* London, Methuen.

Ball, S. J. (1990) Introducing Monsieur Foucault, in Ball, S. J. (ed.) *Foucault and Education: Disciplines and Knowledge.* London, Routledge.

Bangar, S. and McDermott, F. (1989) Black women speak, in Migniuolo, F. and De Lyon, H. (eds) *Women Teachers: Issues and Experience.* Milton Keynes, Open University Press.

Bowe, R., Ball, S. and Gold, A. (1992) *Reforming Education and Changing Schools.* London, Routledge.

Brennan, J. and McGeevor, P. (1990) *Ethnic Minorities and the Graduate Labour Market.* London, Commission for Racial Equality.

Bridges, D. (1989) Ethics and the law: conducting case studies of policing, in Burgess, R. (ed.) *The Ethics of Educational Research.* Barcombe, Falmer Press.

Burton, L. and Weiner, G. (1993) From rhetoric to reality: strategies for developing a social justice approach to educational decision-making, in Siraj-Blatchford, I. (ed.) *'Race', Gender and the Education of Teachers.* Buckingham, Open University Press.

Cockburn, C. (1989) Equal opportunities: the long and short agenda, *Industrial Relations Journal*, Autumn, 213–25.

Cockburn, C. (1991) *In the Way of Women: Men's Resistance to Sex Equality in Organisations.* London, Macmillan.

Cottrell, P. (1992) Fairer university image, *Times Higher Education Supplement*, 20 November.

Davies, L. (1990) Women and educational management in the Third World. Paper presented to the conference on Equal Advances in Education Management, Vienna, December.

Farish, M. and Weiner, G. (1992) Staffing policies in further and higher education: setting the scene. Paper presented at the Equal Opportunities and Management Symposium, CEDAR Annual Conference, University of Warwick, April.

Foucault, M. (1974) *The Archaeology of Knowledge*. London, Tavistock.

Gerver, E. and Hart, L. (1990) Surviving in a cold climate: women and decision making in Scottish education. Paper presented to the Conference on Equal Advances in Education Management, Vienna, December.

Grambs, J. D. (1987) Are older women teachers different?, *Journal of Education*, 169(1), 47–64.

Handy, C. and Aitken, R. (1986) *Understanding Schools as Organisations*. Harmondsworth, Penguin.

Hansard Society (1990) *Report by the Hansard Society Commission on Women at the Top*. London, Hansard Society.

Harding, S. (1986) *The Science Question in Feminism*. Milton Keynes, Open University Press.

Harding, S. (1990) Feminism, science and the anti-enlightenment critiques, in Nicholson, L. J. (ed.) *Feminism/Postmodernism*. New York, Routledge.

Heward, C. and Taylor, P. (1993) Effective and ineffective equal opportunities policies in higher education, *Critical Social Policy*, 37, 75–94.

Hill Collins, P. (1990) *Black Feminist Thought*. New York, Routledge.

Hitchcock, G. and Hughes, D. (1989) *Research and the Teacher: a Qualitative Introduction to School-based Research*. London, Routledge and Kegan Paul.

Holsti, O. R. (1968) Content analysis, in Lindzey, C. and Aronson, E. (eds) *The Handbook of Social Psychology*, vol. 2, 2nd edn. Reading, MA, Addison Wesley.

Hoyle, E. (1988) Micropolitics of educational organizations, in Westoby, A. (ed.) *Culture and Power in Educational Organizations*. Milton Keynes, Open University Press.

Jackson, D. F. (1990) Women working in higher education: a review of the position of women in higher education and policy developments, *Higher Education Quarterly*, 44(4), 297–324.

Jenkins, R. and Solomos, J. (eds) (1989) *Racism and Equal Opportunity Policies in the 1980s*, 2nd edn. Cambridge, Cambridge University Press.

Jewson, N. and Mason, D. (1986) The theory and practice of equal opportunities: liberal and radical approaches, *Sociological Review*, 324, 307–34.

Jewson, N. and Mason, D. (1989) Monitoring equal opportunities policies: principles and practice, in Jenkins, R. and Solomos, J. (eds) *Racism and Equal Opportunity Policies in the 1980s*, 2nd edn. Cambridge, Cambridge University Press.

Jones, A. (1993) Becoming a 'girl': post-structuralist suggestions for educational research, *Gender and Education*, 5(2), 157–66.

Lather, P. (1991) *Getting Smart: Feminist Research and Pedagogy with/in the Postmodern*. New York, Routledge.

Leithwood, K., Steinbach, R. and Begley, P. (1991) The nature and contribution of socialization experiences to becoming a principal in Canada. Paper presented to the International Congress on School Effectiveness, Cardiff.

Lewis, M. (1990) Interrupting patriarchy: politics, resistance and transformation in the feminist classroom, *Harvard Educational Review*, 60(4), 467–88.

Lundgren, V. P. (1986) *Att Organisera Skolan*. Stockholm, Liber.

McKellar, B. (1989) Only the fittest will survive: black women and education, in Acker, S. (ed.) *Teachers, Gender and Careers*. Barcombe, Falmer Press.

MacLure, M. (1993) Arguing for your self: identity as an organising principle in teachers' jobs and lives, *British Educational Research Journal*, 19(4), 311–22.

McPake, J. (1992) Equal opportunities policy documents in further and higher education: some reflections. Paper presented at the Annual Conference, British Educational Research Association, Stirling University, August.

Maguire, M. and Weiner, G. (1994) The place of women in teacher education: discourses of power, *Educational Review*, 46(2), 121–39.

Measor, L. (1985) Interviewing: a strategy in qualitative research, in Burgess, R. (ed.) *Strategies of Educational Research: Qualitative Methods*. London, Falmer Press.

Morgan, G. and Knights, D. (1991) Gendering jobs: corporate strategy, managerial control and the dynamics of job segregation, *Work, Employment and Society*, 5(2), 181–200.

Nicholson, L. J. (ed.) (1990) *Feminism/Postmodernism*. New York, Routledge.

National Union of Teachers (1990) *Promotion and the Woman Teacher – Ten Years on.* London, NUT.

OECD (1985–6) *Women in educational management.* Statistical update to the conference on Equal Advances in Education Management, Vienna, December.

Ouston, J. (ed.) (1993) *Women in Educational Management*. London, Longman.

Ozga, J. (ed.) (1993) *Women in Educational Management*. Buckingham, Open University Press.

Polytechnics and Colleges Funding Council (PCFC) (1991) *Widening Participation in Higher Education*. London, PCFC.

Powney, J. (1992) Every which way: comments on researching institutional policy. Paper presented at the Annual Conference of the British Educational Research Association, Stirling University, August.

Powney, J. and Weiner, G. (1992) *Outside of the Norm: Equity and Management in Educational Institutions*. London, South Bank University.

Queen's University of Belfast (1992) *Equal Opportunities Code of Practice*. Internal university document.

Ranger, C. (1988) *Ethnic Minority School Teachers*. London, Commission for Racial Equality.

Riley, K. (1994) *Quality and Equality: Promoting Opportunities in Schools*. London, Cassell.

Scott, J. W. (1990) Deconstructing equality-versus-difference; or the uses of poststructural theory for feminism, in Hirsch, M. and Fox Keller, E. (eds) *Conflicts in Feminism*. New York, Routledge.

Shakeshaft, C. (1990) Gender and supervision. Paper presented at the conference on Equal Advances in Educational Management, Vienna, December.

Smith, D. (1978) A peculiar eclipsing: women's exclusion from man's culture, *Women's Studies International Quarterly*, 1, 281–95.

SOED (1992) *Scottish Higher Education Statistics: Statistical Bulletin*. Edn./72/1992/18.

Stake, R. (1994) Case studies, in Denzin, N. K. and Lincoln, Y. S. (eds) *Handbook of Qualitative Research*. Thousand Oaks, CA, Sage.

Stanley, L. (ed.) (1990) *Feminist Praxis: Research, Theory and Epistemology in Feminist Sociology*. London, Routledge.

Stanley, L. and Wise, S. (1990) Method, methodology and epistemology in feminist research processes, in Stanley, L. (ed.) *Feminist Praxis: Research, Theory and Epistemology in Feminist Sociology*. London, Routledge.

Summers, D. (1993) Another battle of the sexes, *Financial Times*, 3 February.

Tripp, D. (1994) *Critical Incidents in Teaching.* London, Routledge.

Troyna, B. and Hatcher, R. (1992) *Racism in Children's Lives.* London, Routledge.

Walkerdine, V. (1990) *School Girl Fictions.* London, Verso.

Watson, L. E. (1982) The management of education in its social setting, in Gray, H. L. (ed.) *The Management of Education.* Barcombe, Falmer Press.

Webb, E. J., Campbell, D. T., Schwartz, R. D. and Sechres, L. (1966) *Unobtrusive Measures: Nonreactive Research in the Social Sciences.* Chicago, Rand McNally.

Weedon, C. (1987) *Feminist Practice and Poststructural Theory.* Oxford, Basil Blackwell.

Weiner, G. (1986) Feminist education and equal opportunities, *British Journal of Sociology of Education,* 7(3), 265–74.

Weiner, G. (1993) A question of style or value? Contrasting perceptions of women as educational leaders. Paper presented at the Women in Leadership Conference, Perth, Australia, December.

Weiner, G. (1994) *Feminisms in Education: an Introduction.* Buckingham, Open University Press.

Williams, J., Cocking, J. and Davies, L. (1989) Words or deeds? A review of equal opportunities policies in higher education. Occasional paper, Commission for Racial Equality, London.

Wright, A. (1994) A sisterly hand up the ladder, *Times Higher Educational Supplement,* 24 June, 13.

Yeatman, A. (1993) The gendered management of equity-orientated change in higher education, in Baker, D. and Fogarty, M. (eds) *Gendered Culture.* Victoria University of Technology.

Index

The Society for Research into Higher Education

The Society for Research into Higher Education exists to stimulate and coordinate research into all aspects of higher education. It aims to improve the quality of higher education through the encouragement of debate and publication on issues of policy, on the organization and management of higher education institutions, and on the curriculum and teaching methods.

The Society's income is derived from subscriptions, sales of its books and journals, conference fees and grants. It receives no subsidies, and is wholly independent. Its individual members include teachers, researchers, managers and students. Its corporate members are institutions of higher education, research institutes, professional, industrial and governmental bodies. Members are not only from the UK, but from elsewhere in Europe, from America, Canada and Australasia, and it regards its international work as among its most important activities.

Under the imprint *SRHE & Open University Press*, the Society is a specialist publisher of research, having some 45 titles in print. The Editorial Board of the Society's Imprint seeks authoritative research or study in the above fields. It offers competitive royalties, a highly recognizable format in both hardback and paperback and the world-wide reputation of the Open University Press.

The Society also publishes *Studies in Higher Education* (three times a year), which is mainly concerned with academic issues, *Higher Education Quarterly* (formerly *Universities Quarterly*), mainly concerned with policy issues, *Research into Higher Education Abstracts* (three times a year), and *SRHE News* (four times a year).

The Society holds a major annual conference in December, jointly with an institution of higher education. In 1992, the topic was 'Learning to Effect', with Nottingham Trent University. In 1993, it was 'Governments and the Higher Education Curriculum: Evolving Partnerships' at the University of Sussex in Brighton, and in 1994, 'The Student Experience' at the University of York. Future conferences include in 1995, 'The Changing University' at Heriot-Watt University in Edinburgh.

The Society's committees, study groups and branches are run by the members. The groups at present include:
  Teacher Education Study Group
  Continuing Education Group
  Staff Development Group
  Excellence in Teaching and Learning

Benefits to members

Individual

Individual members receive:

- *SRHE News*, the Society's publications list, conference details and other material included in mailings.
- Greatly reduced rates for *Studies in Higher Education* and *Higher Education Quarterly*.
- A 35 per cent discount on all Open University Press & SRHE publications.
- Free copies of the Proceedings – commissioned papers on the theme of the Annual Conference.
- Free copies of *Research into Higher Education Abstracts*.
- Reduced rates for conferences.
- Extensive contacts and scope for facilitating initiatives.
- Reduced reciprocal memberships.

Corporate

Corporate members receive:

- All benefits of individual members, plus
- Free copies of *Studies in Higher Education*.
- Unlimited copies of the Society's publications at reduced rates.
- Special rates for its members e.g. to the Annual Conference.

Membership details: SRHE, 3 Devonshire Street, London, W1N 2BA, UK. Tel: 0171 637 2766 Fax: 0171 637 2781
Catalogue: SRHE & Open University Press, Celtic Court, 22 Ballmoor, Buckingham MK18 1XW. Tel: (0280) 823388